DRAFTING WILLS AND TRUSTS

DRAFTING WILLS AND TRUSTS

By

Lucy A. Marsh

Professor of Law
University of Denver Sturm College of Law

VANDEPLAS PUBLISHING

UNITED STATES OF AMERICA

Published by:

Vandeplas Publishing – June 2009

801 International Parkway, 5th Floor
Lake Mary, FL. 32746
USA

www.vandeplaspublishing.com

To my sister,
Mary Marsh Zulack

a wonderful, practical
teacher of law

PREFACE

No longer should drafting be relegated to first-year writing courses, or to the law reviews. It is too important.

Drafting is one of the most important skills needed by anyone in the practice of law. Particularly in the area of wills, trusts and estates, effective drafting is crucial.

Including drafting as a component of a traditional course in Wills, Trusts and Estates is feasible and important. Comprehension of the substantive material is significantly increased once drafting becomes a component of the course. When a student learns how to draft a particular document effectively, far greater understanding of the document is achieved.

This book is designed to provide a means by which a component of drafting may be added to substantive courses in Wills, Trusts and Estates – without seriously increasing the workload for either students or faculty. In this way, practical, useful comprehension of the area should be significantly increased.

Students who take a course on wills should be able to draft an effective will by the end of the course. Theoretical knowledge and practical application of that knowledge should be combined – for the benefit of all.

I hope that this book will be of help to students as they learn the necessary drafting skills.

As I wrote this book, by far the most valuable editorial assistance came from my mother, Susan Marsh, a professional musician, author, and wonderfully supportive person, who somehow managed to remain cheerful while having a husband and two daughters all turn out to be law professors.

Special thanks also, to Donna Hughes, who did an outstanding job of pulling everything together. And to my son, Neil Yee, for help in tracking down the wills.

Now, best wishes to everyone who undertakes the challenge of effective drafting!

January, 2009   Lucy A. Marsh

TABLE OF CONTENTS

INTRODUCTION

This book is designed to help law students learn the drafting skills needed for writing wills and trusts. Too often students are asked to study only small bits and pieces of cases—dealing with particular problems involving wills or trusts. The big picture of what a will is, how it works, and how it should be drafted is too often lost in all of the little details. The goal of this book is to make the big picture predominate—so that students will learn how to draft wills and trusts effectively.

When you have finished the book you should have gained a sense of confidence—that you understand the big picture of how wills work, how trusts can be used effectively, and how to draft the necessary documents.

This practical, hands-on approach has made learning considerably more effective—and more fun—for my students for many years. Hopefully, it will do the same for you.

HOW TO USE THE BOOK

To use this book effectively, you should start by reading the full, complete wills of Elvis Presley, Georgia O'Keeffe, and Mark Rothko, found in the Appendix. You will then have a good idea of what a real will looks like—and how the pieces fit together.

Nearly all of the rest of the book is devoted to studying the major components of a will—what the major components are, how they work, and how to draft them effectively. Each chapter contains numerous SAMPLES taken from the actual wills of well-known Americans, so that you can see how real people handled various problems.

As you go through the book you will find there are various drafting exercises which help you to try your hand at applying the concepts you have studied in that section of the book. If you have time—or if your professor assigns them—DO these exercises. Working something out for yourself always makes learning far more effective—and more fun, in the long run.

But even when you do not have time to DO a particular drafting exercise, READ about it, anyway. Considering the practical problems presented by the drafting exercises, and thinking about the Pointers for Drafting which follow each exercise, will give you a far better understanding of the various theories discussed.

Above all, try to make the most of this opportunity. Try out the various tools which will be available to you as a lawyer—when you are drafting wills designed to meet the special, individual needs, goals and aspirations for your clients.

OUTLINE OF THE BOOK

The book starts with a chapter on what happens if a person dies without a will, and some of the reasons it may be better to have a will.

The next section of the book deals with some of the issues which may arise in determining whether your client has the mental capacity to make a will, and if so, how to draft a will which is as strong as possible.

Most of the remainder of the book is devoted simply to helping you learn to understand and to use the various tools available for writing good, effective wills and trusts.

The final chapter of the book includes samples and discussion of three supplementary documents which clients normally want when they come in for a will. The three supplementary documents are: Durable Power of Attorney for Health Care; Durable Power of Attorney for Financial Matters; and "Living Will." All three of these documents go into effect <u>before</u> a client dies. They are designed to make a person's final months, or years, considerably more comfortable for everyone involved. Any lawyer who writes wills or trusts should also be prepared to offer his or her clients appropriate versions of the three supplementary documents discussed in Chapter 11.

WARNING

Those of you who are clerking in law firms may observe that many lawyers today simply try to squeeze their client's individualized needs and goals into standardized forms—the same basic forms the client could have bought for himself or herself for about $10 at any office supply store, or could have downloaded, free, from some source on the internet. That "one size fits all" approach is not acceptable when the client expects—and is paying for—individualized assistance from a competent LAWYER—not just a secretary who can fill in the blanks of a form will.
Word processors are wonderful tools, and should be used effectively. Likewise, forms are a valuable resource to be consulted. Yet the basic structure of any will drafted by a competent LAWYER MUST be the result of INDIVIDUALIZED discussions with the client—to ascertain his or her particular goals, aspirations and family situation. Then the appropriate documents must be appropriately drafted for that client.

Only if you have not taken the time necessary to get to know your client will you believe that your client is adequately served by having his or her needs squeezed into a standardized form.

The goal of this book is to help you to learn the skills needed to write appropriate, effective wills and trusts for individual clients. The drafting skills thus acquired should also be of great value to you in any other area of the practice of law.

FUNDAMENTALS OF GOOD DRAFTING

As with any other skills, drafting improves with practice. Yet there are certain fundamental principles of good drafting that should make it possible for any good lawyer to draft documents effectively.

There are five fundamental steps for good drafting; Perceive, Organize, Write, Stop, and Redraft. (POWSR). Each of the five steps is necessary and should be performed in the specified order.

1. PERCEIVE

First, you must perceive—or understand—what your client would like to accomplish with the will, or any other document you are drafting. This means talking to your client, asking questions, and LISTENING to your client's concerns and ideas. When your client first begins describing his or her goals, the client's plan may be clear and complete; or fuzzy, incomplete, and inconsistent. It is impossible to draft a good document unless the underlying plan is complete and clear. It is your job to ask questions and offer suggestions until your client's plan becomes clear to you—and to the client.

Normally, anyone who takes the time to make an appointment to discuss a will has some basic idea of what he or she wants to accomplish. Yet rarely will a client have any idea of the wide range of options available. Nor is your client likely to have thought about what might happen if various beneficiaries die at unexpected times—such as a younger person dying before an older person—or before the testator.[1]

After you have asked the appropriate questions and have described the various possibilities, you will begin to get a sense for what your client really would <u>like</u> to do in various situations. Once

---

[1] "I never thought of that!," is almost always a client's response when asked, "What would you like to have happen to your property if your daughter, [or son], should die before you do?" Almost always, people assume that friends and relatives will generally die in order of age—as they usually do. But when drafting a will, you should try to anticipate as many of the vagaries of life as reasonable.

your client's goals seem relatively clear, you may be able to suggest the use of various tools—such as trusts, powers of appointment, and the like—to accomplish those goals.

In discussions with your client, always REMEMBER, however, that your client is NOT interested in a law school-type lecture! (When buying a car would you really want a lecture on the details of what makes every part work?) Your job when writing a will is simply to find out your client's wishes; to describe the available possibilities; and then to translate your client's choices into the necessary legal wording. You do NOT have to give your client a mini-course in wills. Nor, at the other end of the spectrum, is it appropriate for you just to cram your client's individual plans into some "one size fits all" type of will form.

So the first step is to talk with your client, until, by means of questions, answers, suggestions, and LISTENING, you clearly PERCEIVE the goals of your client and have figured out the appropriate tools to use to meet those goals.

2. ORGANIZE

The second step is to ORGANIZE the document—to sort out your ideas. Just as you probably put knives and forks in different parts of your kitchen drawer, so, too, you should sort out the different components of the will or trust.

Figure out what the big concepts are that are to be included in the document. Then, set up a special compartment of the document for each concept. Make each compartment complete and clear—and consistent with all of the other components of the document.

In a will, for example, your first compartment usually consists of identification—who the testator is,[2] where he or she lives,[3] names of the spouse and children,[4] and the like. Next, there will

---

[2] John Lennon's will, for example, begins, "I, JOHN WINSTON ONO LENNON, [will signed November 12, 1979]. Benjamin Franklin, who signed his will on July 17, 1888, had a bit more flourish to the first paragraph of his will, which read: "I, Benjamin Franklin of Philadelphia, Printer, late Minister Plenipotentiary from the United States of America to the Court of France, now President of the Sate of Penn. Do make and declare my last Will and Testament as follows:"

For more typical clients, this introductory part of the will is a good place to put the various names by which your client may be known, especially the names in which the client may hold property. If a woman holds some property in her married name and other property in her maiden name, for example, both names should be included in this introductory paragraph. Just ask your client how he or she usually signs an important document—then use that name as the first name in the will—and include all of the other name variations simply as "also known as."

[3] The reason for including a statement of where the client lives—usually just by stating the name of the city and state—is to show domicile. Domicile is important to help prove that the will was executed, (i.e. signed), in accordance with the requirements of the state where the client was domiciled at the time the will was signed.

[4] Naming the spouse and children may be surprisingly important in some circumstances. The movie star, John Wayne, for example, in the first article of his will states, "I and all of my said children except Mary Antonia La Cava and Melinda Ann Munoz are sometimes also known by the surname "Morrison." [will of John Wayne, signed October 5, 1978. Emphasis added.] In the same article of his will, John Wayne also stated the full name and birth date of each of his seven children, which is the standard practice. Dates of birth certainly are not required, however.

If you DO include dates of birth, just be VERY sure that the dates are accurate. It is very easy for a typist, who does not know the children, to make a mistake on birth dates. And that is one mistake which even a very careful lawyer is unlikely to catch. In real life, clients who have adult children, or who have quite a number of children, frequently have difficulty remembering the exact year of each child's birth. And that is not

usually be one paragraph indicating how the testator's debts and taxes are to be paid.[5] The third compartment of a will normally includes a list of specific bequests—gifts of particular items to special people. BE SURE that these specific bequests go EARLY in the will!

One error frequently made by inexperienced attorneys is to say, for example, that "all of my personal property goes to my spouse," and FOLLOWING THAT to try to give specific items of personal property to others. Remember, YOU CAN'T GIVE ANYTHING AWAY MORE THAN ONCE!

So be sure that you compartmentalize your client's wishes, (specific gifts in one compartment; residuary gifts in another compartment), and then arrange the various compartments in a logical order!

Avoid the temptation just to start writing—and put in ideas as they come along. That type of drafting, without planning, usually leads to unclear, inconsistent documents. Plan how your document will fit together and then use the plan.

3. WRITE

The third step is the actual writing of the will. If you have developed a good pattern for the document, and have sorted things into appropriate compartments, the actual writing should not be too difficult.

As you begin to write, follow your plan. Ask yourself constantly, "What am I really trying to say?" Then, simply say what you mean—in clear, concise language.

Above all, use plain English. A will is not some vocabulary contest, where you get "points" for using big words no one quite understands. It takes far more skill to write a clear statement than it does to write a convoluted, complex statement.

A will is one of the most important documents you client may ever sign. Clear, consistent drafting may help prevent the unfortunate and destructive squabbles which break out all too often among family members after someone has died. Keep in mind, also, that since a will only goes

---

surprising. The day of the year on which birthdays are celebrated is important. A person's exact age—over the age of 21—usually does NOT have momentous significance. Yet to have an INACCURATE date of birth in a will could cause problems relating to testamentary capacity, and possibly even identification.

[5] The normal provision on debts and taxes is that they are to be paid from the residuary estate—without apportionment. That simply means that debts are to be paid first, from the property not specifically devised—rather than trying to deduct a little money from each gift before it is distributed. If a person who dies does not have enough money to pay all the taxes and debts owed, the person's surviving relatives DO NOT have to chip in to pay those debts and taxes. The debts and taxes simply do not get paid. But debts and taxes always WILL get paid from decedent's assets, to the extent possible, before ANY of the intended gifts are made.

5

into effect when the testator dies, it will be impossible for your client to explain, later, what he or she really meant. So clear, accurate drafting is especially crucial for wills.

When drafting, if your sentences begin to get too tangled and complex, simply stop—and start over. Do not be afraid to throw out sentences that really are beyond salvage. Remember, if you have accurately understood your client's goals, in accordance with the first requirement for good drafting, you WILL be able to state the will or trust provisions so clearly that others will understand them, too. Simply work at it, and discard as necessary, until you get it right.

Use lots of short, clear sentences. Probably the most common problem with legal drafting is the tendency to try to get everything into one sentence. You have seen some monstrous examples of that type of drafting in some of the cases you have read. You have probably noticed that in law school you normally do not read cases about well-drafted documents. That is because documents which were well drafted usually do NOT later have to be "translated" by a judge.

So remember that, generally, any provision which had to be "tested by litigation," and thus appeared in a case, was simply not a well-drafted provision originally. So do not copy it!

Your goal is to make the provisions of your documents so clear that no provision in any one of your documents will later have to be "interpreted" by some judge as part of a costly and uncertain lawsuit. If you find yourself mentally "explaining" what a sentence means, throw out that sentence and start over. With a little patience, you will learn to say what you mean clearly. Then you will not run the risk of having your document later be "translated" by a court.

Just as you should not fall into the trap of copying a sentence that has been "tested by litigation," so, too, you should avoid the trap of blindly copying a sentence that you find in a form. Some parts of existing forms are good—and some are not.

It may be tempting to copy a sentence in an existing will form just because you think that the sentence in the form must be important, even though you cannot quite understand it. However, it may well be that the reason you are having trouble understanding the particular sentence is really not your problem, but is simply that the provision in the form was poorly drafted. In any case, if YOU cannot understand a sentence, it simply does not belong in any will or trust which you have drafted!

Remember that your client, who probably has not been to law school, MUST be able to understand his or her own will![6] So, simply work at it, and make every sentence clear.

After you have understood your client's wishes; have arranged the components in a logical fashion; and have written the necessary provisions in concise, clear language, you are ready for the fourth step required for good drafting.

4. STOP

The fourth step is simply to STOP and set your drafting aside for some period of time—hopefully overnight. This sounds easy, but it actually is hard—and important.

Just as glue needs time to harden when you are building something, or baked goods need time to rise when you are cooking, so, too, a will needs time to mellow a bit before the finishing touches can be made effectively. Actually, of course, it is your mind which needs the time off. But it is very important for good drafting that you step back from the document for awhile and think about other things.

After you have worked with a document closely, it will seem very clear to you—and beautiful. Surprisingly enough, however, a will which looked perfect on Wednesday night usually does not seem all that spectacular on Thursday morning. Somehow, taking a little time away from a will, (or any other document), lets you see it more clearly. Expect that on Thursday morning, when you come back to your "perfect" will, you will be able to see a significant number of places where it could be improved.

This "next morning" effect is not just you. It happens to virtually everyone. Stopping, stepping back from a document, and then returning to give it a fresh look will allow you to see the problems much more clearly. So the key part of the fourth step is to give yourself some time to step back from the will—to gain the necessary fresh perspective.

5.   RE-WRITE

The fifth step is simply to make the necessary corrections. When a portion of the document reads awkwardly, fix it. If you spot inconsistencies or loose ends, correct them. If the meaning still is not clear, clarify it. You DO get "points" for making improvements on an earlier version of a "perfect" document. And you will nearly always be able to do so.

---

[6] Some lawyers believe it is a good practice, when a client comes into the office to sign a will, to ask the client to describe, briefly, what the client thinks the will OUGHT to say. In any case, the will must be read, completely, to the client, and both lawyer and client must be satisfied that the BIG picture of what is happening is clear to the client.

This means that you must schedule your time appropriately. You must get the initial "perfect" draft of a will done some time in advance, so that you actually have the time to stand back and make the needed improvements.

Such scheduling is not as impossible as it sounds. Just remember that, for good drafting, your drafting time must be divided into at least TWO distinct time slots—with adequate time allowed between the two drafting periods.

First you must do the initial will—making it as perfect as possible. Then you must wait. THEN you must do the final polishing.

CONCLUSION

Drafting does take time, but after you learn how to do it, you should feel a great deal of satisfaction in being able to put your theoretical training from law school to a very practical use.

If, instead of drafting appropriately for your clients, you just cram the client's needs into preexisting forms—using the "one size fits all" theory—you will soon realize that any typist could fill in the blanks in form wills and trusts just as well as you could, and that the high-powered education you paid for in law school is being wasted.

If you do not learn how to do your own drafting, you will lose out on one of the most creative, challenging parts of being a lawyer. And you will not serve your clients as well as they could – and should—be served.

So remember when you give your client a specially drafted, clear and effective will, include with it a little appropriate hype. Both you and your client should feel good about a lawyer who does not give in to the "one size fits all" syndrome, but actually takes the time, and has the necessary skills, to write an effective, individualized will for a special client.

After three or four years of rigorous law school education, you should be entitled to a career that is considerably more challenging and rewarding than merely filling in the blanks in a form!

So, learn to do your own drafting. And enjoy it!

CHAPTER 1.   WHY HAVE A WILL?

A.   WHAT HAPPENS WITHOUT A WILL—INTESTACY

Non-lawyers frequently believe that dreadful things may happen to a person who dies without a will. The specific fear is basically that, "If you die without a will all of your property goes to the state." That simply is not true.

When a person dies without a will, that is called "intestacy." The person who dies without a will is called the "intestate." After the death of an intestate, his or her property will simply be distributed to the closest relatives of the intestate—in accordance with the provisions of the applicable state statute.

State statutes vary, of course. But the basic pattern is that the property of an intestate is distributed in his or her surviving spouse and children. For many people, this is a perfectly acceptable result.

If an intestate dies without surviving spouse or children, then the property is usually distributed to grandchildren of the intestate; if there are no surviving descendants of the intestate, (called "issue"), and no surviving spouse, then the property will usually go to the intestate's surviving parents, brothers, sisters, aunts and uncles, and so forth. A typical pattern of distribution is set forth in footnote 1.[1]

---

[1] Although the statute may be difficult to read, it will provide for full distribution of the property of one who dies intestate. For example, Colorado Statutes, found at C.R.S. 15-11-101, provide as follows:

(1) Any part of a decedent's estate not effectively disposed of by will or otherwise passes by intestate succession to the decedent's heirs as prescribed in this code, except as modified by the decedent's will...

C.R.S. 15-11-102.   Share of Surviving Spouse.

(1) If:

(a) No decedent or parent of the decedent survives the decedent, then the surviving spouse receives the entire estate; or

(b) All of the decedent's surviving descendants are also descendants of the surviving spouse and there are no other descendants of the surviving spouse who survive the decedent, then the surviving spouse receives the entire intestate estate;

(2) If no descendant of the decedent survives the decedent, but a parent of the decedent survives the decedent, then the surviving spouse receives the first two hundred thousand dollars, plus three-fourths of any balance of the intestate estate...

(3) If all the decedent's surviving descendants are also descendants of the surviving spouse, and the surviving spouse has one or more surviving descendants who are not descendants of the decedent, then the surviving spouse receives the first one hundred fifty thousand dollars, plus one-half of any balance of the intestate estate;

C.R.S. 15-11-103. Share of heirs other than surviving spouse. Any part of the intestate estate not passing to the decedent's surviving spouse under section 15-11-102, or the entire intestate estate if there is no surviving spouse, passes in the following order to the individuals designated who survive the decedent:

(1) To the decedent's descendants per capita at each generation;

(2) If there is no surviving descendant, to the decedent's parents equally if both survive, or to the decedent's surviving parent;

(3) If there is no surviving descendent or surviving parent, to the surviving descendants of the decedent's parents or either of them per capita at each generation;

(4) If there is no surviving descendant, surviving parent, or surviving descendant of a parent, to the decedent's surviving grandparents, or any of them, in equal shares;

(5) If there is no surviving descendant, surviving parent, surviving descendant of a parent, or surviving grandparent, to the surviving descendants of the decedent's grandparents per capita at each generation...

The major point is that if a person, (called a decedent), dies without a will, his or her property will go to his or her closest relatives, as determined by the statute of the state in which the decedent was domiciled at death. The people who are determined in this way are called the "heirs" of the intestate. NO PERSON HAS HEIRS UNTIL HE OR SHE DIES, BECAUSE HEIRS ARE ONLY THOSE RELATIVES WHO <u>SURVIVE</u> THE DECEDENT.

Only if <u>no heirs of an intestate decedent can be found</u>, will the decedent's property go to the state. Property which goes to the state in such circumstances is said to "escheat" to the state. But only in very rare circumstances will property actually escheat to the state. Normally, some relative can be found.[2]

So preventing property from escheating to the state is NOT a sufficient reason for writing a will, in most circumstances.

There are, however, many other very good reasons for writing a will, as discussed in the following section.

B.   WHAT CAN BE ACCOMPLISHED BY WRITING A WILL?

For most people, there are a number of very good reasons for writing a will.

Two of the most important things which can be accomplished by a will are: (1) providing for guardians for young children; and (2) distributing the property in the ways most beneficial for a particular family.

1.   GUARDIANSHIPS

For any parent of a young child, the most important single reason for having a will is probably to spell out who is to raise the child—to be the child's guardian—if both parents of the child die before the child has become an adult. Naming a guardian is extremely important for the parents of any young child—whether the parents are wealth, poor, or somewhere in between.[3]

---

[2] The heirs of a decedent are determined by the statue in effect at the time the decedent dies—in the state in which the decedent is domiciled at the time of his or her death. Remember, that may well not be the same state in which the decedent lived for the majority of his or her life.

[3] In many states, it is possible to nominate a guardian without using a will—by complying with the applicable statutory provisions for nominating a guardian. Use of a will is generally preferable, however, because the will can also provide direction as to how the available money is to be allocated in raising the child.

When one parent of a child dies, the child's surviving parent automatically becomes the guardian of the child—regardless of which parent had custody of the child when one parent died.

Used with great care, in an appropriate situation, a will may provide an appropriate vehicle for alerting a court to the fact that the surviving parent would not be a fit person to raise the child—if there have been problems with child abuse, and the like.

In any case, the will of the last parent to die is the document to which the court will look in appointing a guardian for a minor child.

The guardian may be a relative, or just a good friend. The important thing is that the parents of any young child should specify who is to take over, if the parents are not around to raise the child.

SAMPLE ONE—WILL OF JOHN LENNON

The provisions naming the guardian may be simple or complex. In the Sixth paragraph of his will, John Lennon simply said:

> "I nominate, constitute and appoint my wife YOKO ONO, as the Guardian [sic] of the person and property of any children of the marriage who may survive me. In the event that she predeceases me, or for any reason she chooses not to act in that capacity, I nominate, constitute and appoint SAM GREEN to act in her place and stead."

SAMPLE TWO—WILL OF MARK ROTHKO

The American artist, mark Rothko, had an even more concise statement as to guardianship.

For his children, Rothko simply provided, in the Seventh article of his will:

> "In the event of the death of my wife or the simultaneous death of my wife and myself, I appoint as Guardians of my children, MR. and MRS. MORTON LEVINE, of New York."

If you happen to have read the Rothko case, you will have an appreciation for the problems involved with this appointment.[4] But even on its face, the Rothko appointment is insufficient.

First, what happens if either Mr. or Mrs. Levine has died before the death of Rothko? What if both of the Levine's survive Rothko, but then one of them dies a month later? Does Rothko then want the survivor to be the guardian alone? Or was Rothko interested in having his children raised in a two-parent environment?

In addition, what if Mr. and Mrs. Levine had gotten a divorce before Rothko died? Or were divorced after Rothko's death?

---

[4] See In re Rothko, 372 N.E. 2d 291 (1977). The court file for the Rothko will fills twelve filing cabinets—detailing the litigation involved when Rothko's daughter, Kate, decided to sue Morton Levine, among others, for improper administration of her father's estate. After Kate had secured a multimillion dollar judgment against Morton Levine, Levine might not have been an ideal guardian for Kate's younger brother, who was still a minor.

Which one of the Levines was then to raise the Rothko children? Could one child go with each of the Levine's? Or should the children be raised together?

What if both Levine's died in an auto accident the day before Rothko died, or the day after? Then who would raise the children?

Does Rothko have any particular concerns about how his children are to be raised? Are they to be encouraged to go to college? Are they to be encouraged to remain members of any particular religious faith? Are they to be encouraged to become self-supporting? Or are they expected simply to live off the millions of dollars in their father's estate?[5]

No one can accurately foresee the future. But a concerned parent could at least give some guidelines—some aspirations—for how his or her children should be raised.

2.   PROPERTY DISTRIBUTION

Another major reason to write a will is to control the distribution of property. As indicated above, if a person dies intestate, his or her property will simply be distributed to the closest relatives in accordance with the applicable statute. But it may well be that the pattern of intestate distribution provided by statute is not what your client would really like. If the statue for intestate distribution does not match your client's wishes, then your client should have a will.

Clients usually have two major goals for distribution of property. The first goal is simply to control ownership of the PROPERTY.

The second goal is frequently not enunciated by clients, but may be even more important to them than the mere control over ownership of property.

The second, frequently not enunciated, goal of a client may well be to try to CONTROL THE BEHAVIOR OF THE BENEFICIARIES—by means of distribution of property.
Samples illustrating implementation of each of these goals may be helpful.

---

[5] Actually, it is quite clear that Rothko did not expect his children to live off the millions of dollars in his estate. The only monetary gift in the will to the children is found in article FIFTH of the will, which states:

"In the event of the death of my wife or the simultaneous death of myself and my wife, I give, devise and bequeath the sum of Two Hundred Fifty Thousand ($250,000) Dollars together with the real property at 118 East 95th Street, New York, and all the contents thereof, in equal shares to my children, KATE and CHRISTOPHER."

SAMPLE THREE—WILL OF JACQUELINE KENNEDY ONASSIS

An example of a will provision simply controlling distribution of PROPERTY is found in the will of Jacqueline Kennedy Onassis.

In part C of the First article of her will, Mrs. Onassis simply provided:

> "I give and bequeath to my friend ALEXANDER D. FORGER, if he survives me, my copy of John F. Kennedy's Inaugural Address signed by Robert Frost if owned by me at the time of my death."

This gift was not made in an attempt to control the behavior of Alexander Forger in any way. The gift was simply a wonderful remembrance to a very close friend, and a way of controlling, by will, who would end up with ownership of a very special item of property.

By contrast, both Benjamin Franklin and Tennessee Williams were clearly attempting to CONTROL THE BEHAVIOR of beneficiaries by various provisions in their respective wills.

SAMPLE FOUR—WILL OF BENJAMIN FRANKLIN

Benjamin Franklin, in the fourth paragraph of his will, provided:

> "The King of France's Picture set with Four hundred and Eight Diamonds, I give to my Daughter Sarah Brache requesting however that she would not form any of those Diamonds into Ornaments either for herself or Daughters and thereby introduce or countenance the expensive vain and useless Fashion of wearing Jewels in this Country; and that those immediately connected with the Picture may be preserved with the same."

SAMPLE FIVE—WILL OF TENNESSEE WILLIAMS

The great American playwright, Tennessee Williams, in an attempt to control the behavior of his executors, and trustees, and through them the behavior of the ultimate beneficiaries of his will, provided, in Article VII of his will:

> "It is my wish that no play which I shall have written shall, for the purpose of presenting it as a first-class attraction on the English-speaking stage, be changed in any manner, whether such change shall be by way of completing it, or adding

to it, or deleting from it, or in any other way revising it, except for the customary type of stage directions. It is also my wish and will that no poem or literary work of mine be changed in any manner, whether such change shall be by way of completing such work or adding to it or deleting from it or in any other way revising it, except that any complete poem or other literary work of mine may be translated into a foreign language or dramatized for stage, screen or television. I expressly direct that neither my Executors nor my Trustees make or authorize the making of any changes prohibited in this Article VIII. To the extent that I can legally do so, no party who shall acquire any rights in any play, poem or literary work of mine shall have the right to make or authorize the making of any changes in any play, poem, or literary work of mine prohibited in this Article VIII."

This paragraph makes it very clear how Tennessee Williams intends to control both the use of the property, and the conduct of those who would benefit by various provisions of his will.

But could both Franklin and Williams have drafted stronger provisions? Yes. How about adding some penalties—if the wishes of the decedent are not respected? Should gifts to various beneficiaries be made CONTINGENT ON COMPLIANCE with the testator's instructions?

Techniques for doing such things will be discussed in the Pointers for Drafting which follow later in this chapter.

If your client really wants to control the behavior of beneficiaries there must be a system of enforcement—through bribes, or penalties, or both. Basically, a provision using a bribe would say to a beneficiary, "If you do this thing, prior to that time, you will get this property as a reward." A penalty provision, by contrast, might say, "You may have this property for your life, but if, during your life, you do the following act, then the property will be taken away from you, and given to another designated person." Certainly, bribes are easier to enforce than penalties. [It is easier to withhold property until a specific act has been completed, than it is to try to terminate ownership after possession has been transferred.]

In any case, unless the desired conduct would be against the law or against public policy, there is no legal barrier to prevent a testator from trying to use his or her property to try to control the behavior of the testator's friends and relatives—even after the testator has died.[6]

---

[6] One benefit of the common law Rule Against Perpetuities, discussed in Chapter 8, was to put an end to this attempt to control behavior from the grave—eventually.

And, of course, there is nothing to prevent the friends and relatives from simply walking away from the offered gift, and thus not allowing their behavior to be controlled by the decedent.

It is certainly your professional responsibility, as a lawyer, to discuss with your client the possible ramifications of trying to control behavior from the grave. Remember, however, that within the bounds of legality and public policy, it is the client's choice, not yours. And there may be times when a system of bribes or penalties might be entirely appropriate.

The following drafting exercise gives you a chance to try your hand at drafting a provision which might be an appropriate way for a parent to encourage his or her children to finish college.

As you begin doing your own drafting, you may want to check the Pointers for Drafting, which are immediately after the drafting exercise.

C. DRAFTING EXERCISE 1—PROVISIONS TO ENCOURAGE CHILDREN TO FINISH COLLEGE

Your client is a relatively young architect, who has just been diagnosed with cancer. She expects to survive, but is taking this opportunity to get her financial affairs in order, and has therefore come to you to help her write her first will.

Your client is married to a young social worker, who is an excellent father, but will never have a very high earning capacity. Your client and her husband have three young children, ages 8, 6 and 2, and may have one more child in the future—if everything goes well. So far, the children include two sons and a daughter.

Your client believes that if she should die early, her husband would be able to support the children until they are ready for college, but she would like to make sure that half of her own estate is set aside to help pay tuition and expenses for her children while they are in college. (The other half of her estate is to go directly to her husband.)

After discussing the matter, your client has decided that she wants the money which goes to her children to be used only to assist the children with college tuition and expenses. If a child does not go to college, that child is simply not to get a share of the money.

Your client realizes that it may sometimes be educationally beneficial—and financially necessary—for a child to take some time off—before or during college.

Draft a provision to be included in your client's will which would accomplish your client's goals as effectively as possible.

D.   POINTERS FOR DRAFTING

BACKGROUND

The best way for a person to maintain control over money after his or her death is to put the money into a TRUST—which is a separate fund to be managed by someone according to directions in the will. The person who manages the fund is called the TRUSTEE. Because you probably have not yet studied how to create a trust, just assume, for this exercise, that a trust has been properly established. Your job now is just tell the Trustee—the person who manages the trust—how to distribute the money.

SUGGESTIONS

1.   Which children are to be given shares of the money? Right now, your client has three children. But if all goes well, she may have one—or more—additional children. Then she may be so busy that she never takes time to come back and write another will. In any case, it is probably best, now, to write a provision which will include all of the children who may ever be born to your client. (See the next section for issues involving adoption).

2.   Once your client has decided which children are to share in the money, you can simply say that the trustee is to hold and manage the money for the benefit of those children.

3.   The next step is to tell the trustee when and how to distribute the money. In the fact situation of this problem, there already is a six year gap between the oldest child and the youngest child. And that gap may become larger, if there are more children. However, if your client dies before her children are old enough to go to college, and the trust therefore goes into effect, you will know the total number of children your client has had, and how many of them are still surviving, by the time the oldest is ready for college—at about age 17 or 18.

4.   Since you do not want to spend all of the money on the first child to go to college, it may be well to divide the money into shares when the first child is ready to start college—setting aside one share for each child who is alive when the first child starts college.

NOTE: The FIRST child to start college may turn out NOT to be the OLDEST child. The oldest child may decide not to attend college right away—or not to attend college at all. And it must always be remembered that people, including children, may die at unexpected times. So there is no need to divide the money prior to the time when SOME child must be given money for college. It will save trouble, in the end, not to set aside specific shares for specific children until necessary.

However, you DO need to draft some guidelines so that when the first child IS finally ready to start college, it will be clear how much money will be available for that child. So it is probably best to provide that the fund will be divided when the first college payment must be made.

5.   To make the drafting more complex, you could consider trying to vary the size of the shares to compensate for the facts that:

   (a) college tuition will probably increase almost every year—so that the last child to go to college may have considerably higher tuition expenses than the first child who attends college;

   (b) inflation may change the buying power of a dollar;

   (c) money which is being held for younger children in separate shares should be earning interest, and thus be increasing in value; and

   (d) children may select colleges which charge very different amounts of tuition—for example, private schools vs. state schools.

OR, you may just decide that all of the factors listed above will probably balance each other out, to some extent—so that simply setting aside one equal share for each child is sufficient.

6.   What sort of college education does your client have in mind? Only four year liberal arts programs accredited by one of various entities? Or junior colleges? Or technical colleges? Or art or music schools? Or auto mechanic training? Or ballet training? You will need to check this out with your client, and draft accordingly. (For now, you may just assume that your imaginary client has made whatever choices would seem best to you.)

7.   When, and under what conditions, is the money to be paid? When a student starts a semester? When a student completes a semester? With passing grades? With grades in the top 50%--or top 30% of the class?

If your client wants to have quite strict control, from the grave, over her children's college educations, she can go a long way toward doing so—simply by giving financial rewards only for relatively good grades, in particular kinds of courses—or in particular kinds of schools—or both.

Or, your client may want to allow her children great latitude in designing their own educations. (Again, you may just decide this issue for your imaginary client yourself—this time.)

8.   How long is a child to be allowed to drop out of school without losing eligibility for further payments? One year? Five years? Twenty years? Be sure to specify.

9.   Finally, what happens to the money which may be left in the fund—if some or all of the children simply do not go to college, for example? When should that money be distributed, and to whom? If the money is distributed to the children, should higher percentages be distributed to the children who have attended—or completed—college? Should the remaining money, instead of going to the children, be distributed to some favorite college or university?

WARNING: Be sure that the provisions you draft will ensure that the money is all distributed at least by the time all of the children have died. This is good policy just on the basis of common sense, and it will also help you to avoid drafting something which might violate the common law Rule Against Perpetuities—a very complex rule which will be studied in Chapter 8. For now, just be sure that all of the money will be paid—to persons or institutions—by the time all of your client's children die. And in most cases it will probably make sense to have a final distribution long before then.

E.   OMITTING CERTAIN RELATIVES

Sometimes a client, for various reasons, simply wants to omit certain relatives. Generally, with the exception of the surviving spouse, no person has a right to receive property from testator.[7] The property belongs to your client. Your client may distribute it in any way

---

[7] There are a few exceptions. In Vermont, for example, a child under 7, in some circumstances, has a claim against the parent's estate. See Title 14 Sec. 404 of Vermont statutes protecting a child under seven years. And, in Louisiana under C.C. Art. 1621, a child has some protection. A child can only be disowned if:

Art. 1621 Children, causes for disinherison by parents
The just causes for which parents may disinherit their children are twelve in number. There shall be a rebuttable
Presumption as to the facts set out in the act of disinherison to support these causes. These causes are, to wit:

1.   If the child has raised his or her hand to strike the parent, or if he or she has actually struck the parent; but a mere threat is not sufficient.
2.   If the child has been guilty, towards a parent, of cruelty, of a crime or grievous injury.
3.   If the child has attempted to take the life of either parent.

which seems appropriate to him or her—within the limits of the Rule Against Perpetuities, (discussed in Chapter 8), and matters of public policy. Subject to a few statutory modifications[8], a parent, for example, is NOT required to leave anything to a child—even a minor child. So your client need not provide for all of the children or relatives.

When omitting a child, however, it is important to state that the child is being intentionally omitted, so that the child cannot later claim that he or she was simply forgotten.[9]

That is the reason President Calvin Coolidge included the first six words in his remarkably short will, which read, in its entirety:

---

4. If the child has accused a parent of any capital crime, except, however, that of high treason.
5. If the child has refused sustenance to a parent, having means to afford it.
6. If the child has neglected to take care of a parent become insane.
7. If the child refused to ransom them, when detained in captivity.
8. If the child used an act of violence or coercion to hinder a parent from making a will.
9. If the child has refused to become security for a parent, having the means, in order to take him out of prison.
10. If the son or daughter, being a minor, marries without the consent of his or her parents.
11. If the child has been convicted of a felony for which the law provides that the punishment could be life imprisonment or death.
12. If the child has known how to contact the parent, but has failed without just cause to communicate with the parent for a period of two years after attaining the age of majority, except when the child is on active duty in any of the military forces of the United States.

[8] See Vermont and Louisiana, supra, for example.

[9] See, for example, the Uniform Probate Code as amended in 2006 which provides:

Section 2-302. Omitted Children.

(a) Except as provided in subsection (b), if a testator fails to provide in his or her will for any of his or her children born or adopted after the execution of the will, the omitted after-born or after-adopted child receives a share in the estate as follows:

    (1) If the testator had no child living when he or she executed the will, an omitted after-born or after-adopted child receives a share in the estate equal in value to that which the child would have received had the testator died intestate, unless the will devised all or substantially all of the estate to the other parent of the omitted child and that the other parent survives the testator and is entitled to take under the will.

    (2) If the testator had one or more children living when he or she executed the will, and the will devised property or an interest in property to one or more of the then-living children, an omitted after-born or after-adopted child is entitled to share in the testator's estate as follows:

        (i) The portion of the testator's estate in which the omitted after-born or after-adopted child is entitled to share is limited to devises make to the testator's then-living children under the will.

        (ii) The omitted after-born or after-adopted child is entitled to receive the share of the testator's estate, as limited in subparagraph (i), that the child would have received had the testator included all omitted after-born and after-adopted children with the children to whom devises were made under the will and had given an equal share of the estate to each child.

(b) Neither subsection (a)(1) or subsection (a)(2) applies if:

    (1) it appears from the will that the omission was intentional; or

    (2) the testator provided for the omitted after-born or after-adopted child by transfer outside the will and the intent that the transfer be in lieu of a testamentary provision is shown by the testator's statements or is reasonably inferred from the amount of the transfer or other evidence.

(c) If at the time of execution of the will the testator fails to provide in his or her will for a living child solely because he or she believes the child to be dead, the child is entitled to share in the estate as if the child were an omitted after-born or after-adopted child...

SAMPLE SIX—WILL OF CALVIN COOLIDGE

"The White House"

Washington

Will of Calvin Coolidge of Northampton,

Hampshire County, Massachusetts

Not unmindful of my son John, I give all my estate both real and personal to my wife Grace Coolidge, in fee simple. –Home at Washington, District of Columbia this twentieth day December, A.D. nineteen hundred and twenty six. /s/ Calvin Coolidge

SAMPLE SEVEN—WILL OF BENJAMIN FRANKLIN

Benjamin Franklin went into considerably more detail in his will, which contained the following provisions:

To my son William Franklin late Governor of the Jerseys I give and devise all the Lands I hold or have a right to in the Province of Nova Scotia, to hold to him his Heirs and Assigns forever. I also give to him all my books and papers which he has in his Possession and all Debts standing against him on my Account Books, willing that no Payment for nor Restitution of the same be required of him by my Executors. The part he acted against me in the late War which is of public Notoriety will account for my leaving him no more of an Estate he endeavored to deprive me of. [Emphasis added.]

SAMPLE EIGHT—WILL OF HENRY FONDA

Perhaps an appropriate middle-ground was found by Henry Fonda, in the THIRD article of his will, which stated:

I am providing primarily for my wife Shirlee, and my daughter Amy because they are dependent upon me for their support. I have made no provision in this Will for Jane or Peter, or for their families, solely because in my opinion they are financially independent, and my decision is not in any sense a measure of my deep affection for them.

Hopefully, the three preceding examples will be of some assistance to you in drafting appropriate provisions for your clients. Just remember: If your client wishes to omit a close relative, it is safest to include a specific statement to that effect in the will. Generally, it is NOT necessary to give an omitted child "one dollar." Just make it clear that omission of the child is intentional.

And be careful not to include any unnecessary details, which might form the basis for a suit for testamentary libel.[10]

F. WHO ARE THE RELATIVES? POSSIBLITITIES OF ADOPTION
1. INTRODUCTION

Thanks to the increasing, commendable, use and acceptance of adoption, it is important that the possibilities of adoption be considered virtually every time a will is drafted. Otherwise, the application of adoption statutes may cause unexpected and unwanted distribution of a client's property at death—as illustrated by the "What If" chart, included later in this chapter.

Adoption of children is the most common form of adoption. But in most states it is also possible to adopt an adult—of any age. To avoid undesired consequences, therefore, any client who writes a will in this day and age should include clear provisions regarding adoption.

A client cannot control who his or her various friends, relatives, and children may choose to adopt. But your client <u>can</u> determine the distribution of the client's own property—through appropriate provisions in the will.

Once you begin to analyze this matter, you will soon realize that the usual statement that, "an adopted person shall be considered the child of the adopting parent for all purposes," clearly is not sufficient for today's world.

Because each client feels differently about where the lines should be drawn on adoption, you will not be able to use any one, standard adoption clause for all of your clients. Instead, you must ascertain the wishes of each individual client, and then be sure that the client's will is drafted accordingly.

Generally, a client will want his or her own adopted children to be treated equally with the client's biological children. But even this may not be true if your client has adopted step-children. If step-children are involved, does your client want the step-children to receive the same share of the estate as the biological children—<u>even if there later is a divorce, and your client parts company with both the ex-spouse and the step-children?</u>

Remember, statutes <u>may</u> terminate the rights of an <u>ex-spouse</u> to take under provisions of a will when there is a divorce, but such statutes will almost certainly not affect the right of <u>adopted children</u> or <u>step-children</u> who were mentioned in a will. And most people, in the midst of

---

[10] See <u>Brown v. DuFrey</u>, 134 N. E.2d 469 (1956) in which an ex-husband recovered roughly half the estate as damages for testamentary libel because of the statements his ex-wife had made about him in her will.

divorce, simply do not have the time or emotional energy to rewrite their wills. So each will must be drafted to cover as many possible contingencies as practical—including the possible effects of divorce on gifts to adopted children or step-children.

So the first level of inquiry should be designed to ascertain what the client wants to do about gifts to any children or step-children he or she may have adopted, (or may be planning to adopt in the future).

The next level of inquiry is considerably more difficult: to find out what the client wants to do about persons the client's children, (or other friends or relatives), may adopt.

It is quite frequent in wills that clients try to provide for their grandchildren. Or people may leave property, "to my issue, by representation"—which may include descendants of various degrees, including children, grandchildren, great-grandchildren, and so forth. It is important to find out if your client wants to have the terms "grandchildren," or "issue," for example, include more than just your client's own biological grandchildren or issue.

Remember, on matters like this it must be your <u>client's</u> choice, not yours. So it simply is not fair to your client to include a standard adoption clause without first discussing the matter in some detail.

If your client wants to include more than just biological grandchildren, you must ascertain exactly where the client would draw the lines on the "What If" chart. Then you must draft accordingly.

Frequently, a client will want provisions excluding persons who were adopted as adults. Or it may be that your client believes that his or her own children should be permitted to determine for themselves which persons shall be added to the family tree as "grandchildren."

Be especially careful, however, if each grandchild is ultimately to be given an equal share—or if distribution is to be made, "to my issue, by representation." For example, if it happened that after your client died your client's son, A, adopted ten of his best friends, this could be quite unfortunate for the two biological children of your client's other son, B—if all twelve of the "grandchildren" are eventually to take equal shares in a limited fund. So the possibility of unusual adoptions must be appropriately handled by you though clear drafting.

Where adult adoptions are possible, as they are in most states, especially careful drafting is necessary to insure that the goals of your client are accomplished.

The "What if" chart that follows illustrates some of the perhaps unexpected results which may occur because of adoption.

After reading the chart, you may more clearly understand why appropriate drafting is MANDATORY on the issue of adoption!

2. "WHAT IF" CHART-FOR ADOPTIONS

CLIENT

Ann	Bob	Cindy
[biological child]	[biological child]	[adopted child]
		Jeff
		[1]

Dora	Ed	Fran	George	Harry	Isabel
[2]	[3]	[4]	[5]	[6]	[7]

WHAT IF:

1. Jeff is Cindy's HUSBAND, who was adopted by Cindy to try to get a larger part of the estate for her family. (See Minary v. Citizens Bank, 419 S.W.2nd 340 (1967)).

2. Dora was adopted by Ann when she was 3—and is a dutiful, charming grand-daughter.

3. Ed, Ann's step-child, was adopted by Ann when Ed was 15, and Ann was married to Ed's father, Paul. Later Paul divorced Ann in a bitter divorce, quickly married Rhonda, and moved away, taking Ed. Thereafter Ed refused to have anything to do with Ann or any of Ann's relatives.

4. Fran is the child of Ann and Paul, who was adopted by Paul's sister, Teresa, when both Ann and Paul died unexpectedly. (See Hall v. Vallandingham, 540 A.2nd 1162 (1988)).

5. George is Bob's long-time lover, who was adopted by Bob when both Bob and George were 35 years old.

6. Harry is Cindy's biological child.

7. Isabel is Cindy's younger half-sister, who was adopted by Cindy when Isabel was 14 and both of Isabel's natural parents died.

RESULT: If the client's will simply provides that "an adopted person shall be considered the child of the adopting parent for all purposes," then a gift by the client, "to my grandchildren in equal shares," will be shared equally by:

JEFF, DORA, ED, GEORGE, HARRY, and ISABEL—only ONE of whom is a biological grandchild of the client!

FRAN, a biological grandchild of the client will probably be OMITTED, because she has now been adopted into a new family! This is very unlikely to be the distribution the client had in mind.

SAMPLE NINE—WILL OF JOHN WAYNE

Recognizing some of the problems suggested by the preceding "What If" Chart, John Wayne, in Article TWELFTH, Paragraph 5 of his will, included the following provision:

"As used in this will, the term "issue" shall refer to lineal descendants of all degrees, and the terms "child," "children," and "issue" shall include persons adopted before attaining the age of ten (10) years; provided, however, the term "issue" shall include a child born out of wedlock to a male issue of mine only if the male parent who is my issue shall have (i) openly held such child out as his natural child after receiving such child into his home as a permanent resident thereof, or (ii) acknowledged such child as his child by a written instrument delivered to the trustees."

After reading this sample, and considering the "What If" chart which precedes the sample, you may now want to try your hand at drafting an adoption provision for the situation described in Drafting Exercise 2, which follows. The Pointers for Drafting, following the exercise, may assist you in drafting your own provision.

G.   DRAFTING EXERCISE 2—INCLUDING CHILDREN ADOPTED AS
        MINORS: EXCLUDING ADOPTED SPOUSES AND LOVERS

Your client has decided that she wants all adopted children and grandchildren to be included in her will equally with biological children and grandchildren—"As long as they really are adopted as children—you know what I mean?"

She does not simply what to exclude children who are adopted after a certain age because, for example, she thinks that her son may decide to adopt his three step-children, ages 13, 12 and 8, if the natural father of the step-children ever gives his consent—or dies.

Your client is horrified that any of her descendants might ever try to adopt a spouse or lover, and definitely wants to prevent such an adoption from making it possible for an adopted spouse or lover to share in your client's estate.

On the other hand, your client feels that if any of her biological grandchildren should ever be adopted by a step-parent—or anyone else—that such adoption should definitely NOT prevent a biological grandchild from sharing in the property your client wishes to leave to all of her grandchildren. As far as your client is concerned, her biological grandchildren, (and great-grandchildren), will always be members of her family—no matter who happens to adopt them or raise them.

Currently, your client has three adult children, who are all her biological children; plus two darling little grandchildren, who are both the biological children of your client's daughter. Your client hopes and expects that more biological grandchildren and great-grandchildren will be born into her family in the coming years, and she would be happy to accept adopted grandchildren and great-grandchildren—again, "as long as they really are adopted as children."

As you begin drafting this provision you may want to check the Pointers for Drafting which follow.

H.   POINTERS FOR DRAFTING

1.   First, clearly identify who your client wants to include—or exclude.

2.   Next, clearly specify which persons are to be INCLUDED in the provisions of the will— using illustrations and examples, if appropriate. Do not be afraid to include detailed provisions—as long as they are consistent with each other. But do not try to get six different ideas into one sentence. Remember that clarity is crucial.

3.   Specify clearly which adopted persons are to be EXCLUDED from sharing in any property distributed under the will. Again, illustrations and examples may be appropriate.

4.   Remember that your client's will may be controlling the distribution not only of your client's own property, but also property over which your client may have been given a POWER OF APPOINTMENT[11] by another person's will or trust. For example, your client's husband may have given your client something called a general testamentary POWER OF APPOINTMENT. That would give your client, by her will, the power to specify who is to get various items of property which were included in her husband's

---

[11] Powers of appointment are discussed in Chapter 7.

estate or trust. So the definitions included in your client's will should apply to ANY property distributed by your client's will—regardless of the source of that property.[12]

5.   Avoid tying your definitions regarding adoption to particular state statutes.[13] The statutes may be changed—before or after the death of your client. And, as you would guess, adoption statutes vary from state to state.[14] Simply write whatever definitions you need into your client's own will.

6.   Check your drafting against the "What If" chart included at Section A of this chapter. Are all of the possibilities illustrated on the chart covered in a way which is consistent with your client's wishes?

7.   Are the biological children and grandchildren properly included? What happens if a biological child or grandchild is later adopted into another family? Have you made it clear that such an adopted biological child or grandchild is still to share in your client's estate?

8.   Check your drafting for clarity and consistency. Will EVERY reader clearly understand which adopted persons are to be included, and which adopted persons are to be excluded? Are all of the provisions you have drafted consistent with each other—and with the wishes of your client?

---

[12] If there is a definition of adoption in the instrument which created the power of appointment, that definition should, of course, prevail for the appointive property.

[13] Specific existing statutes may be used if an existing statute of a specific state is specified. For example, it would be effective to tie your definitions to "the statutes of Texas in effect at the time I sign this will," if those statutes clearly and completely satisfied the wishes of the particular client.

[14] Compare, for example, the adoption statutes of California, and Texas set forth below.

California Probate Code Sec. 6451 (added 1993).
Sec. 6451. Adoption
(a) An adoption severs the relationship of parent and child between an adopted person and a natural parent of the adopted person unless both of the following requirements are satisfied:
(1) The natural parent and the adopted person lived together at any time as parent and child, or the natural parent was married to or cohabitating with the other natural parent at the time the person was conceived and died before the person's birth.
(2) The adoption was by the spouse of either of the natural parents after the death of either of the natural parents.
(b) Neither a natural parent nor a relative of a natural parent, except for a whole blood brother or sister of the adopted person or the issue of that brother or sister, inherits from or through the adopted person on the basis of a parent and child relationship between the adopted person and the natural parent that satisfies the requirements of paragraphs (1) and (2) of subdivision (a), unless the adoption is by the spouse or surviving spouse of that parent.
(c) For the purpose of this section, a prior adoptive parent and child relationship is treated as a natural parent and child relationship.

Texas Statutes
Sec. 16.55. Effect of Adoption Decree
On entry of the decree of adoption, the adopted adult is the son or daughter of the adoptive parents for all purposes and of the natural parents for inheritance purposes only. However, the natural parents may not inherit from or through the adopted adults.
[Emphasis added.] As amended, 1975.

CONCLUSION

Now, having ascertained the wishes of your client as to the basic distribution of his or her property, it is important to insure that you have some means of demonstrating that your client has sufficient mental capacity to execute a will. That issue will be discussed in Chapter 2.

CHAPTER 2.   CAPACITY TO MAKE A WILL

INTRODUCTION

Once it has been determined that a client NEEDS a will, the next step is to ascertain whether or not the client has the necessary testamentary capacity, (mental capacity), to make a will. Usually this is easy.

All that is required for testamentary capacity is that the client be able to comprehend "the natural objects of her bounty"; the general extent of her property; and the way in which the will affects the general distribution of her property. Usually five minutes of normal conversation will be sufficient to assure you that a client has sufficient testamentary capacity to make a will.[1]

In a few situations, however, testamentary capacity may become a real issue. Sometimes when a person is very elderly, or very sick, the person may no longer have sufficient testamentary capacity to write a will. REMEMBER: Age and illness do NOT, per se, have any effect on testamentary capacity![2] But with people who are elderly, or ill, it is wise to be especially careful about testamentary capacity.

You, as the lawyer, are the one ultimately responsible for making the call on testamentary capacity. If you do not believe that your client has sufficient testamentary capacity to write a will, then you simply CANNOT draft the will.

(As you make this call, it may help to picture yourself in front it of a judge, somewhere down the line, describing the situation, and explaining why you believed that there was—or was not—sufficient testamentary capacity.)

If it is your decision that the client HAS sufficient mental capacity, but that others might possibly disagree, then you must be sure to document the basis for your belief in the client's testamentary capacity—as described later, in the Pointers for Drafting.

---

[1] No specific questions are necessary. Just be sure that your client is reacting to normal conversation in a normal way. If your client, however, like Russell Edward Herman, a carpenter from Illinois, begins to make casual bequests such as $2.41 billion for national forests...$6 trillion to the Federal Reserve Board to pay off the national debt... and $6 trillion to the U.S. Treasury to get the country back on track, [The Denver Post, 7/10/95], serious investigation of testamentary capacity is mandatory—or a guarantee that the relatives all have a good sense of humor!

[2] State statutes, of course, specify a MINIMUM age a person must reach—usually 18 or 21—before being allowed to write a will. And severe mental illness of various kinds might well be deemed to be sufficient to prevent a person from having the requisite mental capacity. However, just because a person has unusual religious beliefs, unusual beliefs in the supernatural, etc. does NOT mean that the person lacks sufficient testamentary capacity to write a will.

Occasionally, the issue of testamentary capacity simply is a very close question. In that case, if the client has a previous will, parts of which would remain the same in a new document, then it is probably safest just to put the new provisions into a CODICIL, (an amendment), to the old will, instead of risking having the client sign an entirely new will.

The advantage of using a codicil, rather than a new will, is that if a court finally holds that the client did <u>not</u> have testamentary capacity at the time the <u>codicil</u> was signed, then only the <u>codicil</u> fails—and the prior <u>will</u> still remains good.

So remember, when there may be a question of testamentary capacity you have three choices: (1) Do not write the will; (2) Write the will, being careful to document the testamentary capacity; or (3) Use a codicil.

A.   UNDUE INFLUENCE

One of the most subtle factors which may prevent a client from having the necessary testamentary capacity to execute an effective will, or portion of a will, is called undue influence. Undue influence may be asserted over anyone, but it is more likely to be found with people who are elderly or very ill. Undue influence occurs when some "outsider" has so much influence over the client that the will or a portion thereof is really the product of the "OUTSIDER'S" choices—not the choices made freely by the client.

In such a case, the will, (or affected portion), although properly executed, will be held to be INEFFECTIVE, to the extent that it was the product of undue influence exercised by an "outsider."

Note that the "outsider" described here is usually, in fact, a very close friend or relative of the client's, the client's caregiver,—or even the client's priest, rabbi, minister, or attorney.[3]

The "outsider" is usually the person who is in the closest contact with the client at the time the client is writing the will. The "outsider" may well be the person who is taking care of the client's physical needs—who is living with the client in the client's home, or who is allowing the client to live in the "outsider's" home.

---

[3] On April 3, 2009 jury selection began in a highly publicized criminal trial involving a codicil added to the will of philanthropist Brooke Astor, two years before her death at the age of 105. Brooke Astor's only child, Anthony Marshall, (age 84) was charged with grand larceny, (carrying a penalty of up to 25 years in jail), and attorney Francis Morrison, Jr. (age 67) was charged with forgery, (carrying a penalty of up to 7 years in jail), because of allegations that the two conspired to add a codicil to Brooke Astor's will two years before her death, while she was suffering from Alzheimer's disease. The disputed codicil was designed to give the son huge financial benefits from his mother's estate.

So the basic issue usually is: Was the will the result of appropriate gratitude or affection felt by the client toward the "outsider," (making the will valid); or did the "outsider" exercise undue influence over the client, (making the will void to the extent that it was the product of such undue influence)?

Every time you write a will you must first check for the possibility of undue influence.

To give you a better appreciation for the difficulties involved with the issue of undue influence, the following section describes the factors which led to ALLEGATIONS of undue influence regarding the will and codicils of the highly respected artist, Georgia O'Keeffe.

As you read through the materials which follow try to figure out how you, as a lawyer, would handle a similar situation. Part C of this chapter gives you an opportunity to practice appropriate drafting for a situation in which undue influence may be suspected.

B.   PROBLEM OF UNDUE INFLUENCE—GOERGIA O'KEEFFE

After the death of the great American artist, Georgia O'Keeffe, there was considerable controversy over whether some of her testamentary dispositions, particularly those in the Second Codicil, reflected her true wishes, or were instead the result of undue influence by her close friend, John Bruce Hamilton.

Hamilton, also known as Juan Hamilton, was 59 years younger than Georgia O'Keeffe, and had met her in 1973 when he was a recently divorced, poor young artist, working at a nearby ranch.[4]

According to the biography, Georgia O'Keeffe, by Roxana Robinson,[5] O'Keeffe first met Hamilton in 1973 when he knocked on the door of O'Keeffe's house in New Mexico, looking for work. That day O'Keeffe had him crate up a painting for shipment, and thereafter had him do other odd jobs around the house for her, on occasion.

Eventually, Hamilton began to play a larger and larger role in O'Keeffe's life—driving her to appointments, traveling with her, representing her in business dealing, living in her house, and being her companion until her death in 1986.

---

[4] Robinson, Roxana, Georgia O'Keeffe—A Life, Harper & Row, 1989 pp. 523-525.

[5] The background facts for this section are based primarily on Georgia O'Keeffe—A Life, copyright 1989 by Roxana Robinson. Pages 523-560 deal particularly with this aspect of Georgia O'Keeffe's life.

In 1980 Hamilton married a woman his own age, had two children, cared for his family, but also continued to take care of Georgia O'Keeffe.

At one point Hamilton allegedly made each of Georgia O'Keeffe's household servants sign a statement promising never to talk about anything which went on in the house. And it was claimed that Hamilton made it very difficult for friends and relatives of Georgia O'Keeffe's to see her – if Hamilton did not like them. Other friends, whom Hamilton did like, seemed to have had no difficulty in getting in to see O'Keeffe.

O'Keeffe signed a will on August 22, 1979, giving considerable property and influence to Hamilton. On November 2, 1983, and again on August 8, 1984, O'Keeffe added codicils to her will—each time giving Hamilton more property and more control.

When the second codicil was signed, on August 8, 1984, essentially giving full control of the estate to Hamilton, Georgia O'Keeffe was 96 years old, nearly deaf, and essentially blind.

The second codicil, unlike her previous will and codicil, contained a "no-contest" clause – saying that anyone who contested the will or codicils would forfeit any gifts made under the will or codicils – and would receive only $1.

At least one person who was asked to serve as a witness for the Second Codicil refused to do so. According to a biography of O'Keeffe,[6] Judge Oliver Seth, who had been a witness on O'Keeffe's 1979 will, and who had supervised the execution of her First Codicil, in 1983, came to Georgia O'Keeffe's house on the day in 1984 when the second codicil was to be signed. After observing the situation, however, Judge Seth decided not to be part of the execution of the second codicil—and left the house.

At least two witnesses who signed the second codicil, however, were people who had been friends of Georgia O'Keeffe's for thirty years.[7]

Approximately one and a half years after signing the second codicil, Georgia O'Keeffe died—at the age of 98. She had continued to live in the same house as Juan Hamilton and his family until her death.[8]

Because of the great fame—and wealth—of Georgia O'Keeffe, the litigation over her estate received substantial publicity. Most people, of course, are neither as wealthy nor as famous a

---

[6] Id., pp. 549-550

[7] Robinson, supra, at 550.

[8] Actually, O'Keeffe died in the hospital in Santa Fe, New Mexico, while Juan and his family were on vacation in Mexico. But until the day before her death she had lived in the home shared with Juan's family, and had had a nurse constantly in attendance until the end. Id., p. 550.

Georgia O'Keeffe. Yet the factors which suggest the possibility of undue influence in the O'Keeffe case; possible SUSCEPTIBILITY of the testatrix, OPPORTUNITY for the "outsider" to exercise undue influence, and SIGNIFICANT GIFTS TO THE "OUTSIDER," are present in a great many situations.

It is not the least bit unusual for an elderly person to become more and more dependent on the assistance and companionship of a younger person—and then to give that younger person a larger share of the estate than seems appropriate to other friends and relatives.

The favored younger person may be a nurse, housekeeper, minister, priest, rabbi, relative or friend. Sometimes the younger person is simply a con-man (or woman). Sometimes the younger person is nearly a saint. Usually, of course, the truth is somewhere in between. And as with many other situations, it may be nearly impossible to establish what the true motivations were of the people involved—especially since motivations and attitudes of individuals normally are constantly changing.

As you analyze the following excerpts from the will and codicils of Georgia O'Keeffe, try to decide how you, as a judge, would rule on the issue of undue influence if you had to base your decisions only on the documents themselves—combined with the few bits of personal information mentioned above.

Also try to determine what you would do if you, as a lawyer, were called by Juan Hamilton[9] to come to Georgia O'Keeffe's house to draft a new codicil for her, along the lines of the Second Codicil.

What would you do to try to ascertain whether or not Juan Hamilton was exercising undue influence over Georgia O'Keeffe? What would you do if you felt that he probably WAS exercising undue influence?

What would you do if you felt that the codicil truly did reflect the wishes of Georgia O'Keeffe? What steps might you take to decrease the likelihood of litigation over the validity of the Second Codicil?

---

[9] The fact that the <u>client</u> does not call to make the appointment should immediately alert you to the <u>possibility</u> of undue influence.

C.   RECOGNIZING AND PREVENTING UNDUE INFLUENCE—WILL AND CODICILS OF GEORGIA O'KEEFFE

The following materials include parts of the will and codicils of Georgia O'Keeffe. As is usual, the will is much longer than the codicils. All three of the documents are well worth reading—not only for the human interest involved, but also as examples of how various situations were handled in a real will and codicil. And remember that for an issue of undue influence, you must look at a variety of surrounding factors. You will find the full text of Georgia O'Keeffe's will and codicils in the Appendix.

As you read the segments which follow, circle, (or at least notice), which provisions might have suggested the possibility of undue influence. Then, try to figure out how you might have drafted the documents more effectively—particularly the Second Codicil.

Was the increasing power of John Bruce Hamilton the natural result of increasingly closer ties between O'Keeffe and Hamilton—or the result of undue influence?

"LAST WILL AND TESTAMENT

OF

GEORGIA O'KEEFFE"

I, GEORGIA O'KEEFFE, residing in Abiquiu, County of Rio Arriba, State of New Mexico, do hereby make, publish and declare this to be my Last Will and Testament, hereby revoking all Wills and Codicils heretofore made by me.

[Paragraphs FIRST, SECOND AND THIRD, dealing with debts, taxes and gifts to employees are omitted.]

FOURTH: I hereby forgive and cancel any outstanding balance of the indebtedness in the amount of Thirty Thousand ($30,000) Dollars evidenced by the Promissory Note executed by RODALITA AND JOHNNY JARAMILLO in my favor along with any interest thereon. I also forgive and cancel any and all indebtedness owed to me at the time of my death by JOHN BRUCE HAMILTON along with any interest thereon...

FIFTH: I give all my right, title and interest in and to my real property located in Abiquiu, New Mexico .... to either the NATIONAL PARK SERVICE or the NATIONAL TRUST FOR HISTORIC PRESERVATION IN THE UNITED STATES, ... as my Executor, in his sole and absolute discretion shall select. ...

SIXTH: I give all my right, title and interest to my ranch, consisting of a house and acreage located outside of Abiquiu .... to my friend, JOHN BRUCE HAMILTON, or if he does not survive me, to THE UNITED PRESBYTERIAN CHURCH IN THE UNITED STATES OF AMERICA. ...

SEVENTH: If my friend, JOHN BRUCE HAMILTON, shall survive me and qualify as Executor of my estate, I give him the following works of art created by me:
   A. Any six (6) works of art from among my oil paintings on canvas.
   B. Any fifteen (15) works of art from among my drawings and/or water colors and/or pastels.
   C. Notwithstanding the foregoing, JOHN BRUCE HAMILTON, shall make his selection from works of art other than those specifically bequeathed elsewhere in this my Will or any Codicil thereto.

EIGHTH: I give the following works of art created by me, if they are owned by me at the time of my death, as follows:

   ... (careful description of 53 different painting, to go to 8 different museums.   See Chapter 7 for a sample of these bequests.) ....

   J. Notwithstanding the foregoing, I authorize and direct my Executor in his sole and absolute discretion to cancel the bequest of any or all of the works of art bequeathed to any one or more organizations named in this Article EIGHTH and/or to substitute different works of art crated by me for the ones designated herein ....[10]

NINTH: All other works of art created by me, other than those specifically bequeathed in this my Will and other than those which must be sold by my Executor to defray the cost of taxes and administration .... shall be given to such charitable organizations or institutions as shall be selected by my Executor ....[11] I direct my Executor to include the UNIVERSITY OF NEW MEXICO and the MUSEUM OF NEW MEXICO, MUSEUM OF FINE ARTS .... Provided

---

[10] This is an extremely broad power of appointment in her executor, Juan Hamilton, to revise completely the careful list which Georgia O'Keeffe had made. It is easy to see why no art museum was likely to do anything which might annoy Juan Hamilton while he had such power.

[11] This is an example of a SPECIAL INTER VIVOS POWER OF APPOINTMENT. Juan, or whoever is the Executor, is given authority by this provision to appoint various works of art to a SPECIAL group of beneficiaries—charitable institutions of his choice. Since Juan could NOT appoint the works of art to himself, under this provision, or to his own estate, his own creditors, or the creditors of his estate, this is considered to be a SPECIAL power—which can be exercised on behalf of only the institutions included in the description. It is an INTER VIVOS power because Juan, or any other Executor, is expected to exercise the power while he or she is alive. Whether a power is INTER VIVOS or TESTAMENTARY is determined by how it is to be EXERCISED—not the kind of document in which it is created.

such institutions are willing to comply with the conditions and restrictions which my Executor may impose in accordance with Article TENTH below.[12]

TENTH: I specifically authorize my Executor to impose any conditions or restrictions ...relating to the manner and frequency of the exhibition of the works of arts so bequeathed as well as any other matters related to such works of art ...

ELEVENTH: [Gift of specific photographs to the National Gallery.]

TWELFTH: A. I give all of my letters, personal correspondence and clippings to YALE UNIVERSITY ....
>   B. I give all of the rest of my writings and papers, together with all copyrights thereon and rights of publication thereto to JOHN BRUCE HAMILTON. If he does not survive me, I give the same to YALE UNIVERSITY.

THIRTEENTH: I give all photographs .... not otherwise specifically bequeathed herein, to such charitable organizations or institutions as shall be selected by my Executor ...

FOURTEENTH: A. I give ... all of the balance of my tangible personal property, including any works of art not created by me which are not otherwise specifically bequeathed, to JOHN BRUCE HAMILTON, if he survives me.
>   B. I give to JOHN BRUCE HAMILTON, if he survives me, all of my ... copyrights and ... royalties ....

FIFTEENTH: [expenses of administration]

SIXTEENTH: All the rest, residue and remainder of my estate ... I give to such charitable organization or institution as shall be selected by my Executor ....

SEVENTEENTH:
>   A. I appoint JOHN BRUCE HAMILTON as Executor under this my Will. If JOHN BRUCE HAMILTON fails to qualify or ceases to act, I appoint GERALD DICKLER .... [who was the attorney who supervised the execution of the Second Codicil] ... to act as Executor in his place.
>   B. I direct that JOHN BRUCE HAMILTON shall not be entitled to any commission or other compensation for his services as Executor, notwithstanding the existence of any statute to

---

[12] Evidently, Georgia O'Keeffe had had a running battle with these two New Mexico institutions, both of which had been reluctant to display her paintings –and had been even more reluctant to display any of the pottery which Juan Hamilton created. Again, a provision like this gives tremendous power to an executor—who is charged with distributing a multi-million dollar estate. Robinson, supra., at 531, 547.

the contrary.[13] The bequests made to him in Article SEVENTH are in lieu of all compensations or commissions to which he would otherwise be entitled as Executor.

If JOHN BRUCE HAMILTON fails to qualify or ceases to act as Executor … I direct that his successor … shall be paid a fee of Two Hundred Thousand ($200,000) Dollars for his or her services as Executor and shall not be entitled to any other commission ….[14]

[Paragraphs EIGHTEENTH, NINETEENTH and TWENTIETH dealing with powers of the Executor, and the like, are omitted.]

IN WITNESS WHEREOF, I have hereunto set my hand this 22 day of August, 1979.

Georgia O'Keeffe"

[Witnesses: Louise Talbot Trigg; Jean M. Seth; Adam Seth]
Approximately four years later, Georgia O'Keeffe signed her First Codicil, which follows.

"FIRST CODICIL TO LAST WILL AND TESTAMENT OF GEORGIA O'KEEFFE"

I, GEORGIA O'KEEFFE, residing in Abiquiu, County of Rio Arriba, State of New Mexico, do hereby make, publish and declare this to be the First Codicil to my Last Will and Testament dated August 22, 1979.

FIRST: I hereby revoke Article FIFTH[15] of my said Will and add a new Article FIFTH to read as follows:

FIFTH: I give all my right … to my real property located in Abiquiu … to such charitable organization. … as shall be selected by my Executor …

SECOND: I hereby revoke Article SEVENTH[16] of my said Will and add a new Article SEVENTH to read as follows:

---

[13] Note that a GIFT to Juan, under current tax law would not cause any tax consequences for Juan, while any Executor's commissions paid to him would be taxable as income to Juan. On the other hand, Georgia O'Keeffe's estate could have taken a deduction on either the estate tax or the estate's income tax return for commissions paid to an executor. There would be no tax deduction available for Georgia O'Keeffe's estate for gifts to an individual who was not her spouse, --as opposed to gifts to a charity or to a surviving spouse, which would have been deductible. So this provision makes things somewhat better for Juan financially, and somewhat worse for the estate.

[14] The New Mexico statute at the time (Sec. 43-3.719) would have allowed an executor's commission of roughly 5% of the estate or approximately $2.5 million on a $50 million estate. It seemed consistent throughout Georgia O'Keeffe's will and codicils that she did not want any significant part of her estate going for executor's commissions. Compare this to the $7.9 million awarded April 20, 1995 to the lawyers for Andy Warhol's estate—estimated to be enough to have paid them at the rate of about $2,400 per hour. [The New York Times, April 21, 1995.] Interesting stories of the administration of Andy Warhol's estate are included in Death and Disaster: The Rise of the Warhol Empire and the Race for Andy's Millions, by Paul Alexander, Villard Books, 1994.

[15] Giving her house and land in Abiquiu, New Mexico to the National Park Service or the National Trust for Historic Places.

SEVENTH: If my friend, JOHN BRUCE HAMILTON, shall survive me, I give him the following works of art created by me regardless of whether he qualifies and serves as Executor of my estate:

A. Any six (6) works of art from among my oil paintings on canvas.

B. Any fifteen (15) works of art from among my drawings and/or water colors and/or pastels.

C. Notwithstanding the foregoing, JOHN BRUCE HAMILTON shall make his selection from works of art other than those specifically bequeathed elsewhere in this my Will or any Codicil thereto.

THIRD: I hereby revoke Article SEVENTEENTH paragraph B[17] and add a new Article SEVENTEENTH, paragraph B to read as follows:

C. I direct that JOHN BRUCE HAMILTON shall be paid a fee of Two Hundred Thousand ($200,000) Dollars for his services as Executor and shall—t [sic][18] be entitled to any other commission or compensation for said services, notwithstanding the existence of any statue to the contrary.

If JOHN BRUCE HAMILTON fails to qualify or ceases to act as Executor for any reason whatsoever, I direct that his successor, whether named herein or otherwise appointed, shall be paid a fee of Two Hundred Thousand ($200,000)[19] Dollars for his or her services as Executor and shall not be entitled to any other commissions or compensation for said services, notwithstanding the existence of any statute to the contrary.

FOURTH: As thus amended, I hereby ratify, confirm, redeclare and republish my said Will.

IN WITNESS WHEREOF, I, GEORGIA O'KEEFFE, have hereunto subscribed my name and affixed my seal this 2 day of November, 1983.

---

[16] Giving Juan his choice of 6 oil paintings and 15 drawings or water colors ONLY if he survived Georgia O'Keeffe and qualified as Executor of her estate.

[17] Gift of paintings instead of commission.

[18] On the certified copy of the will this looks very much as if the word "not" had been eliminated—or almost eliminate—by the use of white-out at this place! If the matter had gone to litigation that would have raised <u>serious</u> problems! Was the white-out applied before or after Georgia O'Keeffe signed the codicil?! With an estate the size of Georgia O'Keeffe's the presence—or absence—of the word "not" would have made a difference of several million dollars! [See fn.14, supra.] This clearly illustrates why corrections should NEVER be made in this way on a will! Unless you are in a true emergency situation, HAVE THE WILL RE-TYPED. Even if there IS a true emergency, <u>always</u> take time to have the testator and all of the witnesses put their initials next to the changes made on the will. Or better yet, do a one paragraph <u>CODICIL</u> to make the changes!

[19] Note that an executor <u>other</u> than John is still limited to a fee of $200,000. That would have given John a strong argument that there <u>was</u> supposed to be a difference in the fees paid to him or to others—and that the partially eliminated "not" [if that's what it was], was simply a typist's error. In that case, the lonely "t" would have clearly been chargeable to the LAWYER for letting an incorrect document get to Georgia O'Keeffe for signing!

GEORGIA O'KEEFFE"

The foregoing instrument was executed by the Testatrix and witnessed by each of the undersigned affiants under the supervision of Oliver Seth, an attorney-at-law. [Witnesses: Laurel Seth; Cynthia Black; Mark Dawson Jamison;]

Now, as you read the second codicil, remember that <u>this</u> is the document which was particularly claimed to be the product of undue influence. What is it that makes this document seem so much more "suspect" than the preceding documents?

"SECOND CODICIL TO LAST WILL AND TESTAMENT OF GIEROGIA O'KEEFFE"[20]

I, GEORGIA O'KEEFFE, hereby make, publish and declare this to be the Second Codicil to my last Will and Testament executed by me on August 11, [sic][21] 1979.

FIRST: Paragraph J. of Article EIGHTH is hereby revoked in its entirety.[22]

SECOND: Article NINTH is hereby revoked in its entirety.[23]

THIRD: Article TENTH is hereby re-designated as Article NINTH and the reference therein to Article NINTH is deleted.[24]

FOURTH: Article ELEVENTH is hereby re-designated as Article TENTH.

FIFTH: Article TWELFTH is hereby re-designated as Article ELEVENTH and paragraph B thereof is hereby deleted in its entirety.[25]

SIXTH: Article THIRTEENTH is hereby re-designated as Article TWELFTH.

SEVENTH: Article FOURTEENTH[26] is hereby deleted in its entirety.

---

[20] See complete text in Appendix.

[21] The original will was executed on August <u>22</u>, 1979, NOT August <u>11</u>th—according to the attestation clause, notary clause, and text of the original will. So using the date of August <u>11</u>th was probably just a typo. But serious problems could arise because of an error like this—with people wondering if there had in fact been an August 11th will—and wondering if this codicil were really intended for the August 22nd will, when it stated that it was a codicil for a will executed August 11th. BE CAREFUL about errors like this!

[22] This paragraph had given the Executor power to cancel any of the carefully described gifts of paintings to various art museums—with or without substituting other paintings instead.

[23] Original provision directed that any of Georgia O'Keeffe's paintings which had not been given away, because of cancellation of the gifts in Article Eighth or otherwise, should go to some tax exempt organization selected by the Executor.

[24] Re-numbering articles when one is changed is crucial—and easy to forget—especially internal references to article numbers.

[25] Paragraph B had provided that letters and papers not given to Yale University should go to John Bruce Hamilton.

[26] Article Fourteenth had given the rest of her tangible personal property, including dogs and automobiles, to John Bruce Hamilton.

EIGHTH: Article FIFTEENTH is hereby re-designated as Article THIRTEENTH.

NINTH: Article SIXTEENTH[27] is hereby re-designated as Article FOURTEENTH and amended in its entirety to read as follows:

FOURTEENTH: All the rest, residue and remainder of my estate wherever situated, including any lapsed gifts, shall constitute my residuary estate. I give my residuary estate to my friend, JOHN BRUCE HAMILTON. If John Bruce Hamilton fails to survive me, I direct that my residuary estate shall instead be distributed to such person or persons and upon such estates or conditions in such manner, and at such times as John Bruce Hamilton shall appoint by will.[28] In default of effective exercise of this power of appointment, my residuary estate shall instead be distributed among the heirs of John Bruce Hamilton as if he died intestate.

TENTH: Articles SEVENTEENTH, EIGHTEENTH, NINETEENTH and TWENTIETH are hereby re-designated as Article FIFTEENTH, SIXTEENTH, SEVENTEENTH and EIGHTEENTH.

ELEVENTH: A new Article NINTETEENTH is hereby added which reads as follows:

NINETEENTH:[29] Should any person entitled to share in my estate either as heir at law or as a legatee or devisee under this Will contest or seek to set aside this Will, or establish any legal right to share in my estate other than as herein approved and provided, I hereby give and bequeath the sum of One Dollar ($1.00) only and expressly direct that he shall receive no other or further share in my estate. Any property forfeited by the operation of this article shall be distributed as part of the residue of my estate, to be disposed of by my Personal Representative,[30] and each interest shall pass and vest under this Will in the same manner, as if such contestant had died without issue prior to the date set for the distribution of my estate.

---

[27] The original Article Sixteenth had given the remaining residuary estate to a tax exempt organization to be chosen by her Executor.

[28] Obviously, this is a major change—[worth approximately $50,000,000 according to Robinson, supra., at p. 549]—to give the entire residuary estate to Hamilton, instead of to charities selected by him, with a general testamentary power in Hamilton to appoint the property to anyone he liked. Notice that the gift in default would have given the entire residuary estate to Hamilton's family—who were his wife and children, as of the time the codicil was written.

[29] This is the no-contest clause, which could have been drafted far more effectively. [See points 11 and 12 of the Specifics for Drafting, in this chapter.] This WAS sufficient, however, to prevent any of the museums from contesting the codicil.

[30] Notice that property which might have been forfeited by a museum would have come right back to Hamilton, to be redistributed by him—or KEPT by him, in accordance with the terms of the new Article Fourteenth. Clearly, this no-contest clause was well designed to give as much protection and power as possible to Hamilton. Does the mere presence of a clause like this suggest the possibility of undue influence?

TWELFTH: Except as hereinabove amended, I hereby ratify, confirm and republish my aforesaid Last Will and Testament and prior Codicils thereto.

IN WITNESS WHEREOF, I have hereunto set my hand this 8th day of August, 1984.

GEORGIA O'KEEFFE"

[Witnessed by: Judy Lopez, Benjamin Sanders, Jr.[31] and Ursula Sanders.]

The signature of Georgia O'Keeffe on the Second Codicil is so poor that it can hardly be read, but her signature on the attestation clause which followed is at least as good as her signature on the First Codicil.

Based only on the materials presented, do you believe that the Second Codicil was the product of undue influence? As a judge, what additional evidence would you like to have on this issue? How might the Second Codicil have been better drafted to try to avoid allegations of undue influence?

As you think about these questions, you may want to try your hand at the drafting exercises which follow.

D. DRAFTING EXERCISES 3.A AND 3.B—TO INCLUDE A SPECIAL FRIEND OR LOVER DESPITE FAMILY DISAPPROVAL

Two different fact situations are presented for this drafting exercise. Take your choice in doing either 3.A or 3.B.

DRAFTING EXERCISE 3.A.—SECOND CODICIL FOR GEIORGIA O'KEEFFE

For this drafting exercise you may simply use the facts about Georgia O'Keeffe and John Bruce Hamilton, (a/k/a Juan Hamilton), which were given earlier in this chapter—(plus any other facts you happen to know about these two people).

Assume that Juan Hamilton[32] asked you to come talk with Georgia O'Keeffe about adding a Second Codicil to her will, and that after talking with her you are convinced that Georgia O'Keeffe knows exactly what she is doing, and is not subject to any undue influence.

---

[31] According to Roxana Robinson, supra., page 550, after Oliver Seth had refused to have anything to do with execution of this codicil, "Hamilton then called on Benjamin Sanders and his wife, friends of O'Keeffe's for thirty years, and asked them to witness the document. Sanders found everything in order: he believed O'Keeffe was lucid, and the codicil was read to her before she signed it."

Draft a codicil, changing the provisions of Georgia O'Keeffe's actual will and First Codicil found in Section B of this chapter, to give everything to Juan Hamilton—except the paintings listed in Article EIGHTH of the will.

Your main challenge here is to make the codicil so strong that even disappointed friends, relatives, and museums will be convinced that the codicil DOES represent the wishes of Georgia O'Keeffe. Thus, your codicil should be designed BOTH to accomplish Georgia O'Keeffe's goals, and to do so in a way which will effectively discourage litigation.

DRAFTING EXERCISE 3.B.—CODICIL FOR A MAN WITH AIDS

Assume that your client, Paul, is a 35 year old man who is dying of AIDS. Paul comes from a fairly wealthy family, and at the urging of his father, wrote a valid will when he was 18 years old – leaving various gifts to charities, and giving the remainder of his estate to his two older sisters. For the last fifteen years Paul has seen very little of his sisters, because both of them have made it clear that they do not approve of Paul's life style, and that they will not accept him until he "marries a nice young woman and settles down and raises a family in an appropriate manner."

Paul is a well-respected young research chemist, active in various community organizations, on the Board of the Symphony and United Way, and is liked by nearly everyone. For the last fifteen years Paul has been living with his partner, Larry, a man three years older than Paul, who is a successful Civil Engineer.

Paul has decided to add a codicil to his will, so that the gifts to the charities will remain the same, but that the residue of his estate, instead of going to his sisters, as it now does under Article Eighteen of his present will, shall go instead to Larry.

If Larry does not survive Paul, then Paul wants his entire estate to go to the charities named in his existing will, in equal shares, excluding both of his sisters, and all of his other family members who survive him.

Paul says that it is virtually certain that his entire family will try to contest the validity of the codicil he has asked you to draft. However, Paul feels strongly that he should be able to leave his own property to the person or charities of his choice.

---

[32] Remember, any time a client does not set up his or her own appointment, be especially alert for the possibility of undue influence.

Draft a provision which will accomplish Paul's goals as effectively as possible, and will help to discourage his family from undertaking litigation to have the codicil set aside.

E.   POINTERS FOR DRAFTING

Both of the drafting exercises in this section, 3.A and 3.B. share the same basic problem—the problem of drafting a codicil which will be effective in giving property to a person of the testator's choice—over the objections of some friends and relatives. In both cases, allegations of undue influence are very likely to be made by those who are disappointed by the provisions of the codicil.

Therefore, the following Pointers for Drafting are designed to be used with either Drafting Exercise 3.A or with Drafting Exercise 3.B.

FIRST, WHY USE A CODICIL?

Before the actual drafting of a codicil begins, you should first ask yourself the basic question— WHY USE A CODICIL, INSTEAD OF SIMPLY WRITING A NEW WILL?

In the old days, when each page of a will had to be individually typed each time it was executed, there may well have been some practical, mundane reasons for not typing long, detailed provisions—such as the gifts of specific paintings in Georgia O'Keeffe's will, for example— more often than necessary. Each time a provision was typed, there was the possibility that new errors would creep into the document—not to speak of the strain on the typist's psyche.[33]

Now, however, with the use of word processors, it is extremely easy to take the provisions of an old document, (such as the first will), and simply print them out as part of a new document, (such as a second will)—AFTER checking to be sure that the old provisions are still appropriate! In any case, thanks to word processors, saving typing time, and avoiding the possibility of new errors, simply are no longer valid reasons for using a codicil instead of a new will.

Other factors, however, may provide a valid basis for using a codicil today. One of the most important situations in which it may be best to use a codicil is the situation in which there is likely to be a challenge to the new document—based on testamentary capacity, undue influence, and the like.

In the O'Keeffe case, for example, it might seem very important to preserve the gifts of particular paintings to specific art museums which Georgia O'Keeffe had included in her will

---

[33] To the billionaire, J. Paul Getty, who had 21 codicils to his will, the typist's psyche was probably not of major concern.

with such care. Partly because these gifts followed a pattern which had been established by Georgia O'Keeffe much earlier in life,[34] the provisions of Georgia O'Keeffe's 1979 WILL were probably much less likely to be subject to challenge that the provisions in her 1984 CODICIL.

Also Georgia O'Keeffe had been a "mere" 91 years old when she signed her will, and was 96 years old when she signed the Second Codicil. With elderly people, it may happen that the older the testator gets, the more his or her decisions are subject to allegations of lack of testamentary capacity—or undue influence—whether or not those allegations are true.

So when the validity of an underlying will seems fairly secure, and the validity of the codicil may well be questioned, it is probably wise to use a codicil, instead of a new will—if the testator wants to be sure to preserve important gifts previously included in the will.

Once you have decided that it is appropriate to use a codicil instead of a new will, you may find that the following Pointers for Drafting are helpful. Many of them, of course, include the same considerations which should also be applied to wills.

POINTERS FOR DRAFTING A CODICIL

1. Verify that your client has sufficient testamentary capacity to execute a valid codicil,[35] and that the provisions you have been asked to draft are not the product of undue influence.

2. Be sure that you fully understand what your client wishes to accomplish—and why.

3. How likely is it that the validity of the original WILL might be contested—and who might be likely to bring such a contest?

4. Is there any way that the CODICIL could stand alone—if the validity of the underlying WILL were successfully challenged?[36]

---

[34] Robinson, supra., at 541-542.

[35] See introduction to this chapter.

[36] It would be highly unusual to have a codicil stand alone, yet in an appropriate situation the codicil certainly could be drafted in such a way as to make it possible for it to do so. In nearly all litigation over wills and codicils the court claims that above all, it is looking for the "intent of the testator." So, when appropriate, why not just include a statement at the beginning of the codicil saying, "If for any reason my will of _[date]_ is held not to be effective, then I intend that this codicil shall nevertheless be effective, and shall constitute my will."

A somewhat similar statement was used by the Vermont philanthropist, John Flynn, at the beginning of his will, when he stated, "BE IT KNOWN, THAT I, JOHN J. FLYNN, a resident of the city of Burlington, County of Chittenden, and State of Vermont being of sound and disposing mind and memory do make, publish, and declare this my LAST WILL AND TESTAMENT, hereby revoking any and all wills by me at any time heretofore made. But this revocation with respect to my will of August 16, 1932 with codicil of August 30, 1935 is conditioned upon the allowance of this instrument as my last will and testament." [Will executed September 1, 1937—emphasis added.] Although this specific provision seems to have been designed for use in a situation of Dependent Relative Revocation, discussed in Chapter 10, there is no reason why a

5.   Next, consider WHO is likely to be UPSET by the codicil. Are there certain family members who are bound to be disappointed by the provisions of the codicil? Will some charities or institutions consider themselves to be hurt by the codicil? To whom would the property be distributed if the codicil were not held to be effective?

6.   Who will have standing to sue to contest the validity of the codicil? Basically, to have standing to sue, the plaintiff must have suffered an injury because of the codicil.[37] So figure out who would have taken the property without the codicil. Would these have been takers under the intestate statute? Or takers under the prior will?

CAVEAT! Remember that the issue of STANDING is decided differently in different jurisdictions.[38] And the VALIDITY of the codicil you are drafting may be determined by the laws of the place where you client is domiciled when he or she DIES—not the laws of the place where the codicil is executed. So when you draft a codicil you simply CANNOT know, for sure, what law may be applied, if and when challenges are made to the codicil.

In the contest over Georgia O'Keeffe's Second Codicil, for example, family members were given standing to sue—even though they were NOT contesting the validity of the 1979 will, and they would NOT have gotten anything under EITHER the 1979 will or the Second Codicil.[39]

That was a highly unusual ruling on standing. But over the centuries, the law has been continuously developing because of unusual rulings.

The best you can do, then, is to make a very educated GUESS as to who may have standing to contest the codicil which you are drafting, and what law might be applied.

---

similarly designed provision couldn't be used as a means of making it possible for a codicil to stand alone—if for some reason the validity of the underlying will were successfully challenged.

[37] This is the same basic rule you mastered in Civil Procedure. "The right of a person to contest a will... [or codicil...] is based upon the loss of property or property rights that would result from recognition of an invalid instrument which deprives the person of those rights." In re Estate of Getty, 149 Cal. Rptr. 656 (1978). [Emphasis added.]

[38] See In re Estate of Getty, 149 Cal. Rptr. 656 (1978), which held that the granddaughter of billionaire J. Paul Getty did NOT have standing to contest the validity of the 21st codicil to her grandfather's will because the trust beneficiaries whom she was attempting to represent were actually better off with the codicil. Trustee or executor fees are NOT enough to give a person standing to sue over the validity of a will or codicil. [Especially, as the Getty court noted, when the granddaughter who was attempting to contest the codicil, was already, "the recipient of a princely income from her grandmother's trust,... and enjoys an expectancy of a royal fortune in principal on the termination of that trust."] Id. at 659.

In contrast, the new Mexico courts allowed family members to contest the codicils to Georgia O'Keeffe's will, without contesting the validity of the underlying will itself, even though their positions, had they won, would not have profited them by one cent. Eventually, the litigation was settled, and the settlement agreement sealed. See Robinson, supra., at 551-559 for a fascinating description of the legal maneuvers, gained from interviews with the various participants.

[39] See text of the will and codicils in the Appendix—and Robinson, supra., at 551-559.

7.   Having predicted who is likely to be motivated to contest the codicil, and who might have standing to bring such a contest, try to anticipate the basis for such contests.

Is your client elderly? The fact is that there generally is a widespread, frequently unfair, discrimination based on age alone. So if your client is elderly, that fact alone may well be used against your client by a disappointed relative.

Is your client especially dependent on one or more persons? Does your client have physical impairments, such as loss of sight or hearing? Does your client have some documented mental problems, for which he or she has had treatment of one kind or another? Does your client have—or appear to have—mental problems for which no treatment has been given? In other words, has your client been, or appeared to have been, fairly "spaced out" at times in the past?

It is important that you try to recognize the various facts or allegations which may be used in the future as a basis for claims of lack of testamentary capacity, or undue influence.[40]

8.   Figure out what might be done, in the document itself, to try to meet the likely allegations of undue influence. Should you add some extra wording in the document to try to EXPLAIN why the testator has made the specific choices included in the Codicil? Remember: Be careful in your choice of wording so that your explanations cannot later be turned around to be used against the testator.[41]

9.   Should you explain, as Henry Fonda[42] did, why the testator has not made certain gifts which would normally have been expected? BE CAREFUL on this also. Again, do not say anything which could later be used as the basis for a suit claiming testamentary libel. What if it turns out that the reasons stated by the testator in the codicil were based on beliefs which simply were not true? What happens, it that case, to the gifts which can be proved to have been based on inaccurate assumptions?[43]

---

[40] As with most aspects of law, anticipating the arguments likely to be made by the opposing side will help you realize what the important aspects of your case may be, and will allow you to collect and preserve the existing evidence which may be needed later to prove the validity of your client's case.

[41] For example, if a testator described his affection for, and dependence on the "outsider," the testator's own words may be used to demonstrate the susceptibility of the testator, the confidential relationship, and the opportunity to exercise undue influence—all key components of the proof required to show undue influence.

[42] Paragraph THIRD of Henry Fonda's will provides: "I am providing primarily for my wife Shirlee and my daughter Amy because they are dependent upon me for their support. I have made no provisions in this will for Jane or Peter, or for their families, solely because in my opinion they are financially independent, and my decision is not in any sense a measure of my deep affection for them."

[43] For example, what happens if the testator believes that one of his children has neglected him, or has died, when in fact that child has been prevented from having access to the testator, and is very much alive? Many statutes provide that if a child is excluded from a will solely because the testator believed the child to be dead, when the child was in fact alive, then the child will receive a share of the estate despite the provisions of the will.

10.   Should you include specific, precatory[44] statements REQUESTING that specified family members or institutions refrain from contesting the codicil? Should you just make a general plea that no one should contest the codicil?

11.   Or should you add a "no-contest" clause like the one included in Georgia O'Keeffe's Second Codicil[45]--which has some real teeth, and is not merely precatory?

NOTE: If you DO write a no-contest clause, you should be able to write an even better one than the one included in O'Keeffe's Second Codicil.[46]

But be aware that many states, consistent with the Uniform Probate Code,[47] will NOT uphold a non-contest clause if the court determines that the disappointed friend or relative HAD PROBABLE CAUSE for the contest.

12.   Specific suggestions for a no-contest clause:

A. In the first place, make your no-contest clause clearly applicable to ALL BENEFICIARIES—both humans and institutions—and any possible combinations of groups or institutions which might join together to contest the codicil.[48]

B. Second, have the forfeited gift ultimately devised, as a gift over, to a CHARITY, with the doctrine of "cy pres" to be applied. Under the doctrine of cy pres, if the charity named to take the forfeited gift is no longer in existence when the gift would vest, the COURT will simply give the gift to another, similar charity. That means that there will virtually ALWAYS be some residuary taker for the gifts which were taken away from people or institutions because they contested the codicil.

If a PERSON is used as the residuary taker instead of a charity, you MIGHT end up with no one to take the property—because the named person might have died, causing that gift, (under applicable law), to lapse. If the attempted gift over lapses, then the property might go to the descendants of the named person, if an anti-lapse statute applied, or might simply go to the testator's heirs—by intestacy.

---

[44] "Precatory" words are words which REQUEST that something be done, but do not legally REQUIRE that something to be done. In most circumstances, use of precatory words in a will or codicil would NOT be appropriate. The testator is in a position to make the rules with regard to distribution of his or her own property. And generally all "rules" in a will or codicil should be legally binding—not just "precatory."

[45] See the new article NINETEENTH added by paragraph ELEVENTH of the second codicil, found in the Appendix.

[46] Notice that O'Keeffe's no-contest clause simply takes the gifts away from someone who contests the will, and then would permit whoever was acting as Executor to give the gift right back to another person in the contestant's family!

[47] Sec. 2-517 of the Uniform Probate Code provides: "A provision in a will purporting to penalize an interested person for contesting the will or instituting other proceedings relating to the estate is unenforceable if probable cause exists for instituting proceedings."

[48] See Robinson, supra., pages 551-559 for interesting details about the negotiations involved in the O'Keeffe case with regard to determining which, if any beneficiaries might have the courage to litigate the issue of undue influence in the face of the no-contest clause.

That would be a rather nice result for the testator's heirs—if THEY happened to have been the ones who had instituted the challenge to the will or codicil![49]

So remember, if you draft a no-contest clause, make sure that the ultimate taker will be a charity, and that the court is specifically directed to apply the doctrine of cy pres.

13.   Realize that each jurisdiction has different rules on the extent to which the courts will actually recognize the no-contest clause which you have drafted. Just try to male yours as strong as possible.

14.   Pay special attention to two other crucial factors—the execution of the codicil;[50] and documentation, outside of the codicil, of the testator's mental capacity, as discussed earlier. Video tapes, memos from you to the file, letters from the client, memos from the witnesses, memos from doctors, memos from friends who are NOT included in the codicil, and the like may all be useful in appropriate circumstances to help document testamentary capacity.

---

[49] For example, assume that Grandfather's will provides that the gift of anyone who contests his will shall go instead to Anna, Grandfather's 20-year old "friend" who is to get the residue of Grandfather's estate, according to the terms of the will. If Anna happens to die before Grandfather, then Grandfather's heirs can freely contest any part of the will—including gifts to Anna or anyone else, knowing that whatever falls into the residue of Grandfather's estate will go to the heirs, by intestacy, [under the Uniform Probate Code lapse provisions], rather than to Anna or her heirs.

If Grandfather had provided, instead, that gifts forfeited by beneficiaries who contested the will should go to a charity, with cy pres to be applied, then people who contested the will really would lose the gifts provided for them by the terms of the will.

The key parts of a no-contest clause are: (1) take the gift away, and then (2) give it effectively to some other entity which is sure to be there to take it.

[50] The codicil should be executed at a time when the testator is most likely to be—and seem to be—entirely lucid. And witnesses for the codicil should be carefully chosen. Even though state law might permit beneficiaries to serve as witnesses, the witnesses to a codicil which might be contested should definitely NOT include persons who would be entitled to gifts under the terms of the codicil. Witnesses in this situation, however, SHOULD be persons who really know the testator, and have known him or her for a long time. The usual witnesses—staff members and law clerks who happen to be around the office—are NOT sufficient when there may be a challenge based on testamentary capacity. If possible, it may be a good idea to include witnesses who have professional training in mental capacity, such as the client's doctor or psychologist. Certainly witnesses should be chosen who would have high credibility with a court. Having realized in advance that there might be challenges based on testamentary capacity, you, as the lawyer, must take time to seek out the appropriate witnesses.

CHAPTER 3.   TOOLS AVAILABLE FOR USE IN WILLS AND TRUSTS

INTRODUCTION

As you begin drafting a will or trust for a client you will find that there are a variety of tools available for use in meeting the goals of your client. With drafting, as with any other construction job, it is well to be aware of the basic tools available, and how they work. In this chapter we will discuss some of the basic tools—and the skills involved in using those tools effectively.

A.   SPECIFIC AND GENERAL BEQUESTS

Many times, one of the major reasons a client decides to make a will is to be sure that special friends or family members get certain gifts. The gift of a particular item is usually called a specific bequest. The gift of a sum of money is usually called a general bequest.

1.   SPECIFIC BEQUESTS

Making gifts of treasured items to special friends and family members may be one of the most personal, poignant aspects of a will—as indicated by the first two samples in this section—from the wills of Jacqueline Kennedy Onassis and Cole Porter. Nearly all clients have some special possessions which they would like to leave to specific persons. Be sure that you allow your client time to talk to you about these special bequests. Then be sure that the bequests are drafted appropriately.

Far too many fights break out within families about distribution of items of the decedent's personal property which may have little or no financial value, but are of great importance to the people involved. Careful drafting may help to avoid some of those fights.

In many states there are two major ways in which a person may control distribution of particular items of personal property at death. First, in all jurisdictions, a testator may make specific bequests of special items as part of the will—the method used by both Jacqueline Kennedy Onassis and Cole Porter in the samples below.

Second, in states which have adopted Sec. 2-513 of the Uniform Probate Code, (UPC), a person may mention in a will that he or she intends to leave a memorandum disposing of various items of tangible personal property. Under the terms of the statute, once the possibility of a memorandum has been mentioned in the will, the testator can THEREAFTER write—and revise—a memorandum, or list, of who should get specific items of property—without going back to a lawyer and without having to call in any witnesses. This adds tremendous flexibility to the special gifts of personal property which formerly had to be included in the provisions of the will itself.

In jurisdictions which permit the UPC memo, virtually ALL[1] wills should be drafted to include provisions for such a memo. In addition, clients are frequently grateful if the attorney provides a sample form for the memo—even though no special form is necessary.[2] It is probably wise, in addition, to give the client a short, clear set of instructions on how to use the memo.[3]

In NON-UPC jurisdictions, all specific bequests must be included in the will itself—and clients should be warned NOT to change those bequests—or anything else in the will—without going back to a lawyer and having the appropriate witnesses, and so forth.

There are no set rules for how specific bequests must be worded. Just be sure that the item is described clearly enough to be easily identified by anyone involved with the estate. Then spell out what happens if the intended beneficiary does not survive the testator—in other words, is the gift to lapse, or to go to a relative of the named beneficiary, or to someone else?

And what happens if the testator no longer owns the item when the testator dies? Should the specified beneficiary just be out of luck, (the usual result with a specific bequest), or are there circumstances in which the specified beneficiary should be entitled to payment of a compensating amount of money from the general assets of the estate?

Rules of construction to determine whether bequests are specific or general, whether gifts lapse or not, are usually only necessary when the testator has not SPECIFIED what is to happen under various circumstances. So be sure that with every specific bequest or general bequest that you write, you take time to spell out the necessary provisions.

---

[1] Two important exceptions to this rule are: (1) When a client cannot read, or is blind, and therefore could not independently verify the words of this memo, and (2) When there is serious danger of undue influence, so that the presence of witnesses would be beneficial to help prevent undue influence.

[2] In providing such forms to clients, I have found it safer to use a very general, all purpose form, rather than citing to a particular section number of the will. The reason for this is my overriding goals of trying to minimize the possibility of error. If the sample memo form refers to a particular section number of the client's will, and then the client wants to add a whole new section to the will when he or she comes in for signing—[unfortunately NOT an unusual occurrence]—then there is a danger that the memo form will not be renumbered when sections of the will are renumbered. If the memo form refers to "section 16" of the will, and the relevant section ultimately ends up numbered "section 17" then you have created a problem. Better, in my experience, to minimize the risk of that error by simply not referring in the memo to any particular part of the will. You should also be aware that a client, years down the line, after he or she has signed an entirely new will, may use the same old memo forms provided. The detailed, clear, technical instructions you give a client do not always "soak in" completely. Therefore, I recommend a sample form such as the one included in the Appendix.

[3] See Appendix for sample.

As you read the following samples of specific bequests from the wills of Jacqueline Kennedy Onassis and Cole Porter, try to ascertain, for each one, whether the sample provides, (1) what happens if the beneficiary dies before the testator, and (2) what happens if the testator no longer owns a specific item at the time of death?

SAMPLE ONE—WILL OF JACQUELINE KENNEDY ONASSIS:

The will of Jacqueline Kennedy Onassis begins:

> I, Jacqueline K. Onassis, of the City, County and State of New York, do make, publish and declare this to be my Last Will and Testament, herby revoking all wills and codicils at any time heretofore made by me.

> FIRST: A. I give and bequeath to my friend RACHEL (BUNNY) L. MELLON, if she survives me, in appreciation of her designing the Rose Garden in the White House my Indian miniature "Lovers watching rain clouds," Kangra, about 1780, if owned by me at the time of my death, and my large Indian miniature with giltwood frame "Gardens of the Palace of the Rajh," a panoramic view of a pink walled garden blooming with orange flowers, with the Rajh being entertained in a pavilion by musicians and dancers, if owned by me at the time of my death.

Has Jacqueline Kennedy Onassis adequately described the items to be given to her friend? Yes. Has she specified that the gifts should go to Bunny only if Bunny survives Jackie? Yes. Has Jackie specified what should happen if the special miniatures were no longer owned by Jackie at her death? Yes. So this is a good sample of an appropriately drafted specific bequest. But it probably would have been better drafting if it had been specified, right in this gift, that the gift was to lapse, (fail), if Bunny did not survive Jackie.

SAMPLE TWO—WILL OF COLE PORTER

The following paragraphs were included in the will of Cole Porter:

> FOURTH:... B. I GIVE AND BEQUEATH to each of the following ... organizations the articles of tangible personal property, which I shall own at my death, set forth below opposite the name of such organization:...

> 2.   THE PRESIDENT AND TRUSTEES OF WILLIAMS COLLEGE, Williamstown, Massachusetts, all of the phonograph records (other than

records of my own musical or literary compositions), books ...[with exceptions], and pianos located in the cottage on my Buxton Hill realty.

3.   The UNIVERSITY OF CALIFORNIA AT LOS ANGELES, all of the books ... [with exceptions], and pianos located in the house I occupy in West Los Angeles, California. ...

6.   The MUSEUM OF MODERN ART, New York, New York, all of my cigarette cases; or, if the MUSEUM OF MODERN ART shall refuse to accept this bequest, to the METROPOLITAN MUSEUM OF ART, New York, New York...

Has Cole Porter adequately described the items to be given away? Yes—using the doctrine of Acts of Independent Significance—so that ANY pianos located in his house in West Los Angeles at the time of Cole Porter's death, for example, will be included in the gift to UCLA—even though no specific piano is described at all as to maker, style, color, and the like.

Has Cole Porter provided what should happen if one of the beneficiaries should "die" prior to the death of Cole Porter? Generally not. Institutions, of course, do not "die" in the same way that human beings die. But institutions DO sometimes go out of existence. What if Williams College, for example, just prior to the death of Cole Porter, had gone out of existence—or had merged with Amherst College? In either of those situations, what would have happened to the pianos destined for Williams College? Although the institutions mentioned by Cole Porter all seem very unlikely to go out of existence, such an eventuality should have been covered, someplace in the will.

What if some of the items covered by the provisions in Cole Porter's will had no longer been owned by Cole Porter at his death? Generally, no problem. Part 2 of the sample from Cole Porter's will, for example, only referred to items which were in Cole Porter's house in Massachusetts at the time of his death; items which had once been in the Massachusetts house but were no longer there at his death, simply would not have been included in the gift. And basically, the same thing would have happened if, prior to his death, Cole Porter had simply given away—or sold—his entire house in Massachusetts.

But what about those cigarette cases? If Cole Porter had simply discarded all of his cigarette cases prior to his death, could the Museum of Modern Art (MOMA) have sued for the value of the cigarette cases? Or could MOMA have gotten the cigarette cases back from anyone who had taken them out of Cole Porter's trash can? The answer to this is almost certainly "no." But wouldn't it have been clearer if Cole Porter, like Jackie Kennedy Onassis, had simply included the phrase, "if owned by me at my death," with all of his specific bequests?

2.   GENERAL BEQUEST

The third and fourth samples, from the wills of Humphrey Bogart and Tennessee Williams, are examples of general bequests. General bequests are usually just a designated amount of money to come from general assets. Gifts of money are certainly welcomed by anyone, but they usually do not have the same emotional significance as bequests of special items—and therefore are less likely to cause fights within families.

Drafting a general bequest of a given amount of money is not the least bit difficult. Just remember NOT to say which bank account is to be used to fund the general bequest—or there are likely to be problems if: (a) that bank account has been closed; (b) there is not quite enough money in the designated account to pay the gift; (c) the money which was once in the bank account has been moved to another bank; or (d) the bank has changed names, or gone out of business.

So if your client wants to give a certain amount to money to each grandchild, for example, try to persuade your client just to specify the amount of money to go to each beneficiary, and NOT to say which bank account is to be the source of the money.

Clients frequently come in with a list of bank accounts, stocks, or Certificates of Deposit, (referred to as CDs), which they want to go to certain people, in hopes of making a fairly equal distribution of assets among several beneficiaries. The best thing you can do in such a situation is simply to talk the client out of the idea of specifying particular bank accounts, stocks, or CDs for particular people.

Explain to the client the difficulties and problems which might arise if a CD, for example, matures before the testator dies—or if one stock plummets in value while other stocks gain. Then try to persuade the client just to make a general bequest of a certain amount of money to each person—as in the wills of Humphrey Bogart and Tennessee Williams—OR to say that each beneficiary is to get a certain FRACTION of the total monetary value of ALL of the specified assets—which may be distributed either in cash or in kind, as the executors or beneficiaries prefer.

Remind the client, too, that the value of a specific amount of money may change over time—so that it may be wiser for the client to give fractional shares—or at least to review, every so often, the specific amounts designated. But if changes are to be made in the amounts of money given to various people, remind the client that the changes MUST be made by a properly executed NEW will or codicil.

Then be SURE to discuss with your client the issue of ademption—as covered later in this chapter.

As you read the following samples from the wills of Humphrey Bogart and Tennessee Williams, respectively, try to ascertain whether each sample provides: (1) what happens if the beneficiary dies before the testator, and (2) what happens if the value of the dollar should fall, (or rise), significantly?

SAMPLE THREE—WILL OF HUMPHREY BOGART

Article FIFTH of the will of Humphrey Bogart, signed on June 6, 1956, approximately eight months before his death, provides:

> I give and bequeath:
>
> (a)   To MAY SMITH the amount of two thousand dollars ($2,000);
> (b)   To KATHERYN SLOAN the amount of fifteen hundred dollars ($1,500);
>   provided that said persons, respectively, shall still be in my employ at the
>   time of my decease.

Has Bogart adequately provided what should happen if May Smith, for example, had died before Bogart? Probably. If May Smith had not been living at the time of Bogart's death, then she clearly wouldn't have been "in his employ" at the time of his death. But what if she had had some sort of unusual employment contract which said she was to be paid for a full month of work any time she had put in 20 days of work during the month, and she died two days before Bogart, but after having put in 20 days of work in that month, for which she had not yet been paid? Fairly unlikely scenario, but why risk the chance of litigation? Why not just say, "if she survives me, and is still in my employ at the time of my decease?"

What would have happened if the value of the dollar had fallen dramatically during the time between when Bogart wrote the will, and the time of his death? Would there have been any adjustment—to give May Smith a gift with the same purchasing power as the gift Bogart had originally intended? No. May Smith would have gotten exactly $2,000—regardless of how that compared in purchasing power to the gift Bogart had intended.[4]

SAMPLE FOUR—WILL OF TENNESSEE WILLIAMS

Article V of the will of Tennessee Williams, signed on September 11, 1980, approximately two and one-half years before his death, provides:

1.   Upon the death of my sister, if my friend ROBERT CARROLL shall then be living, my Trustee shall set aside from the corpus of the Trust such assets which in their sole discretion will be sufficient for the said Trustees to pay to my friend ROBERT CARROLL a sum of money up to but not in excess of $7,500.00 per year payable monthly during his lifetime. Upon the death of ROBERT CARROLL the principle amount so set aside … shall be paid …to the WALTER E. DAKIN MEMORIAL FUND.

Has Tennessee Williams adequately provided what should happen if Carroll had died before Williams? Yes. The gift Carroll is to last no longer than Carroll's life—so no problem here.

Has Tennessee Williams specified what should happen if the value of the dollar goes up or down? Partly. Because of the discretion given to the trustees, if the purchasing power of a dollar had increased dramatically, the trustees had ample authority to decrease the number of dollars given to Carroll. But if the purchasing power of $7,500 in 1996 had been only one-half of the purchasing power of $7,500 in 1980, when the will was written, the trustees would NOT have had authority to have made up the difference for Robert Carroll.

By taking a little more time, could this provision have been drafted to give Robert Carroll a gift each year which would have been the equivalent of the purchasing power of $7,500 in 1980? Would that probably have been closer to the intent of Tennessee Williams? If so, then the lawyer who drafted the will of Tennessee Williams should have pointed out the problem to his client, and then have drafted more appropriately.

---

[4] In this case, Bogart probably would have wanted May Smith to have a gift with the same purchasing power which $2,000 would have had at the time the will was written—as determined by the Consumer Price Index, or the like. With relatively larger gifts, the donor might have preferred to specify that the donee was to get a specific fractional share of the estate—thus allowing the specific dollar amount of the gift to be appropriately adjusted for inflation or deflation over time.

3.   LAPSE PROBLEMS AND GIFTS OVER

As indicated by the preceding samples, it is important to remember that any person named in a will—no matter how young and healthy the person may be at the time the will is signed—may die before the testator. That possibility should be reflected in the drafting of every will.

You must NOT count on the testator having the time, inclination, or MENTAL CAPACITY to redraft his or her will, or to add a codicil thereto, every time there is a death or other significant change in the family. You should draft each will so carefully that all major, foreseeable changes are anticipated. Draft as if your client MIGHT walk out of your office, be struck by a car, and live for another 20 years WITHOUT having regained testamentary capacity. In other words, be sure that your drafting anticipates as many future contingencies as practicable.

The will of the great jurist and U.S. Supreme Court Justice, Oliver Wendell Holmes, is well known primarily for his residuary clause, which stated, simply,

> All the rest, residue and remainder of my property of whatsoever nature, wheresoever situate, of which I may die seized and possessed, or in which I may have any interest at the time of my death, I give, devise, and bequeath to the UNITED STATES OF AMERICA.

However, the will, and four codicils, of Oliver Wendell Holmes are also useful in studying the effects of changed circumstances on testamentary dispositions. As you read the excerpts which follow from the will and codicils of Justice Oliver Wendell Holmes, consider in what ways the original WILL might have been more effectively drafted to anticipate the possibility of lapsed gifts, and in what ways the codicils were necessary because of changed conditions which simply could NOT have been anticipated.

SAMPLE FIVE—WILL AND CODICILS OF OLIVER WENDELL HOLMES

In this WILL, signed on November 3, 1931, Justice Oliver Wendell Holmes provided:

> I, OLIVER WENDELL HOLMES, of Washington, in the District of Columbia, make this my last will … I give to my cousins on my father's side as follows:

> To MARY CLARK—FIFTY THOUSAND DOLLARS ($50,000)

… The silver belonging to me and not having come from my wife or my wife's family, and not otherwise disposed of by me, I give to be equally divided between said MARY CLARK and DOROTHY Q. VAUGHN, as also any furniture that has been in my family before it came to my hands ….

I give to ANNIE MARY DONNELLAN, my parlor maid, FIVE THOUSAND DOLLARS ($5,000) …

I give to EARL H. JONES, my indoor man, if in my services at the time of my death, ONE THOUSAND DOLLARS ($1,000).

I give to ARTHUR THOMAS, my messenger, ONE THOUSAND DOLLARS ($1,000) ….

IN WITNESS WHEREOF, I have hereunto set my hand and affixed my seal, this third day of November, 1931.

Oliver Wendell Holmes

On January 14, 1932, only about two months after he had signed his will, Oliver Wendell Holmes signed his FIRST CODICIL, stating:

My cousin, MARY CLARK, having died, I give and bequeath the legacy of FIFTY THOUSAND DOLLARS ($50,000) given to her by said will to her children, in equal shares ….

The silver and furniture belonging to me and directed to be equally divided between my said cousin, MARY CLARK, and DOROTHY O. VAUGHN, I give to be equally divided and delivered one-half to said DOROTHY Q. VAUGHN and the other one-half among the children of said MARY CLARK. I also give to said children of MARY CLARK the portrait of my Aunt, MARY (HOLMES) PARSONS.

I confirm the legacy of ONE THOUSAND DOLLARS ($1,000) given in my will to ARTHUR THOMAS, formerly my messenger.

Approximately six months later, on June 1, 1932, Oliver Wendell Holmes signed a SECOND CODICIL, stating: …

EARLE H. JONES … [Sic: Spelled "Earl" in will and "Earle" in codicil] … having left my service and I having made such provision for him as seems to me fit, I hereby revoke the bequest to him in my said will.

I also revoke the bequest to my former messenger, ARTHUR A. THOMAS, having made such provision for him as seems to me fit …

It was approximately nine months until the next codicil, the THIRD CODICIL, was signed by Oliver Wendell Holmes, on March 9, 1933. It provided: …

I give and bequeath the sum of ONE THOUSAND DOLLARS ($1,000) to CATHERINE McCARTHY, my maid, and the sum of ONE THOUSAND DOLLARS ($1,000) to THOMAS A. JETER, my indoor man, provided they are in my service at the time of my death. …

About seven months later, on October 24, 1933, the FOURTH (AND LAST) CODICIL was added to the will of Oliver Wendell Holmes, stating: …

I give and bequeath to ANNIE MARY DONNELLAN, my maid and nurse, a legacy of TEN THOUSAND DOLLARS ($10,000), in lieu of the bequest of FIVE THOUSAND DOLLARS ($5,000) made to her in my said will. …

[The last codicil also allowed the Executor to keep open the residences which Holmes owned, and to continue paying the employees, "for such time as, in his absolute discretion, he may deem necessary … without any obligation to utilize said residences for the production of income."]

Question: Could many of the provisions in these codicils have been avoided if the original will had been better drafted? With the benefit of hindsight, what changes would you make to the will and codicils?

4.   DRAFTING EXERCISE 4—TO LET SOME GIFTS LAPSE, WHILE OTHERS DO NOT

BACKGROUND

As indicated by the preceding samples from the will and codicils of Oliver Wendell Holmes, the great jurist changed his mind fairly often on how much to leave to various employees. Perhaps this was inevitable, and unavoidable.

However, the possibility of the death of his cousin, Mary Clark, could have been anticipated, and should have been covered by the provisions of the <u>original will</u>. Similarly, after Mary Clark had predeceased Justice Holmes, why did his lawyer not add appropriate lapse provisions for the <u>other</u> gifts to named individuals?!

EVERY will must provide for the possibility that any named beneficiary may predecease the testator. In the following exercise you will have an opportunity to try your hand at drafting such a provision.

FACTS FOR DRAFTING PROBLEM

Assume that your client is very fond of all three of her sisters, but that she cannot stand the husbands two of her sisters have chosen. If all three of her sisters survive her, your client would like to leave $10,000 to each sister.

If your client's oldest sister, Anna, dies before your client dies, your client wants the $10,000 gift to Anna simply to lapse, and to go into the residuary estate. Your client cannot stand Anna's husband—or their loud, ill-behaved children.

If your client's second oldest sister, Beth, predeceases your client, your client wants the $10,000 to go to Clara's kind, thoughtful husband—provided that he and Clara are still married to each other at the death of Clara. If this $10,000 does not end up with either ~~Clara~~ [Beth], or ~~her husband~~ [David], your client wants the money to go to ~~Clara's~~ [Beth] favorite charity, in memory of ~~Clara~~ [Beth].

Draft the appropriate provisions to accomplish the goals of your client. As you begin drafting, you may want to check the following Pointers for Drafting.

5.   POINTERS FOR DRAFTING

The most important part of this drafting exercise has taken place during the interview with the client. Once you, as a lawyer, have raised the issues with your client, and your client has decided what to do about various situations, the actual drafting should not be particularly difficult. <u>Recognizing</u> the potential problems is most important part.

SUGGESTIONS

1.   Make the gift to each sister a separate gift, and put the survivorship contingency in the same sentence as the gift. For example, you might simply say, "If my sister, Anna, survives me, then I give her the sum of $10,000."

2.   Then, in the next sentence, provide what happens if the first taker does not survive—in other words, provide for a "GIFT OVER" to a secondary taker. Obviously, this will require a different provision for each sister.

3.   Are the secondary takers, the beneficiaries of the "gift over," also required to survive the testatrix in order to get the money? Or is the money to be added to the estate of a secondary taker who has predeceased the testatrix? If a secondary taker is required to survive the testatrix what happens to the share of a secondary taker who does not survive the testatrix? The answers to these questions must be clearly stated.

4.   What does your client mean by the term "survive"? For example, if the testatrix and one of her sisters both die as the result of the same automobile accident, but the sister dies approximately five minutes later than the testatrix, what should happen? Would your client want the money to go to a sister who survived her by only five minutes? (And then, probably, through the sister's estate to the sister's husband?)

     As you may know, under the Uniform Probate Code, a person must live for at least 120 hours longer than a decedent to be considered to have survived the decedent. Within the will, you may specify any period of survivorship you like.

     Just remember that the estate cannot be closed until all of the money has been paid to someone. So, generally, survivorship requirements should not extend beyond a period of a few months.

5.   WHENEVER you draft a provision involving survivorship you must consider the effects of long term use of LIFE SUPPORT SYSTEMS. What if your client and one of her sisters, after having been in the same automobile accident, are both plugged in to life support systems—and later are both unplugged and allowed to die, in accordance with the terms of their respective living wills? [See samples of Living Wills in Chapter 11.] Is distribution of the $10,000 to be dependent on which sister is unplugged first? What can you do to draft around that possibility?

6. What happens if a charity specified in the will is no longer in existence when the testatrix dies—or is no longer a tax exempt organization? Should "cy pres" be applied—so that the court may select another charity to receive the gift? Or should the gift simply lapse?

7. Does your client want to put an upper limit on these gifts—of $10,000, for example—and then provide that each gift should be decreased, if necessary, so that no gift constitutes more than 10% of the net estate?

8. What is your client's choice on the issue of ademption? If all of the gifts specified in the will cannot be paid in full, which gifts are to be paid first? Or shall all gifts be decreased by the same percentage?

6. ADEMPTION AND ABATEMENT CLAUSES—FOR GIFTS OF SPECIFIC ITEMS, SPECIFIC SUMS, OR FRACTIONAL SHARES

INTRODUCTION

What happens if the specific items bequeathed or devised in a will are no longer in the testator's estate when the testator dies? Or what happens if there simply is not enough money in the estate to fund all of the gifts described in the will? In such situations the problems of ademption and abatement arise. Even in the largest estates, provisions should be made for these contingencies.

a. ADEMPTION

Ademption occurs when an asset specifically devised or bequeathed in a will is on longer in the testator's estate when the testator dies. As illustrated in the first part of this chapter, particularly in the specific bequest in the will of Jacqueline Kennedy Onassis, a well drafted devise or bequest of specific real or personal property should state clearly what happens if the property is no longer owned by the testator at death. The best way to do this is simply to make any gift of specifically described property contingent upon if the testator still owns the property at death.

b. ABATEMENT

Abatement becomes necessary when there are not enough assets in the estate to fund all of the bequests made in a will.[5] Appropriate directions for what happens if all bequests cannot be paid

---

[5] Abatement may apply to both specific and general bequests. If a specifically devised asset is not in the estate at the death of the testator, that is a matter of ademption, not abatement. But if the specifically devised assets IS in the estate, but must be sold to pay taxes and expenses of administration, then that becomes an issue of abatement—as to which specifically devised assts should be sold first. The normal order of abatement is intestate property first; then property in the residuary estate; then general bequests; and then specific bequests. In some jurisdictions specifically devised land is the last gift to abate. Other jurisdictions treat real and personal property equally. Most jurisdictions will have an

may be somewhat difficult to draft, but should nevertheless be included in every will where the problem may arise.

Even in the will of Jacqueline Kennedy Onassis, provision was made for the possibility that there might not be enough money in the estate to fund all of the gifts made under the will. Any person writing a will with multiple gifts should simply take the time to specify which gifts are most important to him or her. The approach used by Jacqueline Kennedy Onassis is a good one.

SAMPLE SIX—WILL OF JACQUELINE KENNEDY ONASSIS

In Article NINTH, Paragraph B of her will, (signed March 22, 1994), Jacqueline Kennedy Onassis provided:

> Should my Estate, after payment of all of my debts and funeral expenses, the expenses of estate administration and the taxes referred to in this Article NINTH, be insufficient to satisfy in full all of the pre-residuary bequests and devises which I make under Articles FIRST through THIRD hereof, I direct that the bequests and devises in (1) Paragraphs A, B and C of Article FIRST; (2) Article SECOND; and (3) Paragraph A of Article THIRD shall abate last after the abatement of the bequests and devises in Paragraphs D and E of Article FIRST and Paragraphs B, C and D of Article THIRD.

This might have been written more clearly, but the concept is good.

Another good approach to the problem is illustrated by the will of Ira Humphreys, a Colorado philanthropist. As you can see, Ira Humphreys first made various general bequests, and then specified that those general bequests of designated sums of money should be adjusted down, if necessary, so that the amount of money in those gifts would not exceed 10% of the value of the total estate.

SAMPLE SEVEN—WILL OF IRA HUMPHREYS

ARTICLE III of Ira Humphreys' will provided:

A.   In the event the son of my deceased wife, CARROLL T. BROWN, JR., survives me, Two Hundred Thousand Dollars ($200,000) to John L. J. Hart and Claude M. Maer, Jr. both of Denver, Colorado, in trust to pay the said CARROLL T.

---

established order of abatement—and such laws, not unexpectedly—will vary from one jurisdiction to another. Therefore, it is particularly important that you specify the order of abatement in the will itself, since the order specified in the will will normally prevail over any statute.

BROWN, JR., the net income therefrom at convenient intervals for the duration of his life and, upon his death, to pay and deliver the principal and accumulated earnings to his issue with representation, and if no such issue is then living, to my issue with representation.

B.   One Hundred Thousand Dollars ($100,000) each to such of the following who survive me, namely the grandson of my said deceased wife, GERALD S. BROWN, and her granddaughter, MARY REBECCA BROWN, subject to possible trusteeships as provided in Articles VII and VIII.

C.   Notwithstanding anything in the preceding Paragraphs A and B to the contrary, in the event the total payable under said Paragraphs A and B exceeds ten percent (10%) of the value at the date of my death of my residuary estate passing under this Article III of my will, the amounts payable under said two paragraphs shall be decreased pro rata so that they total an amount equal to ten percent (10%) of said value.

It would seem wise to put an adjustment provision like this in virtually every will—so that unexpected turmoil in the stock market, or an unexpected, very large personal injury judgment, for example, would not cause the estate to be distributed in PROPORTIONS quite different from what the testator intended—simply because the estate turned out to be much smaller, or larger, than expected.

Describing gifts as fractional shares, rather than as set monetary amounts, may be a very useful technique—especially for gifts to a surviving spouse, to a church, to other favorite charities, or to distant relatives.

It is possible to combine fractional shares with a specific dollar amount as an upper limit, as in the following sample, from the will of Andy Warhol.

SAMPLE EIGHT—WILL OF ANDY WARHOL

In article Third of his will, (signed March 11, 1982), Andy Warhol combined a fractional share with a MAXIMUM dollar amount, [and a questionable use of a power of appointment]. The concept of the abatement clause, (disregarding the power of appointment), is a good one.

Article Third provided:

> I GIVE such portion of my residuary estate as my friend FREDERICK HUGHES (or, if my said friend shall not survive me, my friend, VINCENT FREEMONT), shall validly appoint in equal shares, to such of my brothers, JOHN WARHOL and PAUL WARHOL, as shall survive me, by the exercise of a power of appointment over such portion of my residuary estate contained in an instrument in writing duly signed and acknowledged by my said friend and delivered to my Executor within six (6) months after the issuance of Letters Testamentary to my Executor; provided, however, that such portion of my residuary estate shall not exceed the sum of Five Hundred Thousand ($500,000) Dollars or if my residuary estate shall be less than Five Hundred Thousand ($500,000) Dollars, my entire residuary estate.[6] I DIRECT that in exercising the power of appointment granted herein, my said friend shall have the power to determine both the portion of my residuary estate disposed of by this Article and whether cash or other property (at the value set for such property in the final determinations of the Federal estate tax on my estate) shall be allocated in satisfaction of the bequests contained herein.[7]

It may also be appropriate to specify a specific dollar amount as a LOWER limit. Specifying a minimum, lower limit might be especially appropriate in providing basic support for a relative—when the testator wants the relative to have at least a certain amount, no matter what, and then more if the estate turns out to be large enough to provide for a larger gift.

In any case, specific drafting is needed to meet the goals of the client. Hopefully, the preceding samples have given you an idea of how some lawyers have handled the issue.

Another technique sometimes used as a means of indicating the relative importance of various gifts is the inclusion of precatory words, discussed in the next section.

---

[6] The brothers threatened a will contest regarding these provisions, but reached a settlement with the estate attorneys before their objections were filed. Securing this settlement, as well as one with Bianca Jagger in England, were among the commendable actions by the attorneys for the estate which the Surrogate held entitled the attorneys to $7.2 million—which was estimated to be equivalent to paying the attorneys at a rate of $2,400 per hour! [NY Times, 4/21/95].

[7] Giving the named friends the discretion as to which property should be used to fund the bequest to the brothers may be an appropriate use for the power of appointment—though such discretion is normally just given to the executor. IF the donee of the power also had discretion to appoint a grand total of 50 cents to each brother, that would also be an appropriate use of the power of appointment. However, appointing "in equal shares" is NOT an appropriate use of a power of appointment! If the donee of the power is to have no discretion as to the objects of the power to which the appointment is to be made, or the percentage of the property which must go to each object of the power, then there is no reason to use a power of appointment for the division of property. The significance of a power of appointment—and the justification for its use—are in the DISCRETION granted to the donee of the power! Here there appears to be no discretion left to the donee as to objects or percentages of the appointment—although there is discretion on how little may be appointed to the brothers.

7.   PRECATORY WORDS

Precatory words are words which request but do not require that something be done. Normally, precatory words have no place in a will! If the client wants something to be done, clear words of command should be used for that purpose. However, if, in an unusual situation, precatory words are appropriate, be sure to indicate that the words are, indeed, intended to be merely precatory.

SAMPLE NINE—WILL OF ALFRED HITCHCOCK

The following sample from the will of ALFRED HITCHCOCK, (signed August 8, 1963), demonstrates what may be an appropriate use of precatory words.

Article VII of Alfred Hitchcock's will provided:

> It is my desire that my sister, MRS. NELLIE INGRAM, of … London, England, shall receive from my estate ten (10) English pounds sterling each and every week beginning at the date of my death and ending five (5) years after the date of my death; provided, however, that such payments shall be made only so long as and to the extent that my estate shall be financially able to make such payments without unreasonably depriving my wife and my daughter. To that end, I _request_ my executors, my Trustees, my wife and my daughter to make the foregoing payments for such five (5) year period from my estate during administration thereof, from the trust hereunder during the continuance thereof, and thereafter from funds available therefore originating from my estate, of said sum of (10) pounds per week to my said sister, but I do not hereby impose upon any of them the legal obligation to make such payment. [Emphasis added.]

Now that you have seen samples of various abatement clauses, and what may have been an appropriate use of precatory words, you may want to try your hand at using some of these tools in the following Drafting Exercise.

8.   DRAFTING EXERCISE 5—TO INSURE THAT GIFTS TO CHARITIES AND DISTANT RELATIVES DO NOT BECOME TOO LARGE A PERCENTAGE OF THE TOTAL ESTATE

Like many people, your client is interested in making some gifts in his will to various charities, and also to some distant relatives. He would like the gifts to the charities to total approximately 20% of his net estate, with not less than 10% of his net estate going to his church, (synagogue or mosque), and with not less than $5,000 going to each church or charity he mentions in the will.

If the estate is large enough, the church and charities should get more money—until 20% of the estate has been given to charity. But no matter what the size of the estate, each church or charity is to get at least $5,000.

As for the distant relatives, your client feels that it is the <u>idea</u> of the remembrance itself, rather that the amount of money involved, which is important. Therefore, your client wants to leave no more than a total of 5% for his net estate to the relatives, collectively, with the gift to each relative not to exceed $1,000.

Draft a provision which will meet the goals of your client. As an additional challenge, you may include some precatory suggestions on how the gifts are to be used, if you like.

You may list any three charities which seem interesting to you—and include as many named or described relatives as you like—as long as all of the relatives, combined, get no more than 5% of the testator's estate after payment of all debts, taxes, and expenses of administration, and no relative gets a payment of more than $1,000.

9.   POINTERS FOR DRAFTING

First, notice that you have two separate problems here.

The first provision to be drafted is to insure that each church or charity gets at least $5,000. Then, those gifts are to be INCREASED until the total amount given to the church equals 10% of the net estate, and the total amount given to the church and charities combined equals 20% of the net estate.

The second provision to be drafted is to insure that each named relative gets NO MORE THAN $1,000, and that the gifts to relatives, collectively, are to be DECREASED, as necessary, until they equal no more than 5% of the net estate.

SUGGESTIONS

1.   Define the term "net estate." It will probably be defined as the probate estate, less all debts, taxes and expenses of administration. But your client may want to have the term defined in another way—for example by saying that the net estate is to be considered to be the probate estate, less gifts to a SURVIVING SPOUSE, and debts, taxes and expenses of administration. In other words, the fractional share for charities and distant relatives may be set aside from part, or all of the probate estate, depending on the wishes

of your client. For this exercise you may use whatever definition of net estate you consider to be the most appropriate.

2.   Draft the charitable provisions in one section, and the family provisions in another section.

3.   Clearly state the maximum—or minimum dollar amount to be received by each beneficiary

4.   Then state the circumstances under which the stated dollar amount is to be increased or decreased.

5.   What happens to the share of a named relative who does not survive the testator?

6.   What happens if a named charity is no longer in existence at the death of the testator? Is the doctrine of cy pres to be applied? Or is the share of the charity which is no longer in existence to go to one of the other named charities? What if one of the entities named in the will is no longer a charity for tax purposes—because it has engaged in too much political activity, for example? Be sure that you spell out what is to happen in each of these situations.

7.   If you have used precatory words, have you made it clear that the words are only precatory?

B.   ACTS OF INDEPENDENT SIGNIFICANCE--FLEXIBILITY

The doctrine of Acts of Independent Significance is accepted in virtually all states. Basically, it allows acts or events which occurred AFTER the execution of the will to determine who gets various gifts described in the will—IF the events had INDEPENDENT SIGNIFICANCE—beyond just determining who gets the testator's property.

It is frequently easier to understand the concept of Acts of Independent Significance if you see a few samples. By observing how effectively both Cole Porter and Georgia O'Keeffe used the concept of Acts of Independent Significance in their respective wills, you may come to appreciate what a useful concept it is.

SAMPLE TEN—WILL OF GEORGIA O'KEEFFE

The following paragraph was included in the Third article of the will of Georgia O'Keeffe:

THIRD: ...D. I give the sum of One Thousand ($1,000) Dollars to each person who shall be in my employ in Abiquiu, New Mexico at the time of my death (other than those named above in this Article THIRD) provided that such person shall have been in my employ for a continuous period of one year prior to my death.

Note that employing a new person at Abiquiu would have been an Act of Independent Significance—to get more help—rather than just as a means of giving someone $1,000. So the gift would have been good.

SAMPLE ELEVEN—WILL OF COLE PORTER

Cole Porter in his will used the concept of Acts of Independent Significance in a slightly different way. The following paragraphs were included in the will of Cole Porter:

FOURTH: ... B. I GIVE AND BEQUEATH to each of the following ... organizations the articles of tangible personal property, which I shall own at my death, set forth below opposite the name of such organization: ...

3.   The UNIVERSITY OF CALIFORNIA AT LOS ANGELES, all of the books [with exceptions] ..., and pianos located in the house I occupy in West Los Angeles, California.

4.   The Juilliard SCHOOL OF MUSIC, New York, all of the pianos located in my apartment in New York, New York.

5.   YALE UNIVERSITY, New Haven, Connecticut, (i) all of the books ...[with exceptions] ...located in my apartment in New York, New York; (ii) (for the use of the School of Music of said University) all original manuscripts and all phonograph records of my own musical and literary compositions, wherever located; and (iii) all books, wherever located, of clippings relating to me, my personal or family affairs or theatrical and other productions in which I have participated ...

Note that if Cole Porter had purchased more books or pianos for his house in West Los Angeles after he signed his will those purchases would have had significance APART from giving the new books and pianos to U.C.L.A.—so purchase of the new books and pianos would have constituted an Act of Independent Significance—and the items would have gone to U.C.L.A. under the terms of the will.

Likewise, if, after writing his will, Cole Porter had MOVED a piano from West Los Angeles to New York City, then Juilliard, rather than U.C.L.A. would have been the recipient of that piano, under the terms of the will—because moving a piano across the country would surely have been done for some significant reason OTHER THAN benefiting Juilliard.

On the other hand, if Cole Porter, in a NON-UPC JURISDICTION, after the execution of his will, and without witnesses, had typed and signed a NOTE stating that his estate was to give Juilliard a specific piano then in Los Angeles, the note would NOT have been given effect, and Juilliard would NOT have been entitled to the piano—even if the note were proved to have been typed and signed by Cole Porter—because the note would have had NO significance other than giving the piano to Juilliard and would not have been properly executed for a will or codicil.

The important point here is that the NOTE would have had no INDEPENDENT significance and therefore would have been ineffective. A typed, signed note, with no witnesses, by which a person attempts to give away property after death, is simply ineffective under the usual Wills Act.[8]

Just be sure that when you draft a will like Cole Porter's or Georgia O'Keeffe's, which relies on the doctrine of Acts of Independent Significance, that the acts involved really would have accomplished something significant, during the life of the testator, (such as hiring an employee or moving a piano), and would NOT merely have constituted a writing ineffectively attempting to get around the Wills Act.

1. DRAFTING EXERCISE 6—PROVIDING FOR PEOPLE WHO HAVE CARED WELL FOR TESTATOR AT THE END OF TESTATOR'S LIFE—ACTS OF INDEPENDENT SIGNIFICANCE

BACKGROUND

Sometimes, because of Alzheimer's disease, or various other problems, it becomes increasingly difficult to care for people as they near the end of their lives. More physical care is often needed, and, perhaps because of their increased physical and emotional pain, elderly people sometimes

---

[8] In a jurisdiction which accepts the UPC memo provisions discussed at the beginning of this chapter with respect to specific bequests, the note might have been effective—unless, the state applied UPC I, (approved in 1990), and the piano was excluded from being given away by memo because it was considered to be property used in a trade or business.

develop rather difficult personalities. So finding skilled, caring people to provide the necessary assistance for an elderly person may be a challenge.

The following drafting exercise is designed to provide a method by which an elderly person can reward those who have assisted him or her at the end of life. It might also serve as something of an incentive—if the elderly person has friends or relatives to whom he or she discloses the terms of the will prior to death.[9]

FACTS FOR THIS DRAFTING EXERCISE

Assume that your client has a great deal of money, but in this case, that she has no particularly close friends or relatives. Your client has never had any children, and most of her close friends from earlier days have died. She realized that it is becoming increasingly difficult for her to make new friends, because she has become increasingly impatient when anything does not go exactly as she had hoped. Having watched the difficulties of her own parents in their final years, your client would like to do what she can, by means of provisions in her will, to be sure that at the end of her life she is well cared for, in her own home, for as long as possible.

Like nearly all elderly people, your client has concerns about running out of money before she dies—if medical and living expenses become extraordinary. But she is even more concerned with the possibility of being taken advantage of by a "con-man," or a "gold-digger," who might cheat her out of her money. Yet she wants to maintain control of her own money herself for as long as possible—hopefully until she dies.

Your client is willing to spend up to 50% of her entire estate—as a reward, or an incentive, or both—to try to insure proper care for herself in her final years. The rest of her estate will be going to various charities.

Draft a provision which will be as effective as possible in helping your client to accomplish her goals.

---

[9] However, the friends and relatives, hopefully, should be aware of the fact that the elderly person could revoke his or her will—or change it entirely—up until the moment of death, as long as the elderly person had testamentary capacity!

2. POINTERS FOR DRAFTING

BACKGROUND

Note: In real life, a revocable inter vivos trust, with provisions for someone to take over as trustee if your client becomes incapacitated and provisions that the trust should then become irrevocable would probably be a better solution for this problem. But if your client, like many real life clients, is resistant to the concept of a trust, and is determined not to part with ANY control of her assets prior to death, then you must simply do the best you can with provisions to be included in your client's will.

This is an extremely difficult, yet realistic problem. In fact, in real life, the problem would usually be even more difficult because there would usually be less money available.

To develop an appropriate solution for this problem, first you will need to define the care for the elderly person which would be deemed appropriate. Second, you will need to select a person or institution to determine whether or not the appropriate care has been provided. Third, you will need to develop an effective method for encouraging and then rewarding the people who have provided appropriate care.

The underlying theory of this drafting exercise is that the provision of appropriate care for an elderly person should be described in such a way as to constitute an Act of Independent Significance—which will ultimately trigger financial rewards under the terms of the will.

SUGGESTIONS

1. Define the kind and degree of care which would be deemed appropriate. Using examples, illustrations, and statements of intent may help in defining the goals of your client effectively. Remember that, as the years go by, your client's mental and physical health are quite likely to change. Medical technology and public and private resources for the elderly are also likely to change. So, specific details may be of limited use compared to broader statements of intent and goals. Yet the standard of care required MUST be spelled out with sufficient precision to allow someone to ascertain whether or not the standard has been met.

2. Above all, try to avoid a situation in which an elderly person is being maintained on painful, expensive life support systems SOLELY to provide financial benefit for those who may ultimately take under the will.

3. In determining whether or not appropriate care has been provided, try to find some person or institution which could monitor the care while the testator is still alive, and would be motivated to try to have inadequate care givers replaced. Remember, however, that this provision is to be included in a WILL, not a trust, so legally the will does not become effective until the testator has died. And then it would be a little late to initiate a replacement of the care givers.

4. Perhaps, in attempting to assure adequate care, you could develop some system under which care givers would share in the ultimate distribution of the estate ONLY to the extent that they had been awarded certificates during the testator's life indicating completion of, for example, a three month period of care certified to have been appropriate at that time for the testator.

    If you are able to find some appropriate person or institution to monitor the care while the testator is alive, that person or institution could be designated as the one whose "compliance certificates" could later be converted to cash from the testator's estate, in an appropriate amount—by the testator's executor.
    You may well be able to come up with better ideas for tying inter vivos monitoring to ultimate rewards provided by the estate. But as you can appreciate, it is a very difficult problem.

5. However rewards are to be determined, the concept of Acts of Independent Significance can provide a good legal basis for such rewards. But try to make it as clear as possible what the relevant acts of independent significance must be—in other words, what the exact standards are which must be met before rewards are given.

6. Consider designing some way in which the other beneficiaries under the will—in this case the various charities—may increase their own shares if they can prove that appropriate care was given to the testator during her last years. Is there some realistic way to play the charities off against each other in a way which makes ALL the charities strive to be sure that the testator is comfortable in her later years?

7. Consider giving wide discretion to the executor of the will as to the persons to whom rewards for care should be given, and the amounts of such rewards. But if you give such

discretion to the executor you will still need the best guidelines you can draft for the executor. And make sure that there will not be a conflict of interest for the executor!

Trying to insure appropriate care, through provisions in the will, requires very skillful drafting to implement effectively an idea which many laymen have tried on their own. The issue involved with this problem is understandably of major concern to the elderly.

C. INCORPORATION BY REFERENCE

Incorporation by reference is an extremely useful tool for granting powers to fiduciaries such as executors, personal representatives, and trustees. Rather than laboriously spelling out each power of the fiduciary—such as power to sell, power to invest, power to distribute—and so forth, nearly all wills today simply "incorporate by reference" an existing Fiduciaries' Powers Act.

To use the technique of incorporation by reference, two things are required. First, the document to be incorporated must be in existence at the time it is incorporated into the new document—in other words, the document to be incorporated must be a pre-existing document.
Second, the document to be incorporated must be clearly identified. It must be clear which document is intended to be incorporated by reference.

So, to use the doctrine of incorporation by reference you simply need to have a pre-existing document, which is clearly identified. Then you can incorporate it into a new document simply by reference—instead of actually typing it into the new document.

Does incorporation by reference really make that much difference now, when use of a word processor would make it so easy simply to reprint the pre-existing document? Yes. Incorporation by reference is still an extremely useful tool. Once you have read through the Fiduciaries' Powers Act in virtually any state you will see why you probably do not want that much detail and clutter in anyone's will.

Note, however, that some of the provisions authorized by statute may NOT be appropriate for wills for individual clients.[10] At some point, you should go through the Fiduciaries' Powers Act of your state very carefully, modify the powers as appropriate for the majority of your clients, and then in future wills just incorporate the Act by reference—SUBJECT TO the modifications

---

[10] See, for example, the conflicts of interest specifically permitted by C.R.S. 15-1-804 (2) granting the fiduciary power "(d) To acquire an undivided interest in an estate or trust asset in which the fiduciary, in a fiduciary or individual capacity, also holds an undivided interest ... [and] (g) (II) To lease ...[property] even for a term extending beyond the duration of the administration of the estate or trust...[and] (p) To borrow money from any source, including the commercial department of a corporate fiduciary." [Emphasis added.] There are good reasons why conflicts of interest of this sort should simply be avoided.

you have determined to be appropriate and including additional changes which may be necessary for an individual client.

Most lawyers, however, just trustingly incorporate the whole Fiduciaries' Powers Act by reference.

The following sample from the will of Elvis Presley is representative of the standard use of Incorporation by Reference.

SAMPLE TWELVE—WILL OF ELVIS PRESLEY

In ITEM XII (a) of his will Elvis Presley authorized his Trustees:

> To exercise all those powers authorized to fiduciaries under the provisions of the Tennessee Code Annotated, Sections 35-616 to 35-618, inclusive, including any amendments thereto in effect at the time of my death, and the same are expressly referred to and incorporated herein by reference. [Emphasis added.]

Is this a successful use of Incorporation by Reference? Probably. Are there any problems? Yes. If the doctrine of Incorporation by Reference requires that the incorporated document be in existence—that it be a pre-existing document—are the amendments which may be made <u>after</u> Elvis signs, but before he dies, really preexisting documents?

That depends on when Elvis's will really becomes a "document." Is it when Elvis and the witnesses sign? Or when Elvis dies? Technically, for the purposes of Incorporation by Reference, it should be at the time Elvis and the witnesses <u>sign</u>. Otherwise, the testator could continue writing little notes until the date of his death, and claim that they were all incorporated by reference in his will because they would all have been in existence prior to his death. That would not work. Incorporation by reference cannot be stretched that far.

So, the amendments made after the signing of the will technically cannot be included by using Incorporation by Reference. Is there any other doctrine which could be used to save this provision and make it effective? Answer: Yes. Acts of Independent Significance. The Tennessee Legislature probably would have had some independent reason for changing the provisions of the Act after Elvis signed his will—some reason independent of just changing some of the powers granted by Elvis's will. So the amendments would have been effectively included in Elvis's will—as Acts of Independent Significance.

So the provisions in Elvis's will, probably would work—and it is such standard practice that no one is even likely to question it. But is it wise?

Despite the fact that "everybody does it," is there really any reason for your client blindly to accept laws which have not yet been made? Probably <u>not</u>. If there really are additional powers which you would like the fiduciaries to have, you should simply give them such powers specifically, in the will. Blindly accepting future amendments may be convenient for the future fiduciaries—but those fiduciaries really are <u>not</u> the client you are supposed to be representing.

So a preferable and more accurate use of Incorporation by Reference would simply be to incorporate by reference the Fiduciaries' Powers Act <u>as it exists at the time the will is</u> <u>signed</u>. That same rule should be applied to any other documents which are intended to be incorporated by reference.

D.   RESIDUARY ESTATE

Clearly, every will must have what is referred to as a residuary clause—to provide for disposition of what is called the residuary estate. The residuary estate is considered to be everything which is left over after payment of all debts, expenses, taxes, specific and general bequests, and specific devises. It has been held that omission of a residuary clause is malpractice per se—no explanations or excuses permitted.[11]

No one knows exactly how much he or she will own at the time of death. So there must always be provisions for a residuary estate. It would be impossible—as well as highly impractical—to try to make specific bequests of every item owned by the testator or testatrix.

So the general pattern for wills is: first, especially important items are given away; then general bequests are made; then the residue is distributed. Depending on the client, and the assets involved, the residuary estate may contain very few of the total assts of the estate, or the residuary estate may contain the vast majority of the assets in the estate. Residuary "clauses" may go on for several pages, if the client has decided to give most of his estate away by means of fractional distributions of the residuary estate to various friends, relatives, or charities.

In many estates, it may be wise to have a charity as the final beneficiary of the residuary estate— in case there simply are no close relatives alive at the time for distribution. As discussed earlier,[12] the doctrine of cy pres may be applied to prevent failure of an ultimate gift to charity.

---

[11] <u>Knupp V. Schober</u>, Civ.A.No. 89-0895 (RCH), U.S. District Court, District of Columbia, July 14, 1992.
[12] See Chapter 3.A.9.

Two interesting samples of short, thoughtful residuary clauses follow.

SAMPLE THIRTEEN—RESIDUARY CLAUSE OF OLIVER WENDELL HOLMES

Near the end of his will, (which had no paragraph or section numbers), Oliver Wendell Holmes, as you may recall, stated simply:

> All of the rest, residue and remainder of my property of whatsoever nature, wheresoever situate, of which I may die seized and possessed, or in which I may have any interest at the time of my death, I give, devise and bequeath to the UNITED STATES OF AMERICA.[13]

SAMPLE FOURTEEN—RESIDUARY CLAUSE OF HENRY FONDA

Another very interesting residuary clause is found in paragraph SEVENTH of the will of Henry Fonda, in which he stated:

> If … [my wife] is not living 90 days after the date of my death, then I give the aforesaid residue of my estate to the Omaha Playhouse, at Omaha, Nebraska, to be used for such capital improvements, and for the maintenance and operations thereof, as the governing body of said Playhouse deems proper, this gift to be known as 'The Henry and Shirlee Fonda Bequest.'

The final gift in a residuary clause provides an opportunity for a client to make a gift to an institution about which he or she cares deeply, rather than letting the property go by intestacy—possibly to very distant relatives who may be of little concern to the client.

CONCLUSION

Now that you have had an introduction to some of the major tools available for constructing wills and trusts—and have had an opportunity to try using some of those tools in practical situations, it is time to go on to learn about the types of Trusts—both testamentary and inter vivos—which may be designed with the help of these tools.

---

[13] See Chapter 4.G. for a summary of the saga of Congressional attempts to decide how to use this money.

CHAPTER 4.   TRUSTS

A.   OUTLINE FOR TESTAMENTARY AND INTER VIVOS TRUSTS

1.   REASONS TO USE A TRUST

Trusts provide a wonderfully flexible means for retaining control over investment and distribution of assets even after death, and for providing a safety net for special beneficiaries. By putting assets into a TRUST, to be managed by a person or institution called a Trustee, an individual is able to secure unified, skilled management of trust assets, usually preserving the assets intact for the duration of the trust, while providing an income for the designated BENEFICIARIES of the trust.

Trusts can be designed in a multitude of different ways, and used for a great variety of different purposes. As the following samples illustrate, Elvis Presley left a tremendous amount of discretion to the trustee of the trust which he established – as to management of assets and distribution of income or principal to the beneficiaries.

Tennessee Williams, on the other hand, used a trust first to accomplish very specific protection for a special person, and then to accomplish some charitable goals. At each stage of his trust Tennessee Williams gave very detailed instructions to the trustee, about investments,[1] distributions, and the like.

The important thing for you to remember when you are drafting a trust for one of your clients is to be sure to take the time to design a trust effectively tailored to accomplish the goals of your individual client.

2.   DIFFERENCES BETWEEN INTER VIVOS AND TESTAMENTARY TRUSTS

Your client will normally be the SETTLOR of the trust – the person who sets up and establishes the trust. If the trust is created by a document which becomes effective BEFORE the Settlor dies, it is called an INTER VIVOS TRUST. If a trust is created by a person's will, the trust is called a TESTAMENTARY TRUST. Currently, there are NO FEDERAL TAX ADVANTAGES to setting up an inter vivos trust instead of a testamentary trust – IF the Settlor

---

[1] See Chapter 5.B. for an illustration of the detailed investment provisions included by Tennessee Williams in his will.

retains the power to change or amend the inter vivos trust. Speaking very broadly, if a client retains control over an asset until his or her death, that asset will be taxable in the client's estate.[2]

There may be other reasons for establishing an inter vivos trust – frequently called a "Living Trust." Among the reasons for a Living Trust may be privacy;[3] unified, continuing management of trust assets;[4] and savings on probate fees in some states.[5] As a practical matter, the financial benefits of a Living Trust for most clients will be determined primarily by the fee structure used by the local bar for matters of probate.[6]

There are also some definite disadvantages to establishing Living Trusts. For example if the trustee of a Living Trust tells the Settleor's son that the son is not included in the trust, and therefore has no right to see the trust documents, the son may have no way of forcing the trustee to disclose the provisions of the trust, even though the son may be a beneficiary, and someone should have authority to check on the actions of the trustee.

3.   BASIC STRUCTURE OF TRUSTS

With both Living Trusts and Testamentary Trusts, the fundamental structure of the trust is the same.

As indicated above, the person who MANAGES the assets in the trust is called the TRUSTEE. Family members, good friends, or banks are usually selected as TRUSTEES. Any particular trust may have one trustee, or several trustees acting together – depending on the wishes of the Settlor.

The people or institutions who receive the benefits from the trust are called the BENEFICIARIES. The income and/or principal of the trust may be distributed among the beneficiaries in almost any fashion specified by the Settlor.

---

[2] There may be some tax advantages to setting up an IRREVOCABLE inter vivos trust, but the complexities of such matters is happily left to another course.

[3] Expect in highly unusual cases, all wills which are probated become a matter of public record. That means that anyone, with enough effort, can ascertain the contents of a testamentary trust – because the will establishing the trust is a public record. As a practical matter, this is not of much concern to most clients, since no one except close friends or family members would be interested anyway. But if your client is a particularly wealthy of famous person, the privacy available through use of an inter vivos trust may be a determining factor. In most states, the CONTENTS of an inter vivos trust never become a matter of public record – even though state law may require that the EXISTENCE of the trust be registered.

[4] An elderly person, for example, might establish a trust in which the elderly person and his or her children were all trustees as long as the elderly person was able to participate, with control of the trust gradually shifting over to the children, who would then assume full control on the death of the elderly person. The basic structure of the trust would remain the same – with only a change in trustees at various stages.

[5] In a number of states attorneys will routinely set their fees as a percentage of the probate estate. Since the assets in a living Trust may well not have to go through probate, keeping the trust assets out of the probate estate could well result in substantial savings – by minimizing attorneys fees for probate. Many states, however, now consider it improper and unethical for an attorney to base his or her fees on the size of the probate estate. Instead, attorneys in those states are simply required to charge on an hourly basis for the work actually performed for the probate estate.

[6] When attorneys are permitted to charge only on an hourly basis, it usually will NOT save any money to pay the attorney to set up a Living Trust – instead of just paying the attorney to probate the estate. Although payment of attorneys fees for establishing a Living Trust must be made when the trust is established, payment of fees for probate is postponed until after the death of the Settlor – usually an attractive option for the Settlor.

No magic words are necessary to establish a trust. Just be sure to do three basic things. First, make sure that the property is given TO THE TRUSTEE – IN TRUST. Second, write out the necessary INSTRUCTIONS for the trustee on how to manage and distribute the property during the time the trust exists. Finally, be sure to specify when and how the trust will END – and to whom all of the remaining property in the trust shall be distributed upon termination of the trust.

The Rule against Perpetuities, discussed in Chapter 8, will usually, indirectly, set an outer limit as to how long a private trust may continue. However, common sense will normally dictate a much earlier termination than that required by the Rule Against Perpetuities.

Perhaps the easiest, fastest way to understand how trusts are established is simply to read the following samples of testamentary trusts – and thus to get a feel for the variety of provisions which may be included in a trust.

As you read the following samples, notice how the drafters of the various trusts handled each of the three basic steps – giving the property to the trustee; providing the trustee with instructions; and finally terminating the trust and distributing the assets. The footnotes included with each trust should help you to understand the specific components of the trust.

Also notice that Elvis Presley's trust would be considered a DISCRETIONARY trust, because so much DISCRETION was given to Elvis' father – and successor trustees – as to how much to pay – to which beneficiaries. The trust established by Tennessee Williams is both a SUPPORT trust and a CHARITABLE trust – first providing SUPPORT for his sister, then giving the remainder to a CHARITY – with very specific instructions and very little discretion left to the trustees. Any one trust may have a variety of different components and characteristics, as appropriate for the specific people involved.

Samples of various kinds of trusts follow.

B.   DISCRETIONARY TRUST

As you read the following sample from the will of Elvis Presley, notice the tremendous DISCRETION which Elvis gave to his father, Vernon Presley – and notice that any trustee who might follow Vernon Presley would NOT have such broad discretion.

At what age was Lisa Marie considered to be old enough to handle the millions she could inherit from Elvis? Would there be any conditions under which Lisa Marie might NOT get the money when she reached the designated age?

To what extent, if any, would the millions intended for Lisa Marie be protected from being used by her husband?

Are there any circumstances under which the trust might have ended BEFORE Elvis's grandmother, Minnie Mae Presley, had died? Do you think this was an oversight on the part of Elvis – or his lawyer?

(If you would like to read the entire will of Elvis Presley, it is included in the Appendix of this book – and evidently someone at the Probate Court has added the definitive statement at the top of the will that – Elvis is deceased.)

SAMPLE ONE – WILL OF ELVIS PRESLEY

The following discretionary trust is part of the will of Elvis Presley:

ITEM IV
Residuary Trust

After payment of all debts, expenses and taxes as directed under ITEM I hereof, I give, devise, and bequeath all the rest, residue, and remainder of my estate, including all lapsed legacies and devises, and any property over which I have a power of appointment, to my Trustee, hereinafter named, in trust[7] for the following purposes: [Emphasis added.]

(a)   The trustee is directed to take, hold, manage, invest and reinvest the corpus of the trust and to collect the income there from in accordance with the rights, powers, duties, authority and discretion hereinafter set forth. The Trustee is directed to pay all the expenses, taxes and costs incurred in the management of the trust estate out of the income thereof.

(b)   After payment of all expenses, taxes and costs incurred in the management of the trust estate, the Trustee is authorized to accumulate the net income[8] or to pay or apply so much of the net income and such portion of the principal[9] at any time

---

[7] Notice that whenever assets are transferred to a trustee, it should be specified that the transfer is "in trust." These two key words make it clear that the assets are being given not to the trustee personally, but only to the trustee, as trustee.

[8] This is a somewhat unusual provision – giving the trustee authority to accumulate all of the income. Accumulation of income in perpetuity is, of course, not permitted where the common law Rule Against Perpetuities is in effect. But within the time period covered by this trust it would not be illegal to accumulate all of the income – though it might be unwise to do so – and certainly a disappointment to the beneficiaries!

[9] This broad power to invade principal illustrates the tremendous discretion allowed to the trustee. Since Elvis's father is both a beneficiary of the trust, and the sole trustee at the beginning of the trust, this might open up all kinds of interesting possibilities for him! In your own drafting, you

and from time to time for the health, education, support, comfortable maintenance and welfare of: (1) my daughter, Lisa Marie Presley, and any other lawful issue I might have, (2) my grandmother, Minnie Mae Presley, (3) my father, Vernon E. Presley, and (4) such other relatives of mine living at the of my death who in the absolute discretion[10] of my Trustee are in need of emergency[11] assistance for any of the above mentioned purposes and the Trustee is able to make such distribution without affecting the ability of the trust to meet the present needs of the first three numbered categories of beneficiaries herein mentioned or to meet the reasonably expected future needs of the first three classes of beneficiaries herein mentioned.[12] Any decision of the Trustee as to whether or not distribution shall be make, and also as to the amount of such distribution, to any of the persons described hereunder shall be final and conclusive and not subject to question by any legatee or beneficiary hereunder. [Emphasis added.]

(c)   Upon the death of my father, Vernon E. Presley, the Trustee is instructed to make no further distributions to the fourth category of beneficiaries and such beneficiaries shall cease to have any interest whatsoever in this trust.[13]

(d)   Upon the death of both my said father and my said grandmother, the trustee is directed to divide the Residuary Trust into separate and equal trusts, creating one such equal trust for each of my lawful[14] children then surviving and one such equal trust for the living issue collectively, if any, of any deceased child of mine. …

> The Trustee may from time to time distribute the whole or any part of the net income or principal from each of the aforesaid trusts as the Trustee, in its uncontrolled discretion, considers necessary or

---

may want to include more specific guidelines. And in a taxable estate such as this one, BE SURE to check the tax consequences of the precise wording of a power to invade principal. Making all of the assets of the trust taxable in the estate of Elvis's father would certainly seem unwise!

[10] Who did Elvis have in mind with this provision? Were there specific relatives, whom he did not want to mention by name, but who would be know to his father? Or is this just a general provision for relatives? Note that once again, Elvis's father is given absolute discretion on what payments to make – if any – and to whom any payments should be made. Would a provision like this be a way of providing for illegitimate children – without announcing the fact?

[11] Note that Elvis's father only had the authority to help out the unnamed relatives when they were "in need of emergency assistance."

[12] It is a good idea to have a provision of this sort – specifying which beneficiaries are the most important to the settler – and factors which should be kept in mind in making allocation of the resources of the trust.

[13] This makes these provisions even more interesting! Clearly, it was considered appropriate for Elvis's father to make distributions to the unnamed relatives. But a successor trustee, such as a bank, was NOT given authority to make any distributions to such persons – regardless of whether or not there might be an emergency. Might it have been possible to leave the bank with some discretion – but limit gifts to the unnamed relatives to some designated amount – for example no more than 5% of the net income form the trust each year? [Next time someone sees Elvis, it might be interesting to ask the reason behind this provision.]

[14] Use of the word "lawful" in this paragraph, as well as in paragraph (b), above, turned out to have major significance for Deborah Delanie Presley, who brought suit against the estate, claiming to be the illegitimate daughter of Elvis. The Court of Appeals of Tennessee held that since Deborah could not be considered a "lawful" child of Elvis, then it was proper for the trial court to have granted the motion for summary judgment against her.

desirable[15] to provide for the comfortable support, education, maintenance, benefit and general welfare of each of my children. … [Emphasis added.]

(e)   As each of my respective children attains the age of twenty-five (25) years and provided that both my father and grandmother then be deceased,[16] the trust created hereunder for such child shall terminate, and all the remainder of the assets then contained in said trust shall be distributed to such child so attaining the age of twenty-five (25) years outright and free of further trust.[17]

(f)   If any of my children for whose benefit a trust has been created hereunder should die before attaining the age of twenty-five years, then the trust created for such child shall terminate on his death,[18] and all remaining assets then contained in said trust shall be distributed outright and free of further trust and in equal shares to the surviving issue of such deceased child. …

ITEM VI
Alternate Distributees

In the event that all of my descendants[19] should be deceased at any time prior to the time for the termination of the trusts provided for herein, then in such event all of my estate and all the assets of every trust to be created hereunder (as the case may be) shall then be distributed outright in equal shares to my heirs at law[20] per stirpes….

---

[15] Once again, the trustee is given complete discretion on how much money to distribute – from either income or principal – to any of the designated beneficiaries.

[16] What happens if the child reaches 25 but either Elvis's father or grandmother is still alive? Whenever there is a provision in a trust saying, "If [something] happens," you must be sure to include a matching provision saying "If [something] does NOT happen."

[17] Notice that Elvis has decided that Lisa Marie, or any other child of his, would be old enough to handle the millions without the assistance of a trustee at age 25. Certainly the law, including the Rule Against Perpetuities, would have allowed Elvis to leave some or all of the money in the trust until the child was considerably older. (Any child of Elvis's could have served as his or her own measuring life, so the Rule Against Perpetuities, would have allowed Elvis to leave some or all of the money in the trust until the child was considerably older. (Remember, any child of Elvis's could have served as his or her own measuring life, under the Rule Against Perpetuities, because the child would have been born – or at least conceived – by the time of Elvis's death.)

[18] It is important that assets not be held in the trust for longer than 21 years after a child's death, if the trust is to comply with the common law Rule Against Perpetuities. As explained above, any one of Elvis's children could serve as a good measuring life for the Rule Against Perpetuities. But after the child dies, all interests in the trust "must vest, if at all, within 21 years of" the end of the child's life. In appropriate circumstances, however, it certainly would be possible to keep the assets in the trust while the grandchildren were still under the age of 21 since Elvis's children would have been good measuring lives.

[19] This is the provision which may well have been a mistake! Only Elvis's children, grandchildren, etc. are "descendants." So, if Lisa Marie had died, while Elvis' grandmother was still alive, then all of Elvis's descendants would have been dead, and the trust would have terminated. That would have left Elvis's grandmother with no more benefits from the trust. And as indicated below, Elvis's grandmother might well NOT have been considered to be one of Elvis' heirs. So Elvis's grandmother might well have been left with no legal access to Elvis's millions.

[20] Does this mean Elvis's heirs determined at Elvis's death, (the usual interpretation), or does it mean Elvis's heirs determined as of the date of termination of the trust?

Elvis's heirs determined as of the date of Elvis's death would have included Lisa Marie. So if Lisa Marie had been Elvis's sole descendant, and had died in an auto accident at age 21 her share of the trust assets would have gone into Lisa Marie's estate – and then possibly to Michael Jackson – or whoever happened to be married to Lisa Marie at the time.

If Elvis's heirs were to be determined as of the date of termination of the trust, Elvis's "heirs at law" would have been his closest relatives, and would have included only his father, NOT his grandmother, under the applicable Tennessee statue – and the statutes of nearly all states.

ITEM IX
Spendthrift Provision[21]

I direct that the interest of any beneficiary in principal or income of any trust created hereunder shall not be subject to claims of creditors or others, nor to legal process, and may not be voluntarily or involuntarily alienated or encumbered except as herein provided. Any bequests contained herein for any female shall be for her sole and separate use, free from the debts, contracts and control of any husband she may ever have....[22] [Emphasis added.]

ITEM XI
Executor and Trustee

I appoint as Executor of this, my last will and testament, and as Trustee of every trust required to be created hereunder, my said father.[23]

I hereby direct that my said father shall be entitled by his last will and testament, duly probated, to appoint a successor Executor of my estate, as well as a successor Trustee or successor Trustees of all the trusts to be created under my last will and testament.[24]

If for any reason, my said father shall be unable to serve or to continue to serve as Executor and/or as Trustee, or if he be deceased and shall not have appointed a successor Executor or Trustee, by virtue of his last will and testament as stated-above, then I appoint National Bank of Commerce, Memphis, Tennessee, or its successor or the institution with which it may merge,[25] as successor Executor and/or as successor Trustee of all trusts required to be established hereunder.

---

[21] Spendthrift provisions in trusts are very common, and are intended to protect the assets of the trust from creditors of the trust beneficiaries – until the assets are distributed to the beneficiaries. See Section C of this chapter for fuller discussion of spendthrift trusts.

[22] This is NOT a common provision in a trust! This would have been designed to keep someone like Michael Jackson, or any other husband of Lisa Marie's, from having any claim on her money which came from the trust. As discussed in Section C of this chapter, however, there is no direct way in which Elvis could have controlled what Lisa Marie did with the money once it was distributed to her. But can you think of indirect ways Elvis could have controlled Lisa Marie's behavior even after she got a payment from the trust?

[23] It is fairly common to have the same person appointed both as Executor and as Trustee, but there is no need to do so. The job of an executor, ideally, lasts only a year or two, while the assets of the estate are being collected and distributed in accordance with the terms of the will. The job of a trustee may continue for many years, as the trustee administers the trust, and decides which beneficiaries are to get how much money, and when. Because the trustee's job will normally last for a longer time, and require the exercise of more discretion as to distributions, etc., it may be well that your client will select different people for the two distinct jobs of executor and trustee.

[24] Obviously, Elvis was willing to turn over virtually all control of his assets to his father – including choice of successor executor and/or trustee. It is more usual for the testator himself or herself to list several persons who should act as successor executors or successor trustees.

[25] This is important – to realize that banks may merge, change names, or go out of business entirely. It is wise to make some provision for such an occurrence.

C.   SUPPORT TRUST (WITH A CHARITABLE TRUST)

A support trust is designed primarily to provide continuing financial SUPPORT for one or more designated persons. A support trust differs from a discretionary trust in that the beneficiaries of a support trust have a right to DEMAND payments from the trust.

Under the support trust which follows, Tennessee Williams gave the beneficiary a RIGHT to have certain payments made – as contrasted with Elvis Presley's discretionary trust, under which no beneficiary had a right to any payments until termination of the trust. So the main difference between a support trust and a discretionary trust is whether or not the beneficiaries have a RIGHT to payments.

One drawback of a support trust may be that if the BENEFICIARIES have a right to demand payments, so may the CREDITORS of those beneficiaries – at least to the extent that the creditors have provided goods or services necessary for the beneficiaries' support. This may have some undesired financial consequences. In some cases, for example, it may turn out that assets in a support trust are used to pay nursing home costs which might otherwise have been picked up by public benefits programs – if the beneficiaries had not had a RIGHT to support from the trust.

On the other hand, if the Settlor's primary goal IS to insure support for a special person, then a support trust may well be appropriate. In practice, of course, whenever you draft a trust you must weigh the various alternatives in light of the tax and PUBLIC BENEFIT RULES then in effect - -with the realization that they will UNDOUBTEDLY CHANGE.

The following sample, from the will of Tennessee Williams, illustrates how a SUPPORT trust may be drafted when support for a special person is the overriding concern of the Settlor.

SAMPLE TWO – WILL OF TENNESSEE WILLIAMS

Article III of the will of Tennessee Williams provides:

> All the rest, residue and remainder of my estate, real, personal and mixed,[26] of every kind and nature, and wherever situated, of which I may die seized or possessed, including without limitation, all property acquired by me or to which I may become entitled after the execution of this Will, or over which I may have any power of disposition or

---

[26] Can you define what is meant by "mixed" property? Neither can anyone else. Basically, property is either real property or personal property. So the use of the term "mixed" is unnecessary – and very frequently done.

appointment, and all property herein attempted to be disposed of, the disposition whereof by reason of lapse or other cause shall fail to take effect, I give, devise and bequeath to my Trustees hereinafter named, IN TRUST,[27] NEVERTHELESS. For the following uses and purposes: ...

A. If my sister, ROSE ISABEL WILLIAMS, shall survive me,[28] I direct that my Trustees shall use so much of said income as is necessary for the support and maintenance of my said sister at Stony Lodge Sanitarium in Ossining, New York.[29] In addition to the payment of the normal expenses of maintenance of said Institution, my Trustees shall pay to or for the benefit of my said sister such amounts as they deem necessary or advisable for medical and dental expenses, clothing and her usual customary pleasures as she now enjoys, including shopping trips to New York City, personal spending money, it being my intention that said Trustees shall provide liberally for her not only for her needs but also for her comforts and pleasures.[30] In the event it is not possible for my sister to remain in said Institution, then I direct that my said Trustees shall provide for her in the manner hereinabove provided in another institution or institutions of equal status to which she may be moved.[31]

Clearly, support for his sister was of primary importance for Tennessee Williams, so the first part of his trust is a support trust.

At the termination of the same trust,[32] Tennessee Williams directed that the assets should be directed to a CHARITABLE PURPOSE. By providing, in Article V, that the remaining assets of the trust should go to:

The UNIVERSITY OF THE SOUTH, at Sewanee, Tennessee, to endow a separate fund in memory of my grandfather, WALTER E. DAKIN...for the purposes of encouraging creative writing and creative writers in need of financial assistance to pursue their

---

[27] Notice, once again, that property given to a trustee should be given "in trust," just to make sure that it is clear the property is NOT being given to the trustee as an individual, but only as a trustee.

[28] Notice that this whole part of the trust comes into effect only if Rose survives her brother. This illustrates one of the important aspects of flexibility available with a testamentary trust.

[29] As you will see from other parts of Tennessee Williams' will, he gave very specific directions as to what the trustee should do – including naming the institution at which his sister should reside. Details like this may sometimes be appropriate in wills. But always be sure that your client has considered the possibility of changed circumstances after the death of the testator. What if Stony Lodge had been sold, and the new management had made things very unpleasant for the residents? What if a much better place had become available?

[30] Specific, thoughtful provisions like this are entirely appropriate – and helpful to the trustee. Just be sure to keep them sufficiently open-ended to allow for the trustees to respond to changes in circumstances.

[31] It is important to recognize that Rose might have to be moved to another institution. But what if it were still ["possible"] for her to remain at Stony Lodge, but a far better institution became available? Would the trustee have the authority to have her moved to the better institution? In situations like this it is very important, if possible, to have a concerned family member designated as the one to decide which institution is in fact best for the beneficiary. It may be far too easy for a trustee just to continue with the status quo, without really looking into the quality of care being given to the beneficiary.

[32] Termination of a trust is the third factor to be dealt with whenever you set up a trust. Notice that the beneficiaries at the termination of the trust may be entirely different from the beneficiaries during the term of the trust.

vocation whose work is progressive, original and preferably of an experimental nature.[33]
The use of the funds constituting the WALTER E. DAKIN MEMORIAL FUND shall not
be limited to any particular branch of the literary arts and the recipients thereof need not
be enrolled at the UNIVERSITY OF THE SOUTH.[34]

Thus, with one trust, Tennessee Williams was able to accomplish two important goals – first,
supporting his sister, and second, assisting creative writers. This is part of the wonderful
flexibility of trusts.

Of course, as with any other area of planning, you must always be sure to weigh the various tax
aspects of any decisions you and your client may make when establishing a trust. Particular
format and wording may be crucial for tax purposes. Since tax rules and regulations are
continuously changing, you must simply coordinate your client's plans with the latest word on
taxes – and public benefits.

D.   SPENDTHRIFT TRUST

Any trust may be made into a SPENDTHRIFT trust, and most trusts usually are spendthrift
trusts.

SAMPLE THREE – WILL OF HUMPHREY BOGART

To turn a trust into a spendthrift trust all you need to do is to add a paragraph like the one found
in paragraph NINTH (b) of Humphrey Bogart's will, stating:

> The interests of beneficiaries in principal or income shall not be subject to claims of their
> creditors or others nor to legal process, and may not be voluntarily or involuntarily
> alienated or encumbered.

The purpose of this spendthrift provision is to try to insulate the assets in the trust from all claims
of creditors, so that no matter how deeply in debt the beneficiaries become, they will still have a
secure source of income from the trust. State laws vary widely on how much protection such a
spendthrift clause actually provides. Sometimes CREDITORS who have provided
"NECESSITIES" such as basic food, clothing, shelter, medical care, and the like, frequently
ARE allowed to reach the assets of a spendthrift trust. Or immediate family members who have

---

[33] Notice that fairly specific directions may be included with charitable gifts.

[34] Originally, this fund was to be administered by a committee including the Chairman of the Creative Writing Department at the University of
the South, the chairman of the same department at Harvard, and a "highly represented [sic] and qualified theatrical agent." By his codicil of
December, 1982 Tennessee Williams changed control of the fund to Harvard alone.

claims for support on the trust beneficiary may be able to reach the trust assets. By and large, however, a spendthrift clause will provide some protection for the beneficiaries – UNTIL PAYMENT IS ACTUALLY MADE TO THEM.

Once payment has actually been made to a trust beneficiary, then those assets, in the hands of the beneficiary, are subject to the claims of the beneficiary's creditors just like any other assets of the beneficiary.

Because the creditors of a beneficiary <u>can</u> reach trust assets once they are paid to the beneficiary, many trusts are drafted to include a provision that the trustee may make payments directly to the beneficiary; to others for the benefit of the beneficiary;[35] or to other members of the beneficiary's household.[36] That would permit, for example, payments to the <u>spouse</u> of a beneficiary, if the beneficiary had lots of unpaid creditors, but the <u>spouse</u> did not.

On paper this sounds like a very good deal. In practice, this MAY encourage the same sort of irresponsibility which a child is likely to develop if he or she is constantly "bailed out" by his or her parents, and never has to take responsibility for his or her own actions. In drafting any trust provisions, it may be well to keep in mind the <u>non-financial</u> aspects of the trust – in other words, what effect the trust provisions are likely to have on the <u>emotional</u>, as well as <u>financial</u> well-being of the trust beneficiaries.

In the testamentary trust which Humphrey Bogart established for his children, he seems to have had considerations such as these in mind.

As you read the following provisions from Humphrey Bogart's will, notice how he attempts to protect his children financially in ways which are considerably more sophisticated than the simple, basic spendthrift clause quoted above – and how he provides different degrees of support for his children at different stages of their lives. Notice how Humphrey Bogart eventually allowed his children to grow up – and be responsible for their own decisions. Notice, also, how differently his son and daughter were treated!

[Early in the will, Humphrey Bogart had stated, "I am married to BETTY BOGART (also know as LAUREN BACAL BOGART.")]

---

[35] For example, under a provision like this the trustee could just pay the beneficiary's rent directly to the landlord, or make the house payments directly to the bank. This would ensure that the trust money went directly for housing, for example, rather than to other creditors of the beneficiary – or to "gambling expenses" of the beneficiary. If the beneficiary, for one reason or another, really is not capable of handling his or her financial matters, then having the trust provide, housing and medical care directly may be a wise provision.

[36] By keeping this broad, the trustee could pay the money to the beneficiary's spouse, child, or parent – anyone in the household who did not have creditors attempting to get the money distributed by the trustee.

SAMPLE FOUR – DISCRETIONARY TRUST PROVISION FROM THE WILL OF HUMPHREY BOGART

After establishing a trust for each of his children, Humphrey Bogart provided in Article <u>SEVENTH</u> of his will:

(b)   My trustees shall distribute to, or expend and apply for the benefit of, the child for whom such trust is held, such part or all of the income of such trust and such part or all of the principal thereof, as the trustees shall from time to time deem proper in their absolute discretion. Any income not so distributed, expended or applied shall be accumulated and added to principal. In exercising such discretion my trustees shall take into account the provisions that my wife BETTY shall be able to make for such child from time to time out of funds available to her and shall be guided as near as may be by the standard of living to which said children have been accustomed during my lifetime. It is my desire that their care, comfort and welfare be adequately provided for during their tender years, that they be afforded every opportunity for such higher education as may be appropriate in view of their interest and ability, and that consideration for their support and maintenance after completion of their education shall be secondary. At the discretion of the trustees distributions of income and/or principal during the minority of a child may be made directly to such child or to my wife BETTY, or to such other person as may have actual custody of such child, for application to the use and benefit of such child. Beginning at the age of twenty-three (23) years and thereafter so long as each child shall live, the entire net income of his trust shall be distributed to him at quarterly or other convenient intervals.

(c)   I direct that there shall be paid to each child, on his twenty-third (23rd) birthday or upon his marriage prior to attaining the age of twenty-three (23) years, the amount of twenty-five thousand ($25,000) from the principal of his trust. At any time after a child attains the age of twenty-three (23) years the trustees may in their absolute discretion distribute to such child such portion or portions, up to all, of the principal of the trust being held for such child as the trustees in their absolute discretion may deem proper. I direct that in any event the amounts distributed out of principal of each trust held for a son of mine shall equal at least one-half (1/2) of the original principal value of such son's trust by the time such son attains the age of thirty-five (35) years and that the entire remaining balance of principal of such son's trust shall be distributed to him by the time he attains the age of forty-five (45) years. In the case of each trust held for a daughter of mine, I direct that in any event the amounts distributed out of principal shall equal at least one-half (1/2) of the original principal value of such daughter's trust by the time she attains the age of forty-five (45) years.

Now that you have seen several samples of trusts designed to benefit people who were important to the respective Settlors of the trusts, you may want to try your and at drafting a trust yourself. The following drafting exercise and pointers for drafting may help you in developing the skills necessary for drafting an appropriate trust.

E. DRAFTING EXERCISE 7 – SUPPORT TRUST FOR A CHILD WHO HAS A MEDICAL DISABILITY

Your client is a 35 year old single father who has a 7 year old son with serious medical disabilities. Two years ago the car in which the child was riding was struck by a car driven by an uninsured, drunk driver. The prognosis is that the child will never be able to walk again. Your client's wife was killed in the same accident.

The child seems bright, and is gradually developing a more positive mental attitude, but your client wants to do everything possible to be sure that there will always be a safety net to provide basic food, shelter and clothing for his son, for as long as the son may live. The child now has a life expectancy of approximately 65 more years.

Your client hopes that his son may be able to become a lawyer, engineer, or other professional, and thus be able to be self-supporting. But at the present time there is of course considerable uncertainty about that – and about the child's medical prognosis.

Your client hopes to live long enough to be able to come back to you at various times in future years to update his will and to revise provisions for his son in light of changing circumstances. But he realizes that with the continuing possibility of drunk drivers, and other hazards, the will he writes today may be the last one he is able to sign. Therefore, he wishes to provide for his son as skillfully as possible.

For this drafting exercise you may choose either of two sets of background facts:

A. Your client has inherited a great deal of wealth, so finances are not a problem, but your client has an unusual heart disease which suggests that you client will probably not live past the age of 45; or,

B.   Your client is in excellent health, has a good job as a High School English teacher, and expects to pay off his college loans in about one more year, so that he can then start to build up some modest savings.

After selecting facts A or B, draft an appropriate support trust to be included in your client's will. Do not worry about investment powers for the trustee at this point. Just write appropriate provisions for how the assets in the trust should be distributed, and who should serve as trustee – or successor trustee.

F.   POINTERS FOR DRAFTING

1.   Whenever you draft a trust for a child, it is important to consider the possible psychological, as well as financial aspects of the trust – especially if the trust is to continue for a major part of the child's life. Although all of us would enjoy having a large, steady income from a trust, it must also be realized that having a guaranteed, high income from a trust may in fact undercut a child's own self-esteem and sense of self-worth.

For example, if a child with a brand new job earns a salary which is one-quarter of what the child receives as income from a trust, then the child may well feel that the child's own job – and earnings – are not really very important. Instead of being proud to be able to pay for a small first apartment, for example, the child may instead be constantly reminded that hard as the child is working, the child simply doesn't measure up, financially, to the success of a parent or grandparent. The end results may not be psychologically helpful for the child.

So to the extent possible, a trust such as this support trust should be designed to provide a safety net, not a gold "spirit crusher," for the child.

2.   What assets can you use to fund a trust for a client who, like the English teacher in Drafting Exercise B, has lots of financial responsibilities and virtually no savings?

Frequently, for a young, healthy person, life insurance is a good solution, if it is available at a reasonable price.

From a federal estate tax perspective, it usually makes no difference whether the life insurance is payable to the client's estate or to some beneficiary directly. If the client retains the right to change the beneficiary, the insurance will be subject to federal estate tax[37] regardless of who is listed as beneficiary. So unless there are other countervailing factors, it may be appropriate simply to have the life insurance paid to the client's estate, so that the money will then be controlled by the flexible provisions of the client's will.

3. During the time when the trust exists, there will probably be continuous changes in tax laws, health care provisions, and public benefits, so that it will probably be wise to give the trustee wide discretion – to allow the trustee to take advantage of available public benefits, as appropriate, over the years during which the trust will be in existence.

4. Should the trustee be given the option of making payments either to the beneficiary directly, or to people who have provided goods or services to the beneficiary, or have cared for the beneficiary? In other words, should the grant of authority to the trustee be broad enough to allow the trustee to pay rent, for example, directly to the landlord, or to pay money to a member of the beneficiary's household – instead of directly to the beneficiary?

5. Once the trustee is given broad discretion how can you make sure that the trustee will, in fact, provide adequate support for the beneficiary?[38]

Particularly if the trustee's fees are determined, in part, by how much money is in the trust, the trustee may have a financial interest in keeping the payments to the beneficiary as low as possible, so as to increase the fees of the trustee. [Old Colony Trust v. Rodd, 254 N.E.2d 886 (1970), presents a dramatic example of what may happen when a trustee with broad discretion simply decides to be unconscionably stingy particularly toward beneficiaries who do not have the financial resources to sue the trustee!]

6. Consider providing a minimum level of income or care for the beneficiary – to be met by the trust to the extent NOT provided by public benefits.[39] Do NOT, however, describe this level by a specific dollar amount. The buying power of the dollar, over the years covered by a long term trust, is likely to fluctuate far too much to make a set income, expressed in dollars, appropriate. Could you tie the minimum basic income required from the trust to something like

---

[37] If the estate is one of the very few estates that are actually subject to federal estate tax—roughly only one or two percent of the estates in the country!

[38] Try to find some way of having other family members involved in the decision of what is best for the beneficiary – or other close friends of the beneficiary. But try to avoid built-in conflicts of interest, which might arise if the remainder beneficiaries are also the ones who are deciding what level of care should be given to the primary beneficiary.

[39] This will have to be described in general terms, especially if the trust is likely to continue for a long time. The samples from the wills of Tennessee Williams and Humphrey Bogart illustrate ways of indicating the preferences of the settlor. And much more detail might be appropriate. For example, would you want someone with medical training to be constantly in attendance, as provided for Georgia O'Keeffe in her last years? Is it important that the beneficiary be taken to plays and concerts to the extent possible? Is there a way of ensuring choice for the beneficiary?

the consumer price index, or the federally established poverty level?[40] What if such indexes also change – or are abolished?[41]

7.   Would it be appropriate to provide different levels of minimum support at different stages of the beneficiary's life? Perhaps full support while the beneficiary is completing an education, or when the beneficiary becomes seriously ill or elderly – with decreased support during the time the beneficiary should be developing his or her own career?[42]

8.   When the trust terminates, probably at the death of the beneficiary, what is to become of the remaining assets in the trust? Should the beneficiary be given a GENERAL testamentary power of appointment?[43] Or would such a power be more likely to attract "gold-diggers," rather than true friends? Should the beneficiary be given a SPECIAL power of appointment – for relatives – or for charities?[44] Or does your client simply want to specify where the assets are to go when the trust terminates?

9.   Has an appropriate list of trustees and successor trustees been provided?[45]

10.   Under what conditions, if any, should the beneficiary be able to have a trustee replaced by another trustee if the acting trustee simply is not doing a good job? Should the beneficiary be required to take the matter to court, or should a less expensive means of replacement be provided?

Should the beneficiary be limited to selecting from among trustees on a list provided by the testator? Should two or more outside persons be required to agree with the beneficiary before a trustee may be replaced? What if one or more of the outside persons dies before the termination of the trust?[46]

---

[40] Using an index such as this would help compensate for the constantly changing value of the dollar, and might provide a way in which the distributions of the trustee could be accurately measured – so that both trustee and beneficiary would know if the trustee were complying with the terms of the trust.

[41] When all else fails, it may be appropriate just to say payments must be at least equivalent to the "buying power" of a designated amount of money in the year in which the trust is established. At least this will provide some basis for attempting to change the specific dollar amount of payments in response to changes in the economy.

[42] Humphrey Bogart's trust, included in Section C of this chapter, made some general recommendations along this line. More specific details could be included, in appropriate cases.

[43] This would allow the beneficiary to appoint to anyone – including non-relatives, close friends, creditors, the beneficiary's own estate, charities, and the like.

[44] By limiting the power of appointment to relatives the money would be kept in the family, and this would allow the beneficiary to provide for certain family members who might need special protection. Also, under current law, a special power would not be taxable in the estate of the beneficiary; but a general power would cause all property subject to the power to be taxed in the beneficiary's estate!
REMEMBER: If either kind of power of appointment is used ALWAYS INCLUDE A GIFT IN DEFAULT – specifying who is to get the property if the power of appointment is not effectively exercised!

[45] Normally, a settlor will include at least two or three successor trustees, in case the trustees named earlier on the list cannot, or do not want to serve.

[46] As with all other drafting involving wills, you must always be aware of the possibility that people will not necessarily die in order of age. In addition, what if one of the persons required to agree has lost mental capacity because of age or illness – or for some other reason has become inappropriate as a decision maker? It is certainly easier and less expensive to provide for non-judicial settlement of problems. But when all else fails, the courts are available to solve serious problems involving the administration of trusts.

As you draft provisions for replacement of the trustee, remember that there was some strong reason your client did NOT just give the money outright to the beneficiary. If the beneficiary was considered not to be capable or handling the money alone, the how much control should the beneficiary be given over the selection of the trustee?[47]

Remember also that trustees, like any other group of persons, may be good, capable persons, or persons whose actions need to be carefully watched and regulated. During a period of 65 years, several different types of trustees may serve, and some mechanism for replacement of trustees may be entirely appropriate.

11.   Are there circumstances under which the trust should terminate <u>prior</u> to the death of the beneficiary? What if the trust corpus has become so small that the annual fees for the <u>trustee</u> are 10% or 25% of the value of the corpus? What if the beneficiary has in fact become a responsible, self-supporting adult?

12.   Who decides when there should be an early termination of the trust, and to whom should the money then be given?[48]

G.   POUR OVER TRUSTS

Pour Over Trusts are simply trusts which are designed to "pour over" – or transfer – assets from one entity to another. Assets may be "poured" from an inter vivos trust into a testamentary trust, or the reverse; or assets may be "poured" into or out of an estate in accordance with the terms of any will or trust.

SAMPLE FIVE – WILL OF JOHN LENNON

For example, in Article THIRD of his will, John Lennon, [yes, THE John Lennon], states:

I give, devise and bequeath all the rest, residue and remainder of my estate, wheresoever situate, to the Trustees under a Trust Agreement dated November 12, 1979, which I signed with my wife, YOKO ONO, and ELI

---

[47] Remember, if the beneficiary has full power to select the trustee, then the beneficiary could just shop around until he or she found someone who was willing to act as trustee – and would do just exactly what the beneficiary requested. In that case, the whole point of having a trust would be lost.

[48] This will take some careful thinking – and discussions with your client. If the people who have authority to decide that the trust should be terminated are also the people who would take the corpus of the trust on termination, then the entire trust concept is endangered. Yet if the trustee is the one who is authorized to terminate the trust earlier than it would otherwise terminate, there may be real problems in persuading the trustee to put himself or herself out of a job. The ultimate authority, of course, would be the court. But it is far preferable to find some other, faster and less expensive means of terminating the trust early, if possible.

GARNER as Trustees, to be added to the trust property and held and distributed in accordance with the terms of that agreement and any amendments made pursuant to its terms before my death.

By this provision, Lennon simply "poured over" the remaining assets in his estate into a previously established trust. And that is undoubtedly one of the reasons that Lennon's entire will is only four pages long. All of the details about who gets what, and under what circumstances, are almost certainly contained in the documents establishing the inter vivos trust. And those documents are not a matter of public record.

John Lennon's will was signed on November 12, 1979, the same date on which his Trust Agreement was signed. This close coordination between will provisions and an inter vivos trust is a standard and highly effective method of estate planning. By using the technique of "pouring" assets from his will into a preexisting inter vivos trust, Lennon was able to secure the benefits of privacy offered by an inter vivos trust, while still retaining the flexibility offered by a will.

If, one day before his death, Lennon had changed his mind as to who should have had his residuary estate, he could simply have written a codicil changing the third paragraph of his will – to direct the money elsewhere. This would have been considerably simpler than going through the process of transferring title to various assets from the trustee back to Lennon – or to the new beneficiary.

In a state in which attorneys fees are based on the size of the probate estate, however, this flexibility might have come at considerable expense.

So remember that the technique of "pouring" assets over from one entity to another may serve many beneficial purposes. Just be sure to check all of the financial consequences before using this technique.

H.   CHARITABLE TRUSTS

Establishing a charitable trust is a very attractive means of making a gift to charity. Since the Rule Against Perpetuities, (covered in Chapter 8), does not apply to a solid line of charities, a charitable trust can be designed to last forever.

By using a trust, a settlor can specify exactly how his or her gift is to be used – by ` charities – for centuries. This is tempting – especially to one who may be seeking a form of immortality through charitable giving – but it is usually extremely unwise. The needs of the living are continuously changing – and charities need to be able to respond to those changes.

With the benefit of hindsight, it may be instructive to look at two outstanding charitable gifts – made by Oliver Wendell Holmes and Benjamin Franklin, respectively, and then at a more contemporary charitable trust.

SAMPLE SIX – WILL OF OLIVER WENDELL HOLMES

1.   EFFECTIVE CHARITABLE GIFTS <u>WITHOUT</u> A TRUST

In his will, signed on November 3, 1931, Justice Oliver Wendell Holmes made several charitable gifts – without establishing charitable trusts. Examples of two such generous gifts – which do not seem to have caused any problems – are the following:

> I give to the PRESIDENT AND FELLOWS OF HARVARD COLLEGE, of Cambridge Massachusetts, preferably for the benefit of the Law School but subject to the discretion of the University, TWENTY-FIVE THOUSAND DOLLARS ($25.000).

> I give to the BOSTON MUSEUM OF FINE ARTS, TWENTY-FIVE THOUSAND DOLLARS ($25,000).

2.   <u>PROBLEMS</u> WHEN NO CHARITABLE TRUST IS CREATED

It was Justice Holmes' final, and most famous, outright charitable gift which did, in fact, cause problems. As you may recall, Justice Holmes' final gift simply stated:

> All of the rest, residue and remainder of my property of whatsoever nature, wheresoever situate, of which I may die seized and possessed, or in which I may have any interest at the time of my death, I give, devise and bequeath to the UNITED STATES OF AMERICA.

Justice Holmes' will was admitted to probate on March 9, <u>1935</u>, three days after his death. On June 22, <u>1938</u> Congress approved Resolution No. 124 to establish a <u>committee</u> to make recommendations concerning the use of the bequest. On July 19, <u>1955</u> the House of Representatives voted to establish a "<u>Permanent Committee</u> for the Oliver Wendell Holmes Devise." By the <u>1960's</u> a great deal of time had been spent deciding how to use Holmes' bequest. And some of the money had been spent. Among other things, grants of $10,000 each had been made to various law professors at various public and private institutions to assist them in the novel endeavor of studying the U.S. Supreme Court. Do you think that this was what Oliver Wendell Holmes really intended?!

3.   USE OF CHARITABLE TRUSTS

Benjamin Franklin put a great deal of thought and detail into the charitable trusts which he established, and with the benefit of just over two hundred years of hindsight, it is well worth examining the provisions of those trusts – both for the beauty of the trusts themselves, and for an illustration of how much the world may change in a period of two hundred years.

Now, as you sit back, relax, and enjoy reading part of one of the Franklin trusts, you will be learning some important things about drafting long-term charitable trusts.

SAMPLE SEVEN – WILL OF BENJAMIN FRANKLIN

In his will, executed on July 17, 1788, Benjamin Franklin created charitable trusts for the benefit of Boston and Philadelphia, respectively. Then on June 23, 1789, Franklin added a codicil which starts with the following remarkable provisions:

> I, Benjamin Franklin, in the foregoing or annexed last Will and Testament named, having further considered the same, do think proper to make and publish the following Codicil of Addition thereto.
>
> It having long been a fixed political opinion of mine, that in a democratical State, there ought to be no Offices of Profit, for the reasons I had given in an Article of my drawing in our Constitution, it was my intention when I accepted the Office of president to devote the appointed Salary to some public Uses, accordingly I had already before I made my Will in July last, given large Sums of it to Colleges, Schools, Building of Churches, etc., and in that Will I bequeathed Two Thousand Pounds more to the State for the purpose of making Schuylkill navigable: But understanding since, that such a Sum will do but little toward accomplish such a Work and that the project is not likely to be undertaken for many Years to come; and having entertained another Idea, that I hope may be more extensively useful, I do hereby revoke and annul that Bequest, and direct that the certificates I have for what remain due to me of that Salary be sold towards raising the Sum of Two thousand Pounds Sterling, to be disposed of as I am now about to order.

It has been an opinion that he who receives an Estate from his Ancestors, is under some kind of obligation to transmit the same to their posterity: This Obligation does not lie on me, who never inherited a Shilling from any Ancestor or Relation: I shall however, if it is not diminished by some accident before my Death, leave a considerable Estate among my Descendants and Relations. The above observation is made merely as some apology to my family, for my making Bequests that do not appear to have any immediate relations to their advantage.

I was born in Boston, New England and owe my first instructions in Literature, to the free Grammar Schools established there: I have therefore already considered those Schools in my Will. But I am also under obligations to the State of Massachusetts, for having unasked appointed me formerly their Agent in England with a handsome Salary: which continued some years: and altho' I accidently lost, in their service, by transmitting Governor Hutchinson's Letter much more than the amount of what they gave me, I do not think that ought in the least to diminish my Gratitude.

I have considered that among Artisans good apprentices are most likely to make good Citizens, and having myself been bred to a manual Art Printing, in my native Town, and afterwards assisted to set up my business in Philadelphia by kind loan of Money from two Friends there, which was the foundation of my Fortune, and of all the utility in life that may be ascribed to me, I wish to be useful even after my Death, if possible, in forming and advancing other young men that may be serviceable to their Country in both those Towns.

To this End, I devote Two thousand Pounds Sterling, which I give, one thousand thereof to the Inhabitants of the Town of Boston, in Massachusetts, and the other thousand to the Inhabitants of the City of Philadelphia, in Trust to and for the Uses, Interests and Purposes hereinafter mentioned and declared.

The said sum of One thousand Pounds Sterling, if accepted by the Inhabitants of the Town of Boston, shall be managed under the direction of the Select Men, united with the Ministers of the oldest Episcopalian, congregational and Presbyterian Churches in that Town; who are to let out the same upon Interest at five per cent per Annum to such young married artificers, under the Age of twenty-five years, as have served an Apprenticeship in the said Town; and faithfully fulfilled the Duties required in their Indentures, so as to obtain a good moral Character from at least two respectable Citizens, who are willing to become their Sureties in a Bond with the Applicants for the Repayment of the Monies so lent with Interest according to the Terms herein after Prescribed. All which Bonds are to be taken for Spanish milled Dollars or the value thereof in current Gold Coin. And the Managers shall keep a bound Book or Books wherein shall be entered the Names of those who shall apply and receive the Sums lent, the Dates and other necessary and proper Records, respecting the business and concerns of this Institution. And as these Loans are intended to assist young married Artificers in setting up their business, they are to be proportioned by the discretion of the Managers, so as not to exceed Sixty Pounds Sterling to one Person, or to be less than Fifteen Pounds. And if the numbers of Appliers so entitled shall be so large, as that the sum will not suffice to afford to each as much as might otherwise not be improper, the proportion to each shall be diminished so as to afford to everyone some Assistance. These aids may therefore be small at first; but as the capital increases by the accumulated Interest, they will be more ample. And in order to serve as many as possible in their Turn, as well as to make the Repayment of the principal borrowed more easy, each Borrower shall be obliged to pay with the yearly Interest, one tenth part of the principal, which sums of Principal and Interest so paid in, shall be again let out to fresh Borrowers. And as it is presumed that there will always be found in Boston virtuous and benevolent Citizens willing to bestow a part of their Time in doing good to the rising Generation by superintending and managing this institution gratis, it is hoped that no part of the Money will at any time lie dead or be diverted to other purposes, but be continually augmented by the Interest, in which case there may in time be more than the occasions in Boston shall require and then some may be spared to their Neighboring or other Towns in the said State of Massachusetts who may desire to have it, such Towns engaging to pay punctually the Interest and the Portions of the principal annually to the Inhabitants of the Town of Boston.

If this Plan is executed and succeeds as projected without interruption for one hundred Years, the Sum will then be one hundred and thirty-one thousand Pounds of which I would have the Managers of the Donation to the Town of Boston, then lay out at their discretion one hundred thousand Pounds in Public Works which may be judged of most general utility to the Inhabitants such as Fortifications, Bridges, Aqueducts, Public Building, Baths, Pavements or whatever may make living in the Town more convenient to its People and render it more agreeable to strangers, resorting thither for Health or a temporary residence. The remaining thirty-one thousand Pounds, I would have continued to be let out on Interest in the manner above directed for another hundred Years, as I hope it will have been found that the Institution has had a good effect on the conduct of Youth, and been of Service to many worthy Characters and useful Citizens. At the end of this second Term, if no unfortunate accident has prevented the operation the sum will be Four Million and Sixty one thousand Pounds Sterling, of which I leave One Million Sixty one thousand Pounds to the Disposition of the Inhabitants of the Town of Boston and Three

Million to the disposition of the Government of the State, not presuming to carry my views farther.

Directions then followed for the matching trust for Philadelphia – with the money after the first hundred years to be spent for "bringing by Pipes the Water of Wissahickon Creek into the town, so as to supply the Inhabitants [with good water],…[and] making the Schuylkill completely navigable."

Prior to making the gift for piping the waters of the Wissahickon, Franklin explained that such a project would probably be necessary because of "the covering …[of Philadelphia's] Grand Plat with Buildings and Pavements, which carry off most of the Rain and prevent its soaking into the Earth and renewing and purifying the Springs, whence the Water of the Wells must gradually grow worse, and in time be unfit of use, as I find has happened in all old Cities."

Now, what have you learned by reading the Franklin Trust? In addition to getting a bit more insight into a remarkable man, some things about drafting long-term charitable trusts will have become clear. Obviously, the value of money may change dramatically; career training may be accomplished in different ways; and the needs of society may change.

Providing career training for women may well not have been included in Franklin's goals in 1789, yet there is nothing in Franklin's words themselves to indicate that women were not to be treated on an equal basis with men with regard to loans from the trust.

Franklin <u>did</u> have the foresight to permit the money to be used outside of Boston, if appropriate.[49] Yet in addition to the obvious difficulties of drafting a 200 year trust, some other less predictable problems arose, and the Boston trust was the subject of a fair amount of litigation. For example, during the first hundred years of the trust, Boston changed its form of government, so that there were no longer any "Selectmen." The members of the new Board of Aldermen stepped into the shoes of the Selectmen, with no objections by anyone, <u>until</u> it became time to spend the large sum of money accumulated at the end of the first hundred years. Then Massachusetts courts held that the Alderman were NOT the proper successors, and that the projects authorized by their votes thus had <u>not</u> been properly authorized.

More surprising, perhaps, was the difficulty in deciding which ministers were proper representatives. Sometime during the first hundred years of the trust the Episcopalian church which had been the oldest Episcopalian church ceased being Episcopalian; later the Court had to

---

[49] For a contrast, see <u>Estate of Buck v. Marin Community Foundation</u>, 35 Cal. Rptr. 2d 442 (1994), describing attempts to find a solution caused by the "problem" that the assets in the trust were simply too large to be expended in helping the "poor" of Marin County – one of the richest counties in the U.S.

decide whether or not the oldest Congregational church was still Congregational, or had become Unitarian because of changing religious views with regard to the trinity.

And of course there was a great deal of controversy over how the money should be spent – at the end of the first hundred years, and again at the end of the second hundred years. During the litigation <u>lawyers</u> were authorized by the courts to be paid from the trust funds, despite the fact that Franklin had directed that the <u>trustees</u> should serve without pay.

So, the major, practical, thing to be learned from a study of Franklin's trust is that your usual clients, who may well NOT have the remarkable foresight and intelligence of Benjamin Franklin, should simply NOT attempt to create long-term charitable trusts.

Outright gifts to charities are valuable. Short-term trusts are probably manageable. But until one of your clients seems to be an even more remarkable person than Benjamin Franklin, long-term charitable trusts should probably NOT be attempted.

SAMPLE EIGHT – ANDY WARHOL CHARITABLE FOUNDATION

Turning now to examine a more contemporary trust, it may be interesting to take a look at the charitable foundation established by the American artist, Andy Warhol.

In his nine page will, signed on March 11, 1982, Any Warhol made various gifts, including a gift of $250,000 to his friend, Frederick Hughes, (who was also named as executor);[50] and a gift of not more than $500,000, total, to Warhol's two brothers. Warhol's estate turned out be worth approximately $390 million.

In the Fourth Article of his will, Warhol directed that his executor, (Hughes), establish a chartable foundation "for the advancement of the visual arts." To be called "THE FOUNDATION FOR VISUAL ARTS." The Foundation was the recipient of the remainder Warhol's estate – roughly $389 million.[51]

---

[50] In the absence of undue influence, (discussed in Chapter 2), there is no problem with making a gift to a person who is also named executor in the will. Although a gift of $250,000 seems rather "small" for an estate worth $390 million, based on the rest of the will, this sum may well have been chosen for tax purposes. In 1982 Warhol would have been able to give away approximately $600,000 before incurring any federal estate tax liability. The $250,000 to Hughes, combined with the possible $500,000 to Warhol's brothers, would have reached, (and slightly exceeded), that amount. By giving all the rest of his money to charity, as he did, Warhol would have escaped nearly all federal estate tax. Hughes would come out "all right" under the provisions of the will, because, as indicated later, he would have been entitled to approximately $7.8 million as executor of the estate. That $7.8 million would have been taxable to Hughes as income, while and <u>gift</u> to Hughes would not have been taxable to Hughes. But, perhaps, like a professional athlete, who receives very large payments during prime years, Hughes would have been able to manage the tax on $7.8 million of income.
[51] Article Fifth of Warhol's will.

Despite the enormous sum of money thus given to the Foundation, Warhol's will seems to be entirely devoid of any directions on how the Foundation is to operate – aside from tax issues, and statements naming the initial Directors of the Corporation.

In contrast to Benjamin Franklin, who spelled out his intentions with great care and thoughtfulness, Warhol demonstrated no specific concern for anything – except the tax exempt status of the Foundation.

As it turned out, during the early years of its existence, the Foundation established the Andy Warhol Museum in Pittsburg – which presumably would have met with Warhol's approval.

The Foundation also objected to the legal fees of $12 million being sought by Edward Hayes, attorney for the estate.[52] The trial court ultimately awarded attorneys fees of "only" $7.2 million[53] - said by others to approximate a rate of $2,400 per hour for the work actually done on the estate![54]

Under a New York statute in effect at the time,[55] an executor's commission would have been 2% of all amounts over $5 million [thus at least $7.8 million for this estate];[56] and a New York court had held that a fee agreement of 3% of the gross estate was "facially reasonable"[57] – [which would have led to attorneys fees of roughly $11.7 million in this case].

As it turned out, both the executor and the Foundation considered the requested attorneys fees of $12 million[58] to be excessive, so the matter was litigated. But what might have happened if executors, attorneys, and trustees had remained friends?[59]

With such nebulous, or virtually non-existent, directions on goals for the trust, who would really have had standing to object to diversion of "charitable" gifts to such things as excessive fees for attorneys, executors, and trustees? Who would have been harmed by such diversion?[60]

---

[52] See New York Times for April 21, 1995 and Estate of Andy Warhol, 629 N.Y.S. 2d 621 (1995).

[53] Id.

[54] New York Times, supra.

[55] New York SCPA Sec. 2307.

[56] Being an executor seems to be far more "profitable" than just being a friend!

[57] Matter of Goldstick, 177 A.D. 2d 225, cited in Estate of Andy Warhol, supra.

[58] Estate of Andy Warhol, supra.

[59] According to both the N.Y. Times and Estate of Andy Warhol, supra, on the Sunday Andy Warhol died, Hughes called Hayes and asked him to be the attorney for the estate. The two worked very closely together until Hughes finally fired Hayes as required by a settlement agreement with the Foundation. In Warhol's will, in the Fourth article, he named as the initial directors of the Foundation: Hughes, another friend, Vincent Freemont, and John Warhol. When the same friends are named as both executors and trustees, for a charitable trust which has no clearly stated goals, the potential for abuse is quite real!

[60] Assets held in a charitable trust are generally not subject to taxation, so the public may, to some degree, in effect be subsidizing the activities of a charitable foundation.

What should Warhol have done – if he really did have some charitable goals in mind? How could you have drafted the Warhol trust more effectively? Or would it have been easier just to use some standard <u>form</u> for creating a Living Trust?

If Warhol had been as determined to avoid <u>attorneys</u> fees as he was to avoid taxes, he might have been tempted to put all of his assets into a "Living Trust," while he was alive, to attempt to avoid attorneys fees for probate.

I.   LIVING TRUSTS

The final sample in this chapter is segments from a California LIVING TRUST form. As you read through this sample, try to decide if filling in the blanks in a document like this would have been sufficient if you were representing Warhol – or any other client.

SAMPLE NINE – CALIFORNIA LIVING TRUST FORM

Q: What additional steps should the settlor take to be sure that land, for example, really becomes part of the trust?

Q: When the settlor wants to make a $10,000 gift, without incurring tax liability, must the settlor first <u>remove</u> the money from the trust, and then make the gift? Or could the trustee of the trust make the gift directly?

CALIFORNIA REVOCABLE TRUST FOR SINGLE SETTLOR

CALIFORNIA CONTINUING EDUCATION OF THE BAR, 1984, 1993

ARTICLE ONE

Sole Settlor is Sole Trustee

__[Name of Settlor]__, Settlor…, declares that… [he/she]… has set aside and holds in trust… [the property described in Schedule A attached to this instrument]….

ARTICLE TWO

…Trust Estate

All property subject to this instrument from time to time… [including the property listed in Schedule A]… is referred to as the trust estate and shall be held, administered, and distributed according to this instrument.

ARTICLE THREE

…Payment of Income and Principal to Unmarried Settlor

A.   The Trustee shall pay to or apply for the benefit of the settler… […as much of the trust estate as the settler demands]… in quarter-annual or more frequent installments… [and shall accumulate and add to principal any undistributed net income]….

B.   If the trustee considers the net income of the trust estate insufficient to provide for the settlor's proper health, education, support… [and]… maintenance…, in accordance with the standard of living the settler enjoys at the date of this instrument, the trustee shall pay to or apply for the

Q. How effective will this be while the settlor is the trustee?

settlor's benefit as much of the principal of the trust estate, up to and including the whole of this trust, as is necessary in the trustee's discretion for these purposes... [taking into consideration other funds and assets available to the settler held free of this trust]....

ARTICLE FOUR

...Unmarried Settlor Incapacitated

C.   If at any time..., [either in the trustee's discretion or] ... as certified in writing by two licensed physicians not related by blood or marriage to the settlor or to any beneficiary of this trust, the settler has become physically or mentally incapacitated, whether or not a court of competent jurisdiction has declared ...[him/her]... incompetent or mentally ill or has appointed a conservator, the trustee shall apply for the settlor's benefit the amounts of net income and principal necessary in the trustee's discretion or desirable for the settlor's health, support, comfort, enjoyment, and welfare until ...[either the trustee's determination, or]...the certification in writing by two licensed physicians not related by blood or marriage to the settler or to any beneficiary of this trust, that the incapacity is removed and the settler is again able to manage ...[his/]her]... own affairs. Any income in excess of the amounts so applied for the settlor's benefit shall be added to principal.

Q: What assets would the conservator have outside the trust assets?

Q: If the settlor has a general power of appointment, can the settlor <u>change</u> all the trust provisions by <u>will</u>? What happens in a jurisdiction in which a general residuary clause is assumed to <u>exercise</u> a general power of appointment?

Note: The Family Pot Trust is usually funded by the amount of property which would be exempt from federal estate taxes.

Q: Is it possible that a child who is 25 at the settlor's death will end up getting more money from the trust than a child who was 5 at the settlor's death? What if the 25 year old child becomes the trustee?

If a conservator of the person or estate is appointed for the settlor, the trustee shall take into account any payments made for the settlor's benefit by the conservator

ARTICLE FIVE
…Deceased Settlor's Expenses

A. On the settlor's death,… [and subject to any power of appointment exercised by the settlor],… the trustees may in the trustee's discretion pay out of the principal of the trust estate the inheritance taxes, including interest and penalties arising on the settlor's death….

B(1). Family Pot Trust. On the Settlor's death, and as long as any living child of the settlor is under age 21, the trustee shall pay to or apply for the benefit of all the settlor's children, including those age 21 or older, and to the issue of any deceased child of the settlor, as much of the net income and principal of the exemption trust as the trustee in the trustee's discretion deems necessary for their proper support, health, maintenance, and education, after taking into consideration to the extent the trustee considers advisable any of the children's other income or resources known to the trustee (including but not limited to other trusts held for the their benefit)….

Q: Is it appropriate that the surviving spouse of a deceased child might get more money than a minor child of the settlor? Should any limits be put on distributions to certain people?

B(2). In addition, the trustee, if the trustee considers it advisable, may apply net income and principal of the exemption trust for the support, health, maintenance, and education of the surviving spouse of any deceased child of the settlor, after considering, to the extent the trustee considers advisable, any other income or resources of the surviving spouse of the deceased child known to the trustee (including but not limited to other trusts held for their benefit).

B(3). Any net income not distributed shall be added to principal. In exercising the discretion conferred by this subparagraph, the trustee may pay more to or apply more for the benefit of some beneficiaries than others, and may make payments to or applications of benefits for one or more beneficiaries to the beneficiaries. All payments or applications of benefits under this subparagraph shall be charged against the exemption trust as a whole, rather than against the ultimate distributive share of a beneficiary to whom or for whose benefit the payment is made.

…Division of Trust Into Shares

Q: Is the youngest child at a disadvantage in not getting any income after age 21 except what comes from that child's

C(1). When there is no child of the settlor who is under the age of 21, the trustee shall divide the exemption trust into equal shares, one for each living child of the settlor, and one for each group of the living issue of a deceased child of the settlor. Each share shall be distributed or retained in trust as further provided in this instrument….

Q: If the trust is **not divided into shares** until the youngest child is 21, does it make sense to use the age of 18 here?

Should there be a provision to terminate the trust at <u>any</u> time the total assets fall below a given number – or a specified percentage of the <u>costs</u> of administering the trust?

Note: This power of revocation makes all assets in the <u>trust</u> includable in the settlor's <u>estate</u> for federal estate tax purposes.

Note: This power of amendment also makes all of the trust assets subject to federal estate tax in the settlor's estate.

...Termination When Share Is Small

C(7). If the trust share held for any beneficiary who is over …[e.g., 18]… years has a total value at the end of any calendar year of less than $...., the trustee in the trustee's discretion may distribute the entire trust estate to that beneficiary and may terminate the trust for that beneficiary….

ARTICLE SIX

...Revocation by Sole Settlor

A. The settlor may at any time revoke this instrument in whole or in part by a written instrument. If the settlor revokes this instrument, the trustee shall deliver …[promptly/within … days of receipt of the notice of revocation]… to the settlor or …[*his/her*]… designee all of the designated portion of the trust assets. If the settlor revokes this instrument entirely or with respect to a major portion of the assets subject to the instrument, the trustee shall be entitled to retain sufficient assets reasonably to secure payment of liabilities the trustee has lawfully incurred in administering the trust, including trustee's fees that have been earned, unless the settlor shall indemnify the trustee against loss or expense.

...Amendment

B. The settlor may at any time amend any terms of this trust by written instrument signed by the settlor. No amendment shall substantially increase the trustee's duties or liabilities or change the trustee's compensation without the trustee's consent, nor shall the trustee be obligated to act under such an amendment unless the trustee accepts it.

If a trustee is removed as a result of refusal to accept an amendment, the settlor shall pay to the trustee any sums due and shall indemnify the trustee against liability the trustee has lawfully incurred in administering the trust.

ARTICLE EIGHT

...Broad Investment Powers, Diversification Not Required

To carry out the provisions of the trusts created by this instrument, the trustee shall have the following powers besides those now or later conferred by law:

A. To invest and reinvest all or any part of the trust estate in any common or preferred stocks, share of investment trusts and investment companies, bond, debentures, mortgages, deeds of trust, mortgage participations, notes, real estate, or other property the trustee in the trustee's discretion selects; ...[*to buy stocks or other securities on margin; and to buy or sell options, puts, and calls*]... The trustee may continue to hold in the form in which received (or the form to which changed by reorganization, split-up stock dividend, or other like occurrence) any securities or other property the trustee may at any time acquire under this trust, it being the settlor's express desire and intention that the trustee shall have full power to invest and reinvest the trust funds ...[*in an aggressive manner assuming greater than customary risks of loss*]... without being restricted to forms of investment that the trustee may otherwise be permitted to make by law; and to consider individual investments as part of an overall investment strategy. The investments need not be diversified...

Q: Is it necessary, or wise, for the settlor to give the trustee powers which the legislature adopts after the trust is established?

Q: If safety and moderate growth are the primary objectives, what words should be substituted here?

Q: Is it necessary that the trust charge the settlor's estate interest on a loan? If a trustee who is NOT the settlor lends trust money to himself, who determines what the rate of interest should be?

Q: Does this relieve the trustee from any obligation to make <u>any</u> attempt to discover who is alive or dead? Is this provision mainly for the benefit of the trustee, or might it also help the beneficiaries?

...Power to Lend to Settlor's Probate Estate

...J. to lend money to any person, including the probate estate of the settlor, provided any such loan shall be adequately secured and shall bear a reasonable rate of interest...

...ARTICLE TEN

...Notice to Trustee of Births, Deaths, and Other Events Affecting Interests

B. Unless the trustee has received actual ...[written]...notice of the occurrence of an event affecting the beneficial interests of this trust, the trustee shall not be liable to any beneficiary of this trust for distribution made as though the event had not occurred, provided this clause shall not exculpate the trustee from liability arising from nonpayment of death or generation-skipping taxes that may be payable by the trust on occurrence of an event affecting the beneficial interests of this trust...

Choice-of-Law Clause

E. The validity of this trust and the construction of its beneficial provisions shall be governed by the laws of the State of California in force...[on the date of execution of this instrument] [from time to time]... This ...[*article/paragraph*]... shall apply regardless of any change of residence of the trustee or any beneficiary, or the appointment or substitution of a trustee residing or doing business in another state. Notwithstanding the forgoing, the validity and construction of this trust in relation to any real property located in a jurisdiction outside the State of California shall be determined under the laws of such jurisdiction. If the situs or place of administration of the trust is changed to another state, the law of that state shall govern the administration of the trust.

Q: Is it important, when establishing a trust such as this, to ascertain the law of any jurisdiction in which the trust may own land?

Q: What if the trustee changes the situs of the trust to a jurisdiction in which it would be <u>very</u> difficult for the beneficiaries to sue the trustee?

Q: Is this wise, to leave such broad discretion to the trustee to substitute his or her friends over the trustees selected by the settlor?

Q: Is naming a bank as the final trustee a good idea?

Q: Should the adult beneficiaries have any right to have input as to the choice of successor trustees?

Q: Does it help the <u>beneficiaries</u> for the trustees to be freed from their common law duty of checking on each other?

...ARTICLE ELEVEN

...Trustee Has Power to Designate or Appoint Successor Trustee

A.   Any trustee may resign at any time.   If ...[*name of appointed trustee*]..., for any reason fails to qualify or ceases to act as trustee, ...[name of successor trustee]...of ...[*address*]..., shall act as trustee.

Notwithstanding the preceding paragraph, each person designated or acting from time to time as a trustee of any trust(s) established by this instrument shall have the power to designate successor trustees to act when he or she becomes unable or unwilling to act as trustee of the trust(s).   Each person may designate the same or different persons or entities, including corporate fiduciaries, to act as successor trustee(s) of the trust(s).   If all individuals appointed as trustees and any successors designated by them are unable or unwilling to act as trustee, ...[*name of bank or trust company*]... shall act as trustee of ...[*the/all*]... trust(s).   Any persons acting as trustee of any trust may from time to time revoke any designation of any successor to ...[*himself/herself*]... (whether that designation shall have been made by ...[*him/her*]... or by ...[*his/her*]... antecedent in interest), and that person may designate other persons or entities, or one or more of the same persons or entities, or all the same persons or entities previously designated in a different order, as successor trustee to ...[*him/her*]....   All designations or revocations shall be exercised in writing and are effective on delivery to the ...[*trustee/beneficiaries of the trust(s) for which they are designated*]...

...Successor Trustee's Liability for Predecessor's Acts

D.   No successor trustee shall be liable for any act, omission, or default to a predecessor trustee.   Unless requested in writing within ...[e.g., 60]... days of appointment by an adult beneficiary of the trust, no successor trustee shall have any duty to investigate or review any action of a predecessor trustee.   The successor trustee may accept the accounting records of the predecessor trustee showing assets on hand without further investigation and without incurring any liability to any person claiming or having an interest in the trust....

...ARTICLE THIRTEEN

Trustee's Compensation

The trustee shall be entitle to pay ...[*himself/herself*]... reasonable compensation from time to time without prior court order.

In any event, the trustee shall be entitled to reimburse ...[*himself/herself*]... for any expense of the trust that ...[he/she] has paid.

...ARTICLE FOURTEEN

Name of Trust

The trusts created in this instrument may be referred to collectively as the ...[*full name of settlor and year trust established, e.g. MARY L. SMITH 1982 TRUST*]..., and each separate trust created in this instrument may be referred to by adding the name of the beneficiary....

...Signatures
...When Declaration of Trust...

Executed at ...., California, on......., 20....

-[Signature of Settlor]
_____[Typed name below]_

Trustee

I certify that I have read the foregoing declaration of trust and that it correctly states the terms and conditions under which the trust estate is to be held, managed, and disposed of by the trustee. I approve the declaration of trust in all particulars and request that the trustee(s) execute it.

Dated:_____

_____[Signature of Trustee]
_____[Typed name below]_

Acknowledgement...

Q: What is the reason for securing this written approval by the trustee? Can you think of situations in which a person might refuse to serve as trustee?

CHAPTER 5.   **SPECIAL PROVISIONS REGARDING THE TRUSTEES**

INTRODUCTION

Now that you have studied the various types of trusts available. and have become familiar with the basics on how to establish a trust, it will be useful to think about several other special considerations involved with appointment of trustees – including selection of the trustees, special instructions to the trustees, issues of compensation, and protection of the trustee and the beneficiaries.

Of primary importance, of course, is selection of the trustee.

A. SELECTING THE TRUSTEES

There are three usual categories of trustees – close friends of the settlor; family members; or a bank. There are advantages and disadvantages for each of the categories. Close friends may know the family situation, but may be relatively inexperienced when it comes to making the necessary financial decisions. Family members, in addition to perhaps being relatively inexperienced financially, may have definite conflicts of interest—if the trust is designed primarily to provide support for various members of the family. Banks, and similar institutions, certainly may be expected to have the necessary financial sophistication, but may have very little knowledge of, or concern with, particular needs of family members—and will usually be expected to charge higher fees than close friends or family members would charge.

Because of the strengths and weaknesses of each category of potential trustee, if the trust is large enough to be of interest to a bank, (usually at least $100,000 or more), then it may be beneficial to have a combination of trustees – one a bank, and the other(s) selected from among family members or close friends.

There is no limit to the number of trustees who may be appointed. But as a practical matter, the number should be kept small enough for manageability. There should also be some provision for replacement of trustee(s), as necessary.

SAMPLE ONE – WILL OF NORMAN ROCKWELL

An example of a good provision appointing trustees is found in the will of the popular American artist, Norman Rockwell, who in CLAUSE EIGHTH of his will, as later modified by codicil, stated:

I nominate and appoint my said wife MARY L. PUNDERSON ROCKWELL, my said son THOMAS RHODES ROCKWELL, and BERKSHIRE BANK & TRUST COMPANY, a banking corporation with its principal place of business in Pittsfield, Massachusetts, or any successor, as Trustees of the trusts established under Clauses Fourth and Fifth above. In the event that my said wife shall be unable or unwilling to serve or to continue to serve, I direct that no Trustee be appointed to succeed her. In the event that my said son Thomas shall be unable or unwilling to serve or to continue to serve, I nominate and appoint my son PETER BARSTOW ROCKWELL as successor Trustee, and in the event that my said son Peter shall be unable or unwilling to serve or to continue to serve, I nominate and appoint my son JARVIS WARING ROCKWELL as successor Trustee. In the event that no one of my three sons shall be able or willing to serve or to continue to serve, I direct that the oldest adult grandchild of mine who is willing and able to serve as Trustee hereunder at any time or from time to time until said Trusts have terminated, shall serve as a successor Trustee together with said Bank.

By this provision Norman Rockwell appropriately provided for successors to both the corporate and family trustees. Since all trustees are liable for the acts of any one trustee, this should provide good security for the assets of the trust – and good input from family members as to particular concerns of the family.

In contrast to the relatively simple provision used by Norman Rockwell for appointment of trustees, Benjamin Franklin went into far more detail on appointment of the trustees for his charitable trusts for Boston and for Philadelphia. Perhaps because of the fact that Franklin's charitable trust for Boston actually did last for the intended 200 years, his trust serves as an example of the difficulties which may be encountered with regard to appointment of trustees – especially for a relatively long-term trust.[1] (See Chapter 4, Sample Seven.)

Studying a small segment of the history of Benjamin Franklin's trust for Boston points out the tremendous difficulties involved any time the settlor of a trust is engaged in trying to anticipate the future.

B. INSTRUCTIONS TO TRUSTEES

It is definitely appropriate to give rather detailed instructions to a trustee as to the goals of the trust. Discussion of some such instructions may be found in Chapter 1, with regard to a trust designed to provide college money for the settlor's children.

---

[1] Major changes in circumstances are almost certain to happen over a long period of time. But as we all realize, many major changes may also happen over a very short interval of time. So these same problems might have arisen within five years of the establishment of the trust.

Yet when it comes to the issue of financial instructions to a trustee, or directions on types of investments, too much detail is probably not wise.

Although it may seem quite natural for a person who has done well financially to try to pass on guidelines to his or her successor, (the trustee), this is almost never a good idea.

For example, with the benefit of hindsight, you can see that the following investment directives provided by Tennessee Williams in his will were probably unwise.

SAMPLE TWO—WILL OF TENNESSEE WILLIAMS

In ARTICLE XI of his will, signed on September 11, 1980, Tennessee Williams stated:

> With respect to investments by my Trustees, I direct that as assets of my estate are converted into cash that the same be re-invested in either United States Treasury bills, notes, bonds, or certificates of deposit issued by THE CHASE MANHATTAN BANK OF NEW YORK, New York or such other leading New York City bank, as my Trustee may designate.

Basically, as it turned out, these investment directives by the settlor were simply too restrictive to have permitted appropriate diversification and growth of trust assets during this period.

Generally, it is far better to leave full discretion to the trustee[2] – so that changes in the economy and in investment opportunities may be appropriately handled by one who is on the scene at the time the decisions are to be made.

However, if the trust is <u>small,</u> is to last for a relatively <u>short</u> time, and is to be handled by a family member who has little experience in investments, then specific investment directives may be appropriate. Such a situation, for example, might arise when a grandparent wants to set aside $5,000, or so, to assist a favorite grandchild with tuition for college. In that situation, if no family members have any particular experience with investments, instructions like those contained in the will of Tennessee Williams may be quite appropriate.

For a relatively "small" trust, securing the financial expertise of a bank, or similar institution, may be impractical. Conditions vary from place to place, and from time to time, of course, but generally a bank will not be interested in handling a trust of less than $100,000, and trustee's fees will probably be at least $6,000 per year – plus a percentage of the trust income or principal – or both.

---

[2] State statutes, and case law, may curtail any trustee's discretion considerably – requiring the trustee to meet the standards of the "reasonably prudent man rule," for example.

So designating a bank, for example, as a professional trustee is simply not a reasonable option for a relatively small trust. In that case, specific investment directives to the family member who will be acting as trustee may well be appropriate and helpful.

Another situation in which specific investment directives may be appropriate is the situation in which one of the settlor's primary concerns is for a particular <u>cause</u> – such as protection of the environment, development of solar energy, urban revitalization, development of medical technology, or the like. In that case, the settler may be willing to accept smaller financial gains for the trust – or even losses – if the money is being invested in enterprises which seem to the settlor to be particularly worthy causes.

By limiting investments to a particular segment of the economy, the settlor may be able to use the trust assets BOTH to support favorite causes and to provide some income for members of the settlor's family – or for charities.

Drafting Exercise 8, which follows, allows you to try developing investment instructions for such a trust.

C.   DRAFTING EXERCISE 8—SUGGESTING INVESTMENT GOALS FOR THE TRUSTEE—"GREEN INVESTMENTS"

Your client has devoted a great deal of her life to environmental causes, serving as attorney for various environmental groups within the United States, and doing volunteer work on various environmental projects during many of her vacations. She would like to continue helping environmental causes, financially, after her death.

Because your client has two young children, and an elderly mother, all of whom need some financial support from her, your client is unable to give her money directly to her favorite environmental causes. So she has decided to set up a testamentary trust—to provide necessary support for her children until they both reach 25, and for her mother, for the remainder of her mother's life. In addition, the trust is to be designed, if possible, to do something to help the environment.

Therefore, your client would like to require the trustee to invest the trust funds only in "green" investments—that is, investments in companies which are managed in such a way as to protect or enhance the environment.

Draft investment instructions for the trustee which would be effective in meeting the goals of your client. You may select as trustee either a family member, a close friend, or corporate trustee – or some combination thereof. You may also determine the approximate anticipated value of the trust assets at the client's death. Remember, however, that the value of assets in a trust may increase or decrease dramatically, and unexpectedly, after establishment of the trust.

At the termination of a trust such as this, the trust assets would normally be distributed either to your client's favorite environmental organizations, or to your client's children who are alive at the termination of the trust.

Ultimate distribution of trust assets is not part of this drafting exercise. But if ultimate distribution would affect how you draft the investment instructions, then you may specify any ultimate distribution which seems appropriate to you.

D. POINTERS FOR DRAFTING

1.   First, you must explain carefully what your client means by the term "green" investments.

     What definition should you use? If you are personally an expert in this field, you may be able to rely on your own expertise in defining the term. Otherwise, you may simply have to rely on the expertise and preferences of your client.

     Be sure, however, that any definition is (1) flexible enough to be useful ten or twenty years from now, when conditions may have changed significantly, and (2) clear enough to give real guidance to the trustee – and to the beneficiaries. Probably the last thing your client would want would be to have trust money spent on battles between the trustee and the beneficiaries as to the appropriateness of particular investments. So make it clear what is to be considered sufficiently "green."

2.   At what point should "green" investments be considered to be too much of a loss? What if during a particular year the stock market goes UP by 10% and the "green" investments go DOWN by 15%? Should some or all of the investments then be pulled out of "greens"? What if the same general pattern of losses continues for 5 years? Or 10 years?

3.   Should different rates of loss be tolerated depending on which people are being supported by the trust? Would it be appropriate to tolerate fewer losses while the trust was supporting younger children – and your client's elderly mother – and then more investment losses if the trust were supporting only children who were in their early twenties?

4.   How should the investments be designed? To maximize income? Or to maximize help for the environment? Or something in between? How should the trustee seek to balance the competing interests involved?

5.   When, if ever, would it be appropriate for the beneficiaries and the trustee simply to AGREE to modification of the investment directives? Should some designated third party have authority to approve or disapprove of such modifications – without the necessity of going to court?

6.   Under what circumstances should the trustee, or the beneficiaries, be allowed to seek court approval for changes in the investment guidelines? At that time, what guidelines might be provided for the court in ascertaining the settlor's intent?

7.   Under what circumstances should the trust assets be liable for costs of litigation, or judicial determination, involving the investment directives?

8.   Are your provisions clear enough to protect a trustee from unjustified suit by beneficiaries who are unhappy that the trust has not provided them with more income? Are your provisions clear enough to provide a strong basis for environmental groups to insist on "green" investments?

E.   COMPENSATION FOR FIDUCIARIES: TRUSTEES AND EXECUTORS

As indicated above, banks will probably have standard fees for estate and trust work – though if an estate or trust is large enough, there may well be a possibility of bargaining with the bank over the fees to be charged.[3]

States may also have either mandatory or recommended guidelines for fees which may be charged by trustees, or executors, or both – (collectively called "fiduciaries").

In some cases, however, it may be possible to negotiate the fees to be charged by various fiduciaries – and there is no harm in trying. Particularly with a large estate or trust, the fees charged by fiduciaries may seem inexcusably high to the beneficiaries – especially if the fees are based on a percentage of the estate or trust assets—not on the amount of work actually done by the fiduciaries.

---

[3] See, for example, the litigation involving Kate Rothko's successful challenge to the attorneys fees charged for the extensive litigation against the trustees, and the $7.2 million attorneys fees granted, after extensive litigation, to the attorneys for Andy Warhol's estate.

Fee guidelines in the will, if successful, might help to prevent later litigation among trustees, executors, and beneficiaries over the size of the fees to be charged.

When tax matters are a significant consideration it is well to remember that under current law, basically, the fees charged by either a trustee or an executor will be considered ordinary <u>income</u> to the trustee or executor, but may be <u>deductible</u> for the trust or estate. On the other hand, a <u>gift</u> to an individual is <u>not taxable to the recipient</u>, but will <u>not</u> be deductible for the trust or estate. So within any particular family situation, there may be tax reasons for trying to use trustees or executors fees, instead of gifts – or the reverse.

Both Georgia O'Keeffe and Oliver Wendell Holmes, along with many others, tried to limit the fees to be charged by people serving as trustees or executors.

SAMPLE THREE—WILL OF GEORGIA O'KEEFFE

Georgia O'Keeffe, for example, in paragraph SIXTEENTH, part B of her 1979 will stated:

I direct that JOHN BRUCE HAMILTON shall not be entitled to any commission or other compensation for his services as Executor, notwithstanding the existence of any statute to the contrary. The bequests made to him in Article SEVENTH are in lieu of all compensation or commissions to which he would otherwise be entitled as Executor.

> If JOHN BRUCE HAMILTON fails to qualify or ceases to act as Executor for any reason whatsoever, I direct that his successor, whether named herein or otherwise appointed, shall be paid a fee of Two Hundred Thousand ($200,000) Dollars for his or her services as Executor and shall not be entitled to any other commission or compensation for said services, notwithstanding the existence of any statute to the contrary.[4]

---

[4] In fact as you may remember from Chapter 2 the First Codicil to Georgia O'Keeffe's will probably changed this limitation as to Hamilton – by a <u>partial</u> white out of the word "not." And in any case Hamilton was essentially given full control of the entire estate by the contested Second Codicil. After litigation, Hamilton and O'Keeffe's family concluded a settlement agreement under which Hamilton renounced essentially the entire additional *$50* million which would have gone to him under the Second Codicil. Although executor's commissions on $50 million alone might have been approximately $1 million (based on a very modest fee of 2% of the estate) the difference between charging $200,000 as executors fees, and $1 million as executor's fees pales in comparison to Hamilton's willingness, or perceived need, to give up the $50 million which would have gone to him if the validity of the Second Codicil had been upheld.

As it turned out, as his part of the estate Hamilton received "24 paintings, the Ghost Ranch house, all of O'Keeffe's letters to him, and certain copyrights." <u>Georgia O'Keeffe, A Life</u>, by Roxanna Robinson, supra. p. 55.

Certainly this is a strongly worded, clear provision. Whether or not it would be upheld would depend upon state law. But the beneficiaries under the will would certainly have a strong basis from which to object to any commission or fee in excess of $200,000.[5]

F.   EXCULPATORY CLAUSE FOR FIDUCIARIES

It is standard practice in wills and trusts to try to protect trustees and executors from being sued by unhappy beneficiaries. The extent to which such provisions will be upheld, and the extent to which such provisions are wise, will vary with individual circumstances. It is frequently <u>judicial</u> policy that such exculpatory clauses should only be inserted into a document at the request of the <u>client.</u>

In any case, the following sample, from the will of Elvis Presley, illustrates a standard exculpatory clause for the trustee of a discretionary trust, when Elvis states:

SAMPLE FOUR – WILL OF ELVIS PRESLEY

> Any decision of the Trustee as to whether or not distribution shall be made, and also as to the amount of such distribution, to any of the persons described hereunder shall be final and conclusive <u>and not subject to question by legatee or beneficiary hereunder</u>. [Emphasis added]

Later, in setting forth the powers available to his Trustee, Elvis states:

> Except as otherwise stated expressly to the contrary herein, I give and grant to the said Trustee (<u>and to the duly appointed successor Trustee</u> when acting as such) the power to do everything he deems advisable with respect to the administration of each trust required to be established under this, my last will and testament, even though such powers would not be authorized or appropriate for the Trustee. [Emphasis added.]

This provision is also typical of the type of provision lawyers, (who may someday end up as trustees or executors), normally insert into a will – frequently without any particular discussion with the client. Ethically such provisions should only be included at the specific request of the client.

---

[5] See <u>Old Colony Trust Co. v. Rodd</u>, 254 N.E.2d 886 (1970).

SAMPLE FIVE—WILL OF GEORGIA O'KEEFFE

The 1979 will of Georgia O'Keeffe went even further in attempting to protect both trustees and executors, again, with a fairly standard, "boiler-plate" provision which stated:

> Whenever under any of the provisions of this Will, any fiduciary is authorized in such fiduciary's discretion to take any action or make any determination or decision, any such action, determination or decision shall be final and binding upon any one [sic] interested in my estate or any trust hereunder and <u>such fiduciary shall not be held accountable in any court or to any person with respect thereto</u>. [Emphasis added.]

Georgia O'Keeffe then goes on to try to add additional protection for the trustees and executors—for any bad financial decisions, by providing:

> No fiduciary shall be liable or responsible for the loss or depreciation of any security, investment or other property which may be received, purchased, made or retained by such fiduciary in good faith in accordance with the provisions of this Will, or with respect to any of the funds held by such fiduciary hereunder, or for any loss incurred in any enterprise undertaken or participated in by such fiduciary with respect to any of the funds held by such fiduciary hereunder, or for any act, deed or loss, no matter how incurred, arising from any matter with respect to any such funds, undertaken by such fiduciary in good faith pursuant to the provisions of this Will. [Emphasis added.]

Those provisions are all very nice for the various fiduciaries. But WAIT! For whose benefit are these wills and trusts actually being written?! Who really should be protected—the fiduciaries or the beneficiaries?!

Under the terms of Elvis's will, the successor Trustee, or successor Executor might have ended up being the National Bank of Commerce, in Memphis. Do you really think Elvis would have wanted to protect the bank against any possible suit by his daughter, Lisa Marie? What if the bank is doing dumb things? Why make it so difficult for Lisa Marie to litigate?

Exculpatory clauses are usually included in a will as a standard practice, by the attorney drafting the will—without any real discussion with the client. Yet the justification that, "Everybody else is doing it," is hardly a sufficient basis for including any term in any document.

If an exculpatory clause is used, in fairness to the beneficiaries, who are really the primary persons of concern to the testator, any exculpatory clause which is included should be carefully drawn, with the interests of the beneficiaries protected.

Drafting Exercise 9, in Section H of this chapter will give you an opportunity to try drafting such a clause.

G.   NO BOND REQUIRED FOR FIDUCIARIES

One other "boiler-plate" provision which is usually included in trusts and wills is a provision stating that no fiduciary shall be required to post any BOND. An example of such a provision is found in the will of the American Artist, Mark Rothko.

SAMPLE SIX—WILL OF MARK ROTHKO

The EIGHTH, and final, paragraph of the two page will of Mark Rothko states that:

> I direct that my Executors shall not be required to furnish any bond, undertaking or security for the faithful performance of their duties.

As you may know, the "faithful performance" by Rothko's executors ended up being the subject of extensive litigation, resulting in judgments of between $6 million and $9 million against each one of the three executors, at least two of whom would not have had the remotest chance of being able to pay such judgments from their personal funds.[6]

In hindsight, was the "boiler-plate" elimination of the bond requirement in the Rothko will a wise provision?

True, standard will provisions virtually always provide that bond need not be posted. Under the Uniform Probate Code, unless provided otherwise in the will, bond is NOT required, unless the court decides that in a particular case, having bond posted would be a wise decision.

Bonds for executors and trustees, like bonds in criminal matters, do cost some money. The arguments against requiring bonds for fiduciaries are basically two: (1) saving money for the estate is a "good idea," and (2) if the fiduciary cannot be trusted, then he or she should not be appointed as a fiduciary, anyway.

---

[6] See Dukeninier, Johanson, Lindgren & Sitkoff, Wills, Trusts, & Estates, 7th Ed. Aspen Publishers at pg. 789-790.

Widespread use of personal and professional liability insurance, however, would suggest that in other areas, when individuals are handling large sums of money, such blind faith in the "goodness of human nature" is not considered to be a wise business practice.

Perhaps it is appropriate to waive bond for a professional fiduciary, who is expected to have "deep pockets" and sufficient liability insurance in any case.

Perhaps it is NOT wise to waive bond requirements for friends or family members, like the Rothko executors, who do NOT have particularly deep pockets—and may well NOT have sufficient personal assets or liability insurance to cover major losses to the trust or estate.

In any case, the fact that, "everybody does it," is simply NOT a sufficient reason for including such a provision in documents which you draft for your own clients.

Finding the proper balance between the interests of the beneficiaries, and an appropriate degree of protection for the fiduciaries may prove to be a complex challenge.

Drafting Exercise 9, which follows, gives you an opportunity to try your hand at drafting such a provision—for a client who may—or may not—show up to appreciate your drafting.

H. DRAFTING EXERCISE 9—EXCULPATORY CLAUSE TO PROTECT THE TRUSTEES—AND THE BENEFICIARIES

Using the complete will of Elvis Presley, (found in the Appendix), and whatever you happen to know about Elvis and his family, try drafting an appropriate exculpatory clause to be included in the will of Elvis Presley.

Your exculpatory clause should appropriately protect the trustees and executors, and should also provide appropriate protection for the beneficiaries. You may choose to waive bond requirements for some, or all, of the fiduciaries. Or you may choose to specify that some or all of the fiduciaries are to be bonded.

The following Pointers for Drafting may help you to spot and analyze the major issues involved with this drafting exercise.

I.   POINTERS FOR DRAFTING—EXERCISE 9

1.   First, you should decide whether all of the fiduciaries are to be treated alike. How much should be done to try to protect each of the fiduciaries from suits brought by unhappy beneficiaries? Is it appropriate to give lots of protection to Elvis's father, Vernon, while he is acting as trustee or executor—and then far less protection to any successor trustee or executor—such as the bank?

2.   Next, what sort of protection should be provided? It seems clear from the will that Elvis had tremendous faith in his father's judgment. And it looks as if Vernon might be a particularly likely target for suits by unhappy relatives, because of the provision of the ITEM IV(b)(4) giving Vernon, alone, the discretion to make payments to other living relatives who are "in need of emergency assistance." A provision allowing Vernon such wide discretion may in fact subject Vernon to all kinds of "strike" suits by unhappy persons claiming to be relatives "in need of emergency assistance"—unless good protection for Vernon is provided in the will.

3.   On the other hand, how much financial sophistication and experience does Vernon actually have? And how deep are Vernon's pockets—in case he actually does do something wrong in handling the vast sums of money which will be in his care? Might it be a good idea to require that Vernon post bond—or buy insurance—or provide some other way in which the trust could be reimbursed, if necessary? The expenses of such bond, or insurance, would of course be chargeable to the trust.

4.   Would it also be a good idea to have the bank, whenever acting as successor trustee or executor, also post bond? Or is it sufficient to rely on the "deep pockets" and liability insurance already carried by the bank? Should there be a means of checking how much this pre-existing liability insurance is, at any given time—and whether or not the amount of insurance available actually provides sufficient protection for the specific estate or trust?

5.   While protecting the FIDUCIARIES, what special protections should be given to the BENEFICIARIES? Should the estate or trust assets pay the litigation expenses for an unhappy beneficiary? Whether or not the beneficiary wins? Only if the beneficiary wins? What if the beneficiary sues for $10 million and is given a judgment for a nominal sum such as $5. Is that a "win" or not? Who decides?

6.   Should there be a limit on the number of times a beneficiary can bring suit and still be reimbursed by the estate or trust? Once a year? Once every two years? Or should the beneficiary be able to sue as often as her or she likes—and be reimbursed every time the beneficiary wins?

7.   Should it be easier for the beneficiaries to sue the bank than it is for the beneficiaries to sue Vernon? How might that be accomplished?

8.   Should all of the beneficiaries be treated alike? Or should it be easier for Lisa Marie, or Minnie, to sue the estate or trust?

9.   Under what circumstances should the estate or trust pay the litigation expenses for the FIDICUIARIES? Should litigation expenses be more easily paid for Vernon than for the bank?

10.   Should litigation expenses be available to either side only AFTER good faith NEGOTIATION has failed? How in the world do you ascertain that there has been good faith negotiation?

11.   In an estate the size of Elvis's, there should be plenty of money for all the litigation anyone likes. Yet should there be ways to DISCOURAGE LITIGATION—especially against Vernon—so as to minimize the definite EMOTIONAL strain involved in any litigation? How might this be done?

12.   Has an appropriate balance been struck between the interests of the various beneficiaries, Vernon, and the bank? Are all of your provisions so clearly drafted that they will be easily understood by both laymen and lawyers alike—so that unwarranted SUITS WILL ACTUALLY BE DISCOURAGED?

CHAPTER SIX: PET TRUSTS

Many of the issues discussed in the previous chapter also apply to pet trusts. But there are a number of other, specialized issues to be considered when establishing a trust for the care of a pet.

WHEN Leona Helmsley died in 2007 leaving $12 million to a trust to care for her dog, Trouble, that caught the attention of the public.[1] When the New York Surrogate's Court cut the amount down to $2 million in 2008[2] fewer people noticed. Then in 2009 the New York Surrogate's Court held that "[T]he trustees may apply the trust funds for such charitable purposes and in such amounts as they may, in their sole discretion, determine."[3] And the trustees promptly announced that, "[T]he trust funds [will] be put to optimal use as soon as possible in such areas as **health care, medical research, human services, education,** and various other areas."[4]   So much for the dogs.

Most people consider their pets to be valued members of the family.[5] Therefore, a well drafted will should include provisions for the pets. Clients seem to be happily surprised when a lawyer takes time to ask about the pets.

Probably the best solution is simply to give the pets to a trusted friend or relative who likes animals. The cats go to a cat-lover; the dogs go to a dog-lover. And there should be back-up provisions in case the designated person cannot or will not take the pets.[6]

Clients may enjoy having you put the specific names of the pets in their wills. But ALWAYS remember to say that the named pets, "AND ALL OTHER PETS I MAY OWN AT MY DEATH" are to be included under the provisions of the will.

Now for the details.

Normally, a real dog-lover or real cat-lover will take care of a friend or relative's pets – with or

---

[1] See, for example: New York Times, August 29, 2007, "Leona Helmsley's Unusual Last Will" by Jeffrey Toobin; The New Yorker, Sept. 29, 2008, "Rich Bitch, The legal ballet over trust funds for pets" by Jeffrey Toobin.
[2] Order by surrogate Renee Roth, June 17, 2008.
[3] Order of Surrogate Troy Webber, issued February 18, 2009. Actually, the specific pet trust was called the LEONA HELMSLEY JULY 2005 TRUST. The residuary trust, called The Leona M. and Harry B. Helmsley Charitable Trust, was estimated to be worth closer to $ 8 billion, and was directed to be spent for, "(1) purposes related to the provisions of care for dogs; and (2) such other charitable activities as the Trustees shall determine."
[4] [Emphasis added.] See Press Release, February 25, 2009, by the Trustees of The Leona M. and Harry B. Helmsley Charitable Trust.
[5] In Hurricane Katrina it became clear that many people simply would not leave their pets behind when evacuation became necessary. Therefore, in subsequent large evacuations, such as the fires in San Diego in 2007, and the earthquake in L'Aquila, Italy, in 2009, specific provisions were made for pets by the organizations charged with evacuation and rescue operations.
[6] In the global economic downturn of 2008-2009 very large numbers of pets were left at shelters, or abandoned by their owners – even at pet care establishments which had been serving very wealthy clients.

without any financial payments – just out of love for the deceased friend or relative– and the pets. As always, remember that your client knows his or her friends and relatives better than you do. If the pets and the people have been getting along well while everyone is alive, there should be no big problems.[7]

But there are certain issues which should be considered whenever pets may be involved.

A. NOTIFICATION FOR IMMEDIATE CARETAKER

In ANY situation in which pets may be involved, be sure that specific provision is made for who should start taking care of the pets immediately after the death of the client – and how that person should be notified. Remember that the will itself will probably not be submitted for probate until at least five days after the death of the client. And the personal representative or executor may not be appointed for some time after that. So, while details in the will may be helpful, they are not sufficient. When you specify in the will who is to be the immediate caretaker for the pets, also put the same provisions in a separate, independent document. Send copies of that document to anyone who may be involved. Give copies to the neighbors, with instructions as to how to notify the immediate caretaker, and leave a copy in a prominent place at the client's home – especially if the client is living alone.

Even though in most jurisdictions there probably is no specific statutory authorization for such an independent document, which is designed to be effective either before or after the death of the owner, virtually anyone would comply with the instructions that the client has given for care of the pets – if those instructions were known. And having the same provisions in the will should make everything legally binding in the situation where the owner has died. But as a practical matter, be sure not to depend on the will alone.

Be sure that the instructions for immediate care include a right of access to the pets. Probably having the document notarized – and maybe witnessed as well – will provide added psychological, (if not legal), impact to the independent document. In the absence of a specific statute, the actual legal authority for the provisions will be in the will.

The independent pet care document can provide several valuable protections for the pets. In addition to providing for immediate care for the pets on the death of the owner, it can also provide for emergency care in other situations. While you are drafting such a document you should provide that the named caretaker has authority to take care of the pets not only upon the

---

[7] Certainly if the pet is going into a new household, in which there are already one or more pets, there are likely to be adjustment problems among the pets. But such problems can normally be overcome.

death of the owner, but also during the life of the owner, if the owner is suddenly hospitalized, or for any other reason does not have the capacity necessary to arrange for immediate care of the pets. There is no harm in trying to get a copy of this document into the hands of the client's doctor, or into the medical records. But giving friends, family, and neighbors copies of the document, and leaving a copy for emergency responders, are the most likely ways to make the document effective.

Almost anyone would be willing to make a phone call to insure immediate care for pets. The person just has to know whom to call.

The person(s) listed as immediate caretakers for the pets need not be the same people who will be selected for long-term care of the pets.

B. LONG-TERM CARE FOR PETS

1.   FRIENDS AND RELATIVES WHO LOVE THE PETS

As indicated above, the best solution is to give the pets to someone who already knows and loves the pets. Depending on the circumstances, the client may want to give a lump sum of money to the person who takes care of the pets – just as a thank you for taking care of the pets.[8] The money will help with food, veterinarian bills and the like. But probably anyone who really loves the pets will take care of them – with or without the money. So don't add complex financial provisions which will just involve layers of accounting for the new caretaker.

2.   CARETAKERS WHO MIGHT NOT VOLUNTARILY CARE FOR THE PETS.

If the client is not lucky enough to have friends or relatives who would automatically take care of the pets, then a pet trust may be needed. Some states have specific statutory provisions for pet trusts.[9] Many do not. If the state has a specific statute, follow the statute. Otherwise, just set up a standard trust, with a named human or institutional beneficiary[10] who will get certain payments ONLY while there is compliance with the trust provisions regarding the pets.

Here are some pointers for drafting a pet trust.

---

[8] It should be specified in the will that the money should go to the person who actually ends up with the pets – whether than turns out to be the caretaker listed as first choice, or the caretaker listed as a backup choice for caregiver.
[9] For example, see the Colorado Pet Trust statute at C.R.S. 15-11-901.
[10] Remember that at common law a pet could not be the beneficiary of a trust. And even jurisdictions which permitted an "honorary" trust for the benefit of a pet insisted that the trust comply with the common law Rule Against Perpetuities. So to avoid litigation, just provide that the trust is to last "no longer than the last to die of [eight named people], and that a named person, named successors, and/or a named institution are to beneficiaries of the trust, [in the amount of $100 per year?], for so long as the designated pet survives, and the terms of the trust are met.

C.   PET TRUSTS

Setting up a pet trust like Leona Helmsley's is just asking for litigation. Setting up a rational trust, with a rational amount of money, will make it far safer for the pet.

Remember that it is the best interests of the pet that should be the fundamental consideration for a pet trust. Any pet for whom a trust is to be established has probably enjoyed a great deal of love and companionship while the owner was alive. Try to design the trust so that the pet will continue to be provided with that sort of love and companionship.

There are a number of important issues that should be covered in a pet trust: clear identification of the pet; caretaker and back-up caretaker; physical location for the pet; food and medical expenses; payments to the caretaker; designation of trustee and successor trustee; investment of trust funds; verification of proper care for the pet; authority to litigate on behalf of the pet if necessary; provisions for allowing the pet to be put to sleep when that is in the best interests of the pet; and provisions for distribution of funds remaining in the trust at the death of the pet.

1.   CLEAR IDENTIFICATION OF THE PET

If the pet involved does not already have a micro-chip providing identification, have the client ask the vet to implant some such form of identification. A photograph of the pet might also be useful. This may seem foolish, at first. But if a caretaker is to receive generous pay while taking care of Leona Helmsley's dog, Trouble, then when Trouble gets old, or ill, the caretaker might be tempted to substitute a younger, healthier dog, who looks very much like Trouble. So just use the micro-chip, or some such identification, to try to prevent this. It should be provided in the trust that if the pet does not have a micro-chip or some other good form of identification at the time the pet trust goes into effect, then it is the first duty of the trustee or the caretaker to have such a chip, or other good means of identification, provided.[11]

2.   SPECIFY THE CARETAKER, AND BACK-UP CARETAKER

This pet trust is being established because there is no friend or relative who will simply take care of the pet voluntarily, without pay.

So choice, and supervision, of the caretaker will be important.

---

[11] Yes, there is a danger that the micro-chip might later be taken from one animal and implanted in a younger one. Just provide that the best technology which is financially feasible at the time is to be used.

Sometimes, a friend or relative will be willing to take care of a pet if financial benefits are involved. But remember, it is providing love and companionship for the pet that are most important. Probably no client would want his or her pet to be kept alive in a cage or dog-run just so that the caretaker could continue to collect money. So be very careful on this.

One method sometimes used to select a caretaker is to give the veterinarian who has been taking care of the pet most recently the authority to specify who should be named as caretaker. Veterinarians, informally, have been finding homes for pets in this way for years. If the vet is to select the caretaker be sure to specify that the pet is to continue being taken to the same vet, at least once or twice a year, just so that the vet can check up on the condition of the pet.

But if the vet is not able or willing to select a caretaker, then there are a few other options. For some types of dogs and cats there is a specific "Rescue Society," (the Dalmatian Rescue Society, for example), or some such entity, which takes on the responsibility of finding homes for the specific type of animal involved. That might be a good bet.

Or the client might make out a list of trusted friends and relatives who might take care of the pet – if financial remuneration were involved. If choice of the caretaker is to be made from a list provided by the client, then it is probably best to specify that the first decision as to who should be the long-term caretaker should be made by the personal representative or executor of the will– subject to the specific instructions in the will – so that long-term placement of the pet can be made expeditiously. Then, once the pet trust has been established and funded by the personal representative or executor from the assets specified in the will, the trustee of the pet trust, or some other person specified in the trust, should be authorized to change the caretaker as necessary for the benefit of the pet.

3.   PHYSICAL LOCATION FOR THE PET

It is relatively easy, and important, to specify that the pet shall not be confined to a cage, dog-run, or kennel for any extended period of time. Be sure to specify how long the pet can be left at a kennel, or "day-care" facility, and for what purposes. If appropriate, specify that the pet must live in the household of the caregiver. Should there be limits on how many other pets may live in the same household? When should the pet for whom the trust has been established be removed from the home of the current caretaker?

The next issue is geographical location of the pet. If the pet's regular vet is to check the pet at regular intervals, then the pet needs to live within a few hours' drive of the vet - unless technology improves sufficiently to allow a "video" check-up to be satisfactory. Or the client may be comfortable in allowing the vet to recommend another vet in another city. Just remember that anyone charged with checking up on the living conditions of the pet must have easy access to the pet.

4.   FOOD AND MEDICAL EXPENSES

One of the benefits of a pet trust is that a significant amount of money may be made available for the food and medical expenses of the pet. The trustee may be directed to pay a base amount of money, every month, for care of the pet, plus additional money, as necessary, for other expenses. To insure that the food and expense money really is spent for the pet, it is probably a good idea to have the trustee of the pet trust be someone different from the person named as caretaker for the pet. That way, the trustee can be charged with the responsibility of making sure that any food and expense money spent from the trust actually is spent for the benefit of the pet – not the personal benefit of the caretaker.

5.   PAYMENT FOR THE CARETAKER

In addition to the food and medical expenses for the pet, the trustee may also be directed to pay a set amount per month to the caretaker, during the time that the pet is living in the home of the caretaker. These payments are in the nature of a salary for the caretaker. It is a delicate balance in making the payments high enough to make the caretaker feel appreciated, yet not so high as to attract a person who really just cares about the money – not the pet.

Payments to the caretaker, of course, will stop whenever the pet dies, or the caretaker is replaced by another caretaker.

6.   SELECTION OF THE TRUSTEE(S)

The selection of the trustee, and possible successor trustees, should be made in the same way that any other trustees are selected – but keeping in mind that the trustee of the pet trust, and any necessary successor trustees, should be people who really will be concerned about the welfare of the pet.

7.   INVESTMENT OF MONEY IN THE TRUST

As with other trusts, the trustee should be given authority to make any appropriate investments of trust funds. If the amount in the trust is $10,000 or less, it is probably appropriate just to say that the money is to be kept in an interest-bearing account covered by federal deposit insurance, or whatever similar program is available at the time. It is not important that the value of the trust should increase during the dozen or so years the pet may continue to live. It is just important that the necessary money be reliably available – no matter what happens to the stock market.

If a larger amount of money is to be put into the pet trust, then more liberal instructions on investment may be appropriate. But specify that the welfare of the pet is to be the primary goal for investment, NOT the benefit of whoever will get the assets remaining in the trust when the pet dies.

To be blunt, if there is a chance that significant money may remain in the trust, then be sure that neither the caretaker, the trustee, nor any person or entity directly related to the caretaker or trustee will benefit from the early demise of the pet!

All investments should be made with the goal of insuring steady income while the pet is alive. Investments designed primarily for growth of the assets, for the benefit of the remaindermen, should be prohibited.

Verification and authority to litigate are important issues, as discussed below.

8.   VERIFICATION OF PROPER CARE FOR PET

Some person or entity should be given the responsibility to be sure that the pet is being cared for appropriately. This could be the trustee – who could be given the responsibility to document the living conditions of the pet, and collect periodic reports from the vet certifying the condition of the pet before any payments are authorized. Any breach of these fiduciary duties by the trustee could subject the trustee to personal liability.

Or an independent person or entity could be appointed as the "guardian" for the pet. For example, a friend, who likes animals but is allergic to cats, or lives in an apartment, or is required to travel frequently for work, might be a good "guardian" for the pet. Or a local animal shelter might be appointed.

Certainly, any "guardian", as well as any person named as a potential trustee or caretaker should be given authority to report to the trustee, or the court, if the existing care being given to the pet is inadequate.

And what can be done if there actually are problems regarding appropriate care for the pet?

9.   AUTHORITY TO LITIGATE ON BEHALF OF PET

Some states have specific legislation covering this issue. For example, the Colorado pet trust statute, originally adopted in 1995, provides that, "The intended use of the principal or income can be enforced by an individual designated for that purpose in the trust instrument, by the person having custody of an animal for which care is provided by the trust instrument, by a remainder beneficiary, or, if none, by **an individual appointed by a court upon application to it by an individual.**"[12]

Using this statute as a guide, the pet trust should specifically provide standing to a number of different people or entities to litigate to enforce the terms of the trust. Because litigation is expensive, the trust should provide that anyone who brings successful litigation for the benefit of the pet should be reimbursed for the expenses of litigation – including attorneys' fees.

However, the goal of the pet trust is not to support lawyers! Therefore, try to provide some mandatory steps for dispute settlement before any litigation may be undertaken. Standard arbitration sounds nice – but it has turned out that discovery expenses for standard arbitration can frequently turn out to be almost as high as related expenses for litigation.

So perhaps the chairman of the board of the local animal shelter, or the director of the animal shelter, should be authorized by the trust document to decide any dispute which may arise regarding care of the pet. For major decisions, such as improper investment of trust funds, which should be decided by a court, the chairman of the board of the local animal shelter could be given the authority to certify that the matter should be referred to the courts. The trust document might provide that NEITHER the trustee, nor the person instituting the litigation should be entitled to attorneys fees from the trust in the absence of this prior certification granting authority to sue.[13]

The bottom line is that since the pet itself cannot sue, some person or entity must be authorized to litigate on behalf of the pet – to enforce the specific terms of the trust.

10.   ALLOWING THE PET TO BE PUT TO SLEEP

Virtually all pet owners understand that there may come a time when the suffering of an elderly or severely injured pet should not be prolonged. Pets probably can be kept "alive" for extended times by tube feedings and the like. But the vet, or some other person or entity should be

---

[12] [Emphasis added.] C.R.S. 15-11-901(3)(d).
[13] In effect, this could be like the "Right to Sue" letter issued in cases of employment discrimination covered by federal statutes. Except that this "Right to Sue" letter would be issued by a specified person, or charitable entity, as specified in the pet trust.

authorized to certify in writing when the time has come that for the benefit of the pet, the pet should simply be "put to sleep." When a caretaker is receiving significant monthly payments while the pet is alive, there may be a conflict of interest between the best interest of the pet – and the financial interests of the caretaker. A licensed vet should have a major role in making any necessary decision about putting the pet to sleep, based solely on the best interests of the pet.

11.   DISTRIBUTION OF REMAINING FUNDS

If financial planning has been appropriate, there should be some money left in the trust when the pet finally dies, or is put to sleep. Make CERTAIN that there is no built-in conflict of interest on this issue for the caretaker. You don't want the caretaker to be financially motivated to let the dog play in the street – or chase cars along a busy highway!

Nor do you want the trustee to benefit from the early termination of the trust.

So be sure to provide that the remainder, at the end of the trust, should NOT go to either the caretaker or the trustee. Instead, the remainder might go to an animal shelter, or some other entity which should have no motivation to hasten the death of the pet. And remember that the larger the remainder may be, the more hazardous it may be for the pet.

In Leona Helmsley's trust for Trouble, setting aside $12 million for the care of one dog simply invited expensive litigation. It did not provide the necessary legal framework necessary to insure loving care for the dog.

With careful drafting the pets of ordinary people can be protected much more effectively.[14]

---

[14] For a short, thoughtful article on providing protection for pets see "Basics of Pet Trusts for Estate Planning Attorneys," by Gabriela N. Sandoval, 37 Colorado Lawyer, pages 49-53, May 2008.

CHAPTER 7.   POWERS OF APPOINTMENT

A.   INTRODUCTION TO POWERS OF APPOINTMENT

As you have seen in prior chapters, one of the major difficulties involved with designing a will or trust is trying to anticipate the future. What will the needs of the beneficiaries be, several years down the line? What will the economy be like? Will there be major, unexpected changes in who the family members are who are alive at any given time? Will there be major, unexpected changes in the amount of money available for distribution under the terms of the will or trust?

Try as we may, none of us can accurately predict the future. Once the testator or settlor has died, the terms of the will or trust may become fixed—whether or not they turn out to be sufficiently responsive to changing circumstances.

Therefore, in many situations, use of a POWER OF APPOINTMENT is an extremely useful technique for helping to solve the problem of our inability to predict the future.

How does a power of appointment work? The testator or settlor who sets up the power of appointment is called the "DONOR" of the power. The person to whom the power of appointment is given is called the "DONEE" of the power.

In essence, a power of appointment allows for a two stage process for determining the provisions of a will or trust. First the DONOR declares the initial guidelines for distribution. Then, for the second stage, the DONEE of the power is authorized to MODIFY the distributive terms of the will or trust. If the donee chooses NOT to modify the terms, then the property subject to the power of appointment (the "APPOINTIVE PROPERTY") simply goes in accordance with the terms of a "GIFT IN DEFAULT," which should have been specified by the donor of the power.

Thus, using a power of appointment, the donor can provide a mechanism by which the donee MAY re-adjust the terms of the will or trust at a later date—in accordance with the changes in circumstances that have actually occurred.

Because of the wonderful flexibility this adds to a will or trust, many people use powers of appointment. A husband, for example, might give his wife the income of a trust for her life, and then the power to reallocate, (appoint), the family assets among the children at her death—in accordance with the needs of the children at that time—with a gift in default to the children equally if the wife chooses not to exercise the power.

Or a mother might give her son the income of a trust for life, with a power to appoint the money remaining, (the corpus of the trust), to such of the son's children as might need the money at the time of the son's death (with a gift in default to the son's children equally). In such a situation, the mother's use of a power of appointment would allow the son, at the second stage, to distribute the corpus to his children in the way that seemed most appropriate under the particular circumstances in existence at the <u>son's death</u> rather than limiting the gift to what might have seemed appropriate at the <u>mother's</u> death—possibly a generation earlier.

At the time of the <u>son's</u> death, for example, the son's will might exercise the power of appointment in such a way as to give extra money to one of the son's children who had special medical needs that could not have been foreseeable to the mother at the time of her death. Adding this potential for flexibility at the second stage is highly beneficial for many estates.

Illustrations of various powers of appointment will follow. As you read the illustrations you will notice that there are four kinds of powers of appointment: GENERAL INTER VIVOS; SPECIAL INTER VIVOS; GENERAL TESTAMENTARY; and SPECIAL TESTAMENTARY.

What do those labels mean? Powers of appointment that are set up to allow the donee of the power to exercise the power of appointment by WILL are called TESTAMENTARY powers.

Powers exercisable by an inter vivos instrument, such as a DEED, are called INTER VIVOS powers.

If the donee may appoint to ANYONE, (including the donee, the donee's creditors, the donee's estate, the creditors of the donee's estate—or anyone else), the power is a GENERAL power.

If the donee may appoint only to a SPECIAL CLASS of persons, (NOT including the donee, donee's creditors, donee's estate, or creditors of the donee's estate), the power is called a SPECIAL power.

So, combining the various possibilities, as indicated above, we have four kinds of powers of appointment: General Inter Vivos; Special Inter Vivos; General Testamentary; and Special Testamentary. Illustrations of each of the four kinds of powers are set forth below.[1]

---

[1] In practice, there may be very important tax reasons for using a <u>special</u> power rather than a general power of appointment, since property subject to a <u>general</u> power of appointment is subject to federal estate tax in the <u>donee's</u> estate. And the application of the Rule Against Perpetuities, (RAP), to a General Inter Vivos power is different from the way RAP is applied to the other three powers of appointment. These matters will be discussed later.

B.   GENERAL INTER VIVOS POWER OF APPOINTMENT

In real life, a general inter vivos power of appointment would be extremely rare. Since the donee of such a power would have the ability to appoint the property to himself or herself, at any time, it would be far more likely that the donor would simply skip a step, and give the property directly to the donee—instead of creating a power of appointment.

Basically, for tax purposes, the donee of a general power of appointment is considered to be the owner of the property subject to appointment—whether the power is inter vivos or testamentary, and whether or not the power is exercised. So, for example, there would be no <u>tax</u> advantages in giving a child a general inter vivos <u>power of appointment</u> over specific property, instead of just giving the property to the child.

However, if for some reason a child were considered not to be capable of outright ownership of specific property, such as the portrait of great-grandfather, then the child might be given a life estate in the portrait, instead, subject to a general inter vivos power of appointment in a parent—thus allowing the parent to cut short the child's right to possession of the portrait at any time, should circumstances so warrant.

As indicated above, however, actual use of a general inter vivos power of appointment is very rare.[2]

C.   SPECIAL INTER VIVOS POWER OF APPOINTMENT

A SPECIAL inter vivos power of appointment allows the donee of the power, while alive, to appoint the property subject to the power to one or more members of a designated class. If the donee of the power has the authority to EXCLUDE one or more members of the designated class, then the power is called an EXCLUSIVE power of appointment. If the donee must appoint, at least something to every member of the designated class, then the power is called a NON-EXCLUSIVE POWER, since the donee does NOT have authority to exclude any member of the class. [The same terminology—of exclusive or non-exclusive—is also used with special TESTAMENTARY powers.].

---

[2] One example of a general inter vivos power may be found in a rather complex provision included in the EIGHTH article of the will of the Vermont philanthropist, John Flynn, in which he provided:

"I give...to my niece Lolita Smith Deming the house... in Burlington where I once resided... [t]o have and use the same during the term of her natural life with remainder to <u>such person or persons</u>... as the said Lolita Smith <u>may by</u> will or by <u>deed appoint</u>... It is my earnest hope that she may retain said property during her life but if she shall elect to sell the same and shall appoint the grantee to take the remainder under the power provided in this will said appointment shall be irrevocable, it being my intention that <u>said deed and</u> <u>appointment</u> shall constitute a <u>complete</u> transfer of the right created by this instrument." [Emphasis added.]

Whenever a SPECIAL, NON-EXCLUSIVE power of appointment is created, it is important to specify the minimum amount, (in dollars, percentages, or fractions), which must be appointed to each person,[3] (called an object of the power), who is within the designated class.

Special inter vivos powers of appointment are frequently given to the executors of wills to let the executors make some of the decisions as to which persons, within a designated group, should be given particular items.[4]

SAMPLE ONE—WILL OF ANDY WARHOL

Andy Warhol, in his will, included a special inter vivos power of appointment over millions of dollars. In Article FIFTH of Andy Warhol's will he provided:

> I GIVE the balance of my residuary estate… to the foundation created pursuant to Article FOURTH of this Will or if, for any reason, … the bequest herein shall not be deductible for United States estate tax purposes… I do not GIVE such balance of my residuary estate to such foundation but, instead, I GIVE such balance of my residuary estate to such one or more corporations, associations and organizations for the advancement of the visual arts, bequests to which are deductible under Section 2055 of the Internal Revenue Code of 1954, and in such proportions <u>as my Executor, in his discretion, shall determine.</u> [Emphasis added.]

By the underlined provisions, Warhol gave his executor a special inter vivos power of appointment—to appoint only to a designated group of organizations, (for which gifts would be deductible), and to make those appointments within the lifetime of the executor, (thus making the appointments <u>inter vivos</u> appointments).

Another interesting use of a special inter vivos power of appointment is found in the will of the popular American artist, Norman Rockwell.

SAMPLE TWO—WILL OF NORMAN ROCKWELL

In CLAUSE FOURTH, part (2) of his will, Norman Rockwell provided:

---

[3] With a non-exclusive power, if the appointment made to an object of the power is <u>too small</u>, then the appointment may be held to be "<u>illusory</u>" and thus not a sufficiently large appointment. What a court might consider to be "illusory" is, of course, quite uncertain. So it is important that the <u>donor</u> of the power <u>specify</u> exactly what dollar amount or fractional amount must be appointed to each object of the power if a non-exclusive power is used.

[4] For example, it is quite usual for a will to provide that the executor will have the final decision or distribution of various items of tangible personal property—such as furniture, books, etc. found within the decedent's house. Such a <u>power,</u> to distribute items of personal property among a <u>designated group</u>, would be a <u>special, inter vivos power of appointment</u>.

If my said wife so directs in a written instrument or instruments delivered to the Trustees during her lifetime, the Trustees shall pay to or among any one or more of my sons then living and the issue then living of any of my said sons who has then died, all or any part of the principal of the trust, at such times and in such amounts as my said wife so directs.

By this provision Rockwell gave his wife a <u>special</u> power—exercisable only in favor of one or more of Rockwell's sons or their issue. The power was an <u>inter vivos</u> power, because it could be exercised by Rockwell's wife—during her lifetime.

Note that both samples of special inter vivos powers of appointment were created in <u>wills</u>—but since the powers were <u>exercisable</u> by the donees while the <u>donees were alive</u>, the powers are called <u>inter vivos</u> powers of appointment.

Since all special powers of appointment must be either exclusive or non-exclusive powers, can you figure out whether the powers created by Warhol and Rockwell, respectively, are exclusive or non-exclusive powers?

Answer: Clearly, both powers are EXCLUSIVE powers of appointment, because both give the donee the power to appoint among "ONE OR MORE" of the objects of the powers. Because the ability to appoint to only ONE object of the power allows the donee to EXCLUDE the other objects of the power, both powers of appointment are therefore EXCLUSIVE.

D.   GENERAL TEATAMENTARY POWERS

General testamentary powers of appointment are probably the most frequently used powers of appointment. By means of these powers, a spouse or child may be given the use of assets during life, and then a power of appointment to give the assets away at death in <u>any</u> way the donee of the power may choose.

Note that for the one or two percent of people in the United States who actually have estates large enough to be subject to federal estate tax, the tax consequences of general powers of appointment have been of importance. Prior to the 1982 revisions in federal tax law, property devised to a surviving spouse for life did not qualify for the marital deduction unless the spouse was also given a <u>general testamentary</u> power of appointment over the assets. Since 1982, assets devised to a surviving spouse for life <u>can</u> qualify for the marital deduction—even without a general power of appointment. In addition, as mentioned earlier, property over which a donee holds a general power of appointment is subject to tax in the <u>donee's</u> estate just as if it were property belonging to the donee. So, for the few estates which actually may be subject to federal estate tax, the tax consequences of <u>general</u> powers of appointment should be carefully considered.

For most people, however, the real issue is simply the degree of restriction that the donor wishes to place on appointments to be made by the donee. If the donee is to be restricted to making appointments only to charitable organizations, or to family members, then a <u>special</u> power should be used. If the donee is to be allowed to appoint to <u>anyone</u>, then a <u>general</u> power should be selected.

In part (b) of the SIXTH article of his will, Humphrey Bogart created a general testamentary power of appointment for his wife, Betty—also known as Lauren Bacall. Bogart also, appropriately and commendably, provided for various "gifts in default," (in parts (b) and (c)), in case Lauren Bacall did <u>not</u> exercise the general testamentary power of appointment.

SAMPLE THREE—WILL OF HUMPHREY BOGART

Parts (b) and (c) of the SIXTH article of Bogart's will read as follows:

> Upon the decease of my wife BETTY the remaining principle and any undistributed income of this trust shall go and be distributed <u>to such persons, in such proportions and upon such terms and conditions as she may designate and appoint by her last will</u> and testament. <u>If she shall fail to make such appointment</u> and designation said principle and undistributed income shall, after payment of the expenses of her funeral and last illness (unless such expenses are provided for from other sources), be added proportionately to the share then held in trust, and the share theretofore distributed, pursuant to the provisions of Clause SEVENTH hereof. [Emphasis added.]

> (c)   If distribution cannot be made pursuant to the immediately preceding paragraph (b) because there shall be no issue of my wife BETTY and me then living, this trust shall continue and the net income thereof shall be paid, in quarterly or other convenient installments, to BETTY'S mother, NATALIE GOLDBERG, so long as she shall live, and thereafter in equal shares to BETTY'S cousins, JUDITH DAVIS ORSHAN and JOAN DAVIS, so long as they both shall live, and all to their survivor so long as she shall live. Upon the decease of the last survivor of said three persons this trust shall terminate, and the

principal and any undistributed income thereof shall go and be distributed to THE HUMPHREY BOGART FOUNDATION.

Note that this sample from Humphrey Bogart's will is a particularly good illustration of the care that should be taken in drafting gifts in default—to follow the grant of <u>any</u> power of appointment.

Now, what about the EXERCISE of a general testamentary power of appointment? Are there any particular words that are necessary in order to exercise such a power? MAYBE. It depends on the words used to create the power.

If the instrument that creates the power of appointment states that to exercise the power, specific reference must be made to the document that created the power, then such reference is, indeed, necessary. However, UNLESS limits of this kind are put upon powers of appointment, there are NO SPECIAL WORDS NECESSARY to exercise any power of appointment.

SAMPLE FOUR—WILL OF JACQUELINE KENNEDY ONASSIS

A typical exercise of a general testamentary power of appointment is found in article FOURTH of the will of Jacqueline Kennedy Onassis, which provides:

> FOURTH: Under the Will of my late husband, John Fitzgerald Kennedy, a martial deduction trust was created for my benefit over which I was accorded a general power of appointment. I hereby exercise such power of appointment and direct that, upon my death, all property subject to such power be transferred, conveyed and paid over to my descendants who survive me, <u>per stripes</u>.

Note that by this provision Jackie Kennedy Onassis gave the property directly to her descendants and did not attempt to exercise control over the property for an extended time after her own death.

Because the Rule Against Perpetuities, (RAP), starts to run when a power is CREATED, rather than when the power is EXERCISED, (with the exception of the general inter vivos power), RAP problems may be created when the donee of a power of appointment tries to hold onto control of the property for too long.

For example, the Rule Against Perpetuities began to run on the power of appointment created by President Kennedy at his death on November 22, 1963, even though the power of appointment was not exercised until approximately 32 years later, when the will of Jackie Kennedy Onassis went into effect at her death.

So remember that with any power of appointment, (except a general inter vivos power), RAP starts to run when the power is CREATED. So be particularly careful not to violate RAP when EXERCISING a power of appointment.

E.   SPECIAL TESTAMENTARY POWER

The fourth and final kind of power of appointment is the special testamentary power of appointment, It allows a donor to provide for tremendous flexibility in distribution of the appointive property, while still ensuring that the property will be kept within the family.

Because special powers of appointment are not currently taxable as property of the donee of the power, and because it is no longer necessary to give a surviving spouse a general power of appointment in order to have the property qualify for the martial deduction, the use of special testamentary powers of appointment should become increasingly popular.

For example, the donor of a special testamentary power of appointment might provide in her will that the appointive property is to go to her husband for life, and then to one or more of the couple's issue, as the husband may appoint by will. Creating a special, exclusive, testamentary power of appointment like this would ensure that the donor's property would be available first to her surviving husband, and then to one or more of the donor's issue, (including children, grandchildren, and so forth).

This might be especially appropriate for items of property that have special emotional significance for family members—(such as the portrait of Uncle Harry, for example)—or for types of property which should be managed as one unit—(such as a family farm, family business, or the like).

If sufficient assets were available, for example, a woman might appoint her share of the family farm to her husband for life, then to such of her issue as her husband might appoint by will. When the husband died, perhaps 15 years down the line, he might devise his own share of the family farm to whichever of the children had shown the most interest in farming, and also appoint his wife's share of the family farm to the same child. (And hopefully there would be sufficient assets so that other provisions could be made for the children who had shown less of an interest in farming).

Admittedly, giving the husband a life estate and a special testamentary power of appointment would make it very difficult for the husband to sell the farm during his lifetime. But that might be exactly what the wife had in mind.

If the appointive property in the illustration above were not a particular farm, however, but merely stocks and bonds held in a trust, then sale should not be difficult, since a trustee normally has the power to sell any assets in the trust. If the wife, in her will, gave the husband the income of the trust for life, and then a special testamentary power of appointment exercisable in favor of the issue of the couple, then the assets would end up with the Donor's issue—rather than with the second wife of the husband, for example. And it would be important to add a gift in default— probably to the children of the donor of the power, in equal shares—or possibly to the donor's issue by representation.

F.   GIFT IN DEFAULT

As indicated above, EVERY power of appointment should include a gift in default—in case the donee of the power chooses not to exercise the power, or does not exercise the power successfully. An excellent sample of such a gift in default, from Humphrey Bogart's will, was discussed in Section D of this chapter.

SAMPLE FIVE—WILL OF HUMPHREY BOGART

As you may recall, the gift in default basically provided that,

> If [Lauren Bacall]...shall fail to make such appointment...[then the income from the property] ...shall be paid ... to Betty's mother, NATALIE GOLDBERG, [for life] ...[then] to BETTY'S cousins, JUDITH DAVIS ORSHAN and JOAN DAVIS [for life]... [and then shall be] distributed to THE HUMPHREY BOGART FOUNDATION.

By this provision, Bogart made thoughtful distribution of the assets in case Lauren Bacall did not exercise the power of appointment that he had given her. Bogart might, of course, have shortened the gift in default simply by providing that the assets should go directly to The Humphrey Bogart Foundation. But there is no reason not to include as many details and specifics in the gift in default as your client may wish.

Frequently, if one spouse gives the other spouse a general or special testamentary power of appointment, the gift in default is simply to the issue of the couple, (either <u>per stirpes</u> or <u>by representation</u>).

Sometimes, the provisions of the gift in default may be particularly important. For example, there are instances in which the donee of a <u>general</u> power of appointment may specifically decide NOT to exercise the power of appointment, but to let the assets pass in accordance with the gift in default.

SAMPLE SIX—WILL OF COLE PORTER

In part B of the SECOND article of Cole Porter's will, he states:

> I DO NOT exercise and I HEREBY SPECIFICALLY REFRAIN from exercising any and all powers of appointment, under any will or instrument whatsoever, which I may have at my death.

Nothing appears on the face of Cole Porter's will to explain this decision not to exercise any power of appointment.

In other situations, however, if the donee of a <u>general</u> testamentary power of appointment might end up with an insolvent estate, (because of an unexpected personal injury judgment, for example), then it would be highly unwise for the donee to exercise a general power of appointment—<u>if</u> the gift in default would have provided for satisfactory distribution.

Normally the rule is that if a donee of a GENERAL power of appointment EXERCISES the power of appointment, then EXERCISE of the power makes the appointive property subject to the claims of the donee's CREDITORS—to the extent that the appointive property is necessary to pay the debts of the DONEE.[5]

So before exercising any GENERAL power of appointment, it is important to see what the GIFT IN DEFAOULT would be. For example, there is absolutely NO REASON TO EXERCISE a GENERAL power of appointment in favor of the "TAKERS IN DEFAULT"—the people who would take the property in default of exercise of the power. If the donee of the power simply declines to exercise the power, the takers in default will get the appointive property, as if it came directly from the donor. If the donee of the power EXERCISES a GENERAL power of

---

[5] This rule is frequently stated as the rule that the donee must be "<u>just before generous</u>" in the distribution of the appointive property. In other words, since the donee might have appointed the property to her own creditors, the courts will compel her, when necessary, to be "<u>just</u>," and pay her own debts, before she is "<u>generous</u>" in giving the property away to <u>others</u>.

appointment, however, then the appointive property may end up unnecessarily subject to the claims of the CREDITORS OF THE DONEE!

So, in drafting a gift in default for a GENERAL power of appointment, be especially careful in specifying the takers in default, in case the donee of the power would prefer not to exercise the power.

G. DRAFTING EXERCISE 10—SPECIAL TESTAMENTARY POWER OF APPOINTMENT

Your client is an elderly woman who has three adult children, and six grandchildren—ranging in age from 6 months to 10 years of age. With your help, your client is in the process of drafting a will, to provide financial assistance to each of her three children.

However, your client's main concern is the lovely portrait of her grandfather, which she would like to keep in good hands, in the family, for as long as possible.

Draft an appropriate provision to accomplish your client's goals using a special, testamentary power of appointment. You may make up any names you like for your client's grandfather, children and grandchildren, being aware that more grandchildren and great-grandchildren may be born after your client signs her will.

As you begin your drafting, you may want to check the Pointers for Drafting, which follow.

H. POINTERS FOR DRAFTING—DRAFTING EXERCISE 10—SPECIAL TESTAMENTARY POWER OF APPOINTMENT

This drafting exercise is really quite easy, because the difficult choices are left to future generations—thanks to the use of the power of appointment. All your client has to do is to decide which of her three children is most likely to make wise decisions in the future about ownership of grandfather's portrait.

1.   To create a special power of appointment you must specify the class to whom an appointment could be made—the objects of the power. Remember that this may include persons born—or unborn—at the death of the testatrix.

2.   To make this a testamentary power of appointment, it must be EXERCISABLE in the WILL of the donee of the power.

3. What happens if the original donee of the power fails to exercise the power—or tries to appoint the portrait to a non-object of the power (someone not included in the class of persons to whom the portrait may be appointed)? Should there be an alternate power of appointment, so that another donee might have a chance to do a better job? When might the alternate power of appointment come into existence?

4. Be sure that you provide a good gift in default in case the power or alternate power is not effectively exercised. You may want to draft a complex gift in default—like the one in Humphrey Bogart's will, in Sections D and F of this chapter—or you may feel that a simple gift in default is preferable.

5. Are there any situations in which you would want the portrait simply to go to a museum? If so, be sure to specify which museum—and at least one alternate museum—in case the first museum named goes out of existence—or does not have quite the same interest as your client has in the lovely portrait.

CHAPTER 8.   RULE AGAINST PERPETUITIES (RAP)

INTRODUCTION TO THE RULE AGAINST PERPETUITIES

Virtually every will or trust involves consideration of the Rule Against Perpetuities. So it is necessary to understand the basics of the rule before drafting any such document.

Concededly, the rule is old and complex. Nevertheless, the rule still exists in many jurisdictions, and actually serves the valuable contemporary function of helping to cut off "dead-hand" control. For example, without the rule, it would be much easier for individual landowners, wise or foolish, to tie up use of the land for hundreds of years. That simply is not fair to future generations, who should be allowed to make their own decisions, wise or foolish, on how the land is to be used in light of the understandings, needs and knowledge of their own times.

Although the common law rule has been modified in some states by "cy pres,"[1] "wait and see,"[2] or the relatively new Uniform Statutory Rule Against Perpetuities,[3] it is still necessary to comply with the common law Rule Against Perpetuities if you do not want your drafting to be modified later by some court.[4] Although you may practice in a jurisdiction which has modified, or almost abolished the common law Rule Against Perpetuities, your client may end up dying in one of the numerous jurisdictions which still apply common law RAP. The law of the place of domicile at death will be the law applied to the will. So you need a good, basic understanding of RAP.

---

[1] "Cy pres," used in this context, allows a court to reform an interest which violates the Rule Against Perpetuities, (hereafter called RAP). Normally, "cy pres" is just used to cut down the number of years specified in a document. For example, by applying "cy pres," a court might change a gift to grandchildren "who reach 25" to a gift to grandchildren "who reach 21"—thereby avoiding a violation of RAP.

[2] In a jurisdiction that accepts the principle of "wait and see," no interest is actually held to be void under RAP until the time allowed by RAP has expired. The theory of "wait and see" is that if we use actual events, rather than possible events, many interests that MIGHT have violated RAP will actually turn out not to do so. "Wait and see" sounds very appealing and sensible—until it is actually applied. The case of Estate of Pearson, (275 A.2d 336 (1971)), clearly illustrates some of the problems with "wait and see." In that case, the court decided that the applicable "wait and see" statute required the court to wait until 21 years after the deaths of at least 48 people before deciding whether or not the estate was entitled to a charitable deduction for an attempted charitable gift. Use of "wait and see" can cause similar needless uncertainty with regard to the title to land. Some states have now extended that time to one-thousand years!

[3] The Uniform Statutory Rule Against Perpetuities, known as USRAP, was approved by the National Conference of Commissioners on Uniform State Laws in 1986, and has since been the subject of much academic controversy, but has been adopted in several states. In essence, it provides a period of 90 years during which a court is directed to "wait and see." If, at the end of 90 years, the attempted interest would still violate RAP, then the court is directed to reform the interest in such a way as to bring it within the time allowed by common law RAP, or a period of 90 years for "wait and see," whichever is longer.

[4] "Cy pres" and USRAP both specifically require a court to re-write a provision that is still found to be in violation of RAP. When a court re-writes a provision it is guessing as to what the testator's or settlor's choice might have been in the particular situation. Far better to let the client make that choice for himself or herself! Pure "wait and see," technically, does not require a court to re-write a provision. It simply requires a court to wait for all the lives in being, plus 21 years, to determine, at that time, which interests are good, and which are bad, thus causing increased litigation expenses, uncertainty in title, and delay.

It is NOT that difficult to learn the basics of the Rule Against Perpetuities, (hereafter called RAP). Three clear, direct steps will lead you to the correct answer every time.

As you recall, the basic statement of RAP was made by Prof. Gray:

> No interest is good, unless it must vest, if at all, not later than 21 years after some life in being at the creation of the interest.[5]

A.   CLEAR, QUICK WAY TO APPLY RAP

To apply RAP correctly, simply follow these three steps:

1.   Notice when the interest is created;

2.   Figure out who to use for a measuring life; and then

3.   Check to see if each interest created by the document will either vest or fail within 21 years after the death of the person who is being used as the measuring life for that interest.

1.   STEP ONE—NOTICE WHEN THE INTEREST IS CREATED

    a.   WILLS—interests are created when the will goes into effect—at the death of the testator.

    b.   TRUSTS—interests are created when the trust becomes irrevocable.[6] For a testamentary trust the document becomes irrevocable at the death of the testator.   For an inter vivos, or living trust, the document becomes irrevocable when the settlor gives up all power to change or revoke the trust—either by renouncing the powers to amend or revoke while alive, or by dying. (One who has died can no longer revoke or amend a trust.)

    c.   POWERS OF APPOINTMENT—interests are deemed to be created:

---

[5] J. Gray, The Rule Against Perpetuities Sec. 201, at 191 (4th ed. 1942).

[6] Note that this may or may not be at the time the trust first goes into effect. Basically, RAP does not begin to run until a grantor parts with ownership of the property. As long as a grantor keeps, or could resume, full ownership of property, RAP, in essence, considers it still to be the property of the grantor—so RAP does not begin to run until the grantor has irrevocably parted with full ownership of the property.

1.   FOR A GENERAL INTER VIVOS POWER ONLY, when the power is EXERCISED.[7] Since the donee of the general inter vivos power could appoint the property to himself or herself at any time, RAP considers the property, in effect, to belong to the donee. So RAP is not involved until the donee actually EXERCISES the power.

2.   FOR ALL OTHER KINDS OF POWERS, when the power is CREATED BY THE DONOR of the power—i.e., when the document CREATING the power becomes irrevocable.[8]

2.   STEP TWO—FIGURE OUT WHO TO USE FOR A MEASURING LIFE

a.   <u>IF THE DOCUMENT SPECIFIES A MEASURING LIFE OR LIVES, THEN USE THE SPECIFIED LIFE OR LIVES!</u>

If the gift is to a charity,[9] or other institution, the only measuring lives available will be the human lives specified in the document, because only human lives can be used as measuring lives. If no human lives are specified, then the time allowed by RAP for an institution is simply 21 years. Clearly, if an institution is a beneficiary you cannot use either the beneficiary or the "parent" of the beneficiary as a measuring life, because neither is a human life. So for INSTITUTIONS you will be limited to 21 years or to specified human lives as the measuring lives.

If the gift is to a human, the measuring life or lives may also be specified.

EXAMPLE ONE:

Testator devises property, "To my oldest descendant alive at my son, Tom's death." Tom is the measuring life.

---

[7] Note that this is ONLY for a <u>general inter vivos</u> power—a power which gives the donee the right to appoint to <u>himself or herself immediately</u>, while the donee is still alive.

[8] The three other kinds of powers are: general testamentary, (allowing the donee to appoint to anyone by will); special testamentary, (allowing the donee to appoint by will only to a special class, not including: the donee, the donee's creditors, the donee's estate, or the creditors of the donee's estate); and a special inter vivos power, (allowing the donee to appoint by deed, but only to a special class, not including: the donee, the donee's creditors, the donee's estate, or the creditors of the donee's estate). For the purposes of RAP, all three of these powers are considered to have been created only when the donor's instrument creating the powers became irrevocable—i.e., when the donor actually gave the power of appointment to another and couldn't take it back.

[9] Gifts to a SOLID LINE OF CHARITIES are not subject to the Rule Against Perpetuities. But if a gift to a charity follows a gift to a non-charity, then the gift to the charity is subject to RAP just as any other gift would be, and the charitable exception is not available.

EXAMPLE TWO:

Testator devises property, "To my oldest descendant alive at the death of the last to die of all of my issue alive at my death." Testator's issue alive at his death are the measuring lives.

Note: A person may set up any collection of measuring lives he or she likes, as long as (a) the specified people really are alive at the creation of the interest, and (b) they are not too numerous to be ascertained and followed.[10]

Remember: It has always been permissible under RAP to look at the situation <u>at the time of the testator's death</u>, to see who is then a life in being. Common law RAP simply does not permit one to look at what happens <u>after</u> the time of the testator's death.

>   b.   <u>IF A MEASURING LIFE IS NOT SPECIFIED IN THE DOCUMENT THEN:</u>
>
>   i.   SEE IF THE BENEFICIARIES CAN BE THEIR OWN MEASURING LIVES.

Beneficiaries can be their own measuring lives only if they were alive at the time of the creation of the interest, and were then members of a closed class.[11]

EXAMPLE THREE:

Testatrix leaves property "to such of my children as reach 25." Can the children of the testatrix be their own measuring lives? YES.

All of the children of the <u>testatrix</u> will have been born by the time of her death, so the ones who survive her will be members of a <u>closed class</u>—and <u>lives in being</u> at the death of the testatrix. Thus the gift to the testatrix's OWN children if they reach 25 (or 50), is GOOD, because the testatrix's <u>own</u> children can serve as their <u>own</u> measuring lives.

---

[10] Jackie Kennedy Onassis, for example, had a provision, in Article FIFTH, Part A.1. of her will limiting the applicable time by saying: "In no event, however, shall the Foundation's primary term extend beyond a period of twenty-one (21) years after the death of the last to die of those <u>descendants of my former father-in-law Joseph P. Kennedy who were in being at the time of my death.</u>" [Emphasis added.] By this provision, the entire Kennedy Clan in existence at Jackie's death could be used for the measuring lives.

[11] A closed class means that no one could get into the class later. People may fall out of the class later, by dying, for example, but no new people can get into the class. Again, only humans can be measuring lives.

EXAMPLE FOUR:

Testator leaves property "to C for life, then to such of C's children as reach 25."

Can C's children be their own measuring lives, (and thus save the gift to them)?

YES—IF C HAD DIED BEFORE THE DEATH OF THE TESTATOR!

In that case, if C were already dead at the creation of the interest, (at testator's death), then all of C's children who would ever be born would have been born prior to C's death, and thus prior to the death of the testator. So C's children would be members of a <u>closed class,</u> and those who were <u>alive at the testator's death</u> could serve as their <u>own</u> measuring lives. The gift to C's children would then be GOOD, because it would vest, if at all, within the lifetimes of C's children who were alive at the testator's death, all of whom were thus both <u>lives in being</u> at the creation of the interest, and were members of a <u>closed class</u>—(because C was already dead.[12])

Notice that this would NOT work if C were still ALIVE at the death of the testator. In that case, C might have another child, X, after the death of the testator. The after-born child, X, would NOT have been a life in being at the creation of the interest, and therefore could NOT be used as a measuring life. Might it happen that X would reach 25 more than 21 years after the death of all of the people who were lives in being at the death of the testator? Yes. So because of the <u>possibility</u> that X might be <u>born,</u> and might reach the age of 25 more than 21 years after the death of the lives in being, the <u>whole</u> gift to C's children would <u>fail</u>.[13]

If the beneficiaries <u>cannot</u> be their own measuring lives either because they were <u>not alive</u> at the creation of the interest or because they were <u>not members of a closed class</u> at the creation of the interest, then, to find the measuring life, you should:

---

[12] As you recall, RAP always allows for the period of gestation—if some child were actually in gestation at the applicable time. For example, if C were a man, and his wife was three months pregnant with C's child at the time of C's death, then when C's child was actually born alive, the child's life would be considered to relate back to the time of conception. So C's child, though actually born about six months after C's death, would still be considered to have been a life in being at the time of C's death. The opportunity for posthumous <u>conception</u> of a child by use of a sperm bank is basically disregarded when applying RAP.

[13] As you recall, for the purposes of RAP, people are assumed to be able to have children until the moment they die. They certainly are legally capable of <u>adopting</u> children up until the time of their deaths. Because of the class gift rule—the rule that any class must stand or fall as a <u>whole,</u> the gift fails, as to C's children, even if C's <u>existing</u> children were 19 and 20 at the time of the gift. The two existing children might die before reaching 25, and then the only one of C's children to reach 25 might be the child who was not a life in being at the creation of the interest. That would be too late to comply with the requirements of RAP.

ii.   USE THE RELEVANT <u>PARENT</u> OF THE BENEFICIARIES AS THE MEASURING LIFE!

There is absolutely NO need to run around trying to check out all the lives in being at the creation of the interest! Most of them will have absolutely NO EFFECT on when the intended beneficiaries reach 21, or 25, or whatever. The ONLY person who will have any effect on when the intended beneficiary reaches 21 or 25 is a PARENT of the beneficiary. And generally, only ONE of the potential parents of the beneficiary is of legal significance for RAP!

EXAMPLE FIVE:

Testator leaves property "to my daughter, D, for life, then to such of D's children as reach 21."

The one and only measuring life for this provision is D—if D survived the testator. D's husband can produce all the children he likes, but they will not constitute "D's children" unless D is their mother. So D is the ONLY relevant life for D's children with regard to RAP.

Neighbors, alive at the testator's death can live or die as they like—without having <u>any</u> effect on whether or not <u>D</u> has children! Only <u>D</u> can be the measuring life for this gift to <u>D's</u> children!

EXAMPLE SIX:

Testator leaves property "to my child, C, for life, then to such of my grandchildren as reach the age of 21."

Here the measuring lives are <u>all</u> of the testator's <u>children</u> who are alive at the testator's death—because <u>all</u> of the testator's <u>children</u> are potential parents of the testator's <u>grandchildren</u>. So if the testator actually had three children alive at his death, creatively named A, B, and C, then <u>all three</u> of the testator's children would be measuring lives. The <u>testator's three children</u>, and no one else, will determine when the <u>testator's grandchildren</u> are born. So <u>all three</u> of the testator's children, A, B, and C, are measuring lives, even though two of them, A and B, were <u>not mentioned in the document</u>.[14]

---

[14] It is NEVER necessary for a measuring life to be mentioned in the gift, or to receive any gift under the will. Anyone whose life will affect the vesting of the interest may be a good measuring life.

SUMMARY: To find the measuring life, (1) use the measuring life specified in the document; or (2) use the beneficiaries as their own measuring lives if they were alive and members of a closed class at the creation of the interest; or (3) use the relevant parents of the beneficiaries as the measuring lives.

3.   STEP THREE: CHECK TO SEE IF EACH INTEREST WILL VEST, IF AT ALL, WITHIN 21 YEARS AFTER THE DEATH OF THE PERSON BEING USED AS THE MEASURING LIFE FOR THAT INTEREST.

The easiest way to do this is simply to imagine that the person you have ascertained to be the measuring life is hit by a truck and dies the day after the interest is created. Would it then be certain that within the next 21 years the interests created would either get to the intended beneficiaries, or fail?[15] If it would NOT be CERTAIN—in other words, if, within 21 years after the death of the measuring life you STILL MIGHT NOT KNOW whether or not the intended beneficiaries would get their interests—then those interests are VOID under common law RAP.

EXAMPLE SEVEN:

Testator gives property "to A for life, then to the first of A's children to graduate from law school."

If A is alive at the death of the testator, then A's children are not yet a closed class, and therefore cannot be used as their own measuring lives.[16] Therefore, A will be the measuring life—as the relevant parent of the beneficiaries. If A were hit by a truck the day after the testator died, might it be possible that it would take more than 21 years for one of A's children to graduate from law school? Certainly. So the interest intended for the first child of A to graduate from law school is VOID—as a violation of RAP—UNLESS one child had already graduated from law school at the time the TESTATOR DIED.[17]

Would it make any difference if A had died before the testator? Definitely. Then A's children would be members of a closed class of lives in being at the creation of the interest, and they

---

[15] Remember, all RAP requires is that an interest must vest, "if at all," within the applicable period. It is prolonged uncertainty, not failure of a gift, which is the important concept for RAP.

[16] After the death of the testator A might have another child, Q, who would outlive all of the people who were alive at the testator's death and might then decide to go to law school. Because Q, when he or she graduated from law school, might be the first of A's children to do so, Q would feel entitled to the gift. However, it might have taken Q more than 21 years after the lives in being to qualify for the gift and that is too long to wait, under RAP.

[17] If, at the time of the testator's death, one of A's children, X, had already graduated from law school, and had been the first of A's children to do so, then X would be entitled to the gift immediately upon the death of the testator. Because no period of uncertainty would be required, RAP would not be violated, and the gift would be good.

could be their <u>own</u> measuring lives.[18] It might be that no child of A would ever graduate from law school. But that would not cause a violation of <u>RAP</u>, because we <u>will</u> know whether or not the interest has vested by the time all of A's children, (the measuring lives), actually die. So the interest in "the first of A's children to graduate from law school" would be GOOD under RAP, IF A HAD DIED PRIOR TO THE TESTATOR.

SUMMARY:

To avoid drafting anything which violates the Rule Against Perpetuities, simply: (1) ascertain the date of the creation of the interest; (2) ascertain the measuring life; and (3) be certain that each interest will vest, if at all, within 21 years after the death of the person used as the measuring life.

Now that you understand the fundamentals of the Rule Against Perpetuities, you may be interested in analyzing samples of perpetuities problems in the wills of Alfred Hitchcock and Norman Rockwell in the sections that follow.

B.   VIOLATIONS OF THE RULE AGAINST PERPETUITIES

For each of the following samples, see if you can spot the perpetuities problem and then think of a way it could have been avoided.

SAMPLE ONE—WILL OF ALFRED HITCHCOCK:

Alfred Hitchcock included the following provision in Article V. Sec. 5.(h) of his will:

> If any of said children…, [meaning Hitchcock's future grandchildren], for whom a trust has been established hereunder shall die prior to attaining the age of thirty-five (35) years, his or her trust shall terminate, and the Trustees shall immediately deliver all of the then balance of the principal and accumulated income of such deceased child's trust to his or her then living issue, if any, … or if such child shall leave no then living issue, then to my then living issue …

QUESTIONS:
        WHAT IS WRONG WITH THIS PROVISION?
        HOW COULD IT HAVE BEEN CORRECTED?

---

[18] If A were dead at the death of the testator, then A would not be having any more children. So the children alive at the testator's death would be a closed class and would be good measuring lives.

ANSWERS:

A: WHAT IS WRONG?

The problem with this provision is that it attempts to shift the interest of a grandchild to another person—possibly 34 years after the death of the testator and all measuring lives! The testator is NOT allowed to hang onto control of the property for that long! Because Hitchcock's daughter, Patricia, seems to have been alive at the time the will was written,[19] she might also have been alive at his death. If Patricia survived Alfred Hitchcock, then as of that time it would definitely have been a possibility that some of Alfred Hitchcock's grandchildren might have been born or adopted after his death,[20] so the grandchildren would <u>not</u> have all been lives in being and members of a closed class at Alfred Hitchcock's death, and therefore could not have been used as their own measuring lives. Instead, Hitchcock's daughter, Patricia, (and any of his other children alive at Hitchcock's death), should have been used as the measuring life, (or lives), for the grandchildren. Could it have happened that one of Patricia's children would have lived for more than 21 years after Patricia's death, and then have died, at age 34? Certainly. Therefore, the attempted shifting executory interests[21]—to shift the assets from the 34-year-old grandchild to the then living issue of either the grandchild, or Hitchcock himself, would have been void under the Rule Against Perpetuities.

B.   HOW COULD THE PROBLEM HAVE BEEN CORRECTED?

There are three clear-cut ways to correct this provision.

FIRST: Cut the age limits down to 21 instead of 35. An age limit of 21 for grandchildren, IN A WILL,[22] is safe, because the testator's own children would be good measuring lives. Anything keyed to an age of more than 21 for grandchildren, however, is dangerous.

SECOND: If, at the time the will was written, Patricia, (and other children of Hitchcock), had reached an age where it would be unlikely for any more grandchildren to be born or adopted,[23]

---

[19] This is based on the fact that Patricia is mentioned several times by name in the will, in ways which indicated that she was still alive when the will was written.

[20] RAP assumes that any person is capable of having children until the moment of death. And in any case, regardless of how old Patricia might have been at her father's death, she could still have <u>adopted</u> children, who would then probably have been considered to have been Hitchcock's grandchildren.

[21] These are shifting executory interests because they follow preceding vested estates, and executory interests are the only interests, created in a third person, which can follow a preceding vested estate. These interests are "shifting" interests because they "shift" from one grantee to another—rather than "springing" over a gap of time.

[22] But watch out for such a provision in a deed! As indicated in the answer to Question 6, near the end of this chapter, a gift in a DEED to such of the Grantor's grandchildren as reached 21 might well be VOID under RAP, because the <u>Grantor</u> is still alive at the time of the deed, and may thus be the only good measuring life.

[23] Despite the fact that under RAP anyone is considered to be capable of producing children until the moment of death, in real life, people beyond a certain age are very unlikely to have or adopt any more children.

then Hitchcock might have provided for the existing grandchildren <u>by name</u>. That would have served the function of making the existing grandchildren members of a closed class.[24] Any <u>named</u> grandchild living at Hitchcock's death could serve as his or her <u>own</u> measuring life. Then any age provision for a <u>named</u> grandchild would have been effective under RAP—and the gifts over after the death of a <u>named</u> grandchild would also have been effective.

THIRD: The gifts to grandchildren might have been drafted in such a way as to be vested, with payment postponed. This is probably what Alfred Hitchcock's attorney intended to do—but he or she simply did not do it effectively.[25] To make an effective gift to a testator's grandchild that is vested with payment postponed—without causing a violation of RAP—you must give the assets clearly and irrevocably to or for the benefit of the grandchild—and then just provide that the assets are actually to be handed over to the grandchild at various specified times. For a gift that is vested, with payment postponed, you can delay payment, but you CANNOT TAKE THE GIFT AWAY ENTIRELY without running into problems with RAP. The NEW gift that is made, after the assets are taken away from the first beneficiary, (because he or she dies before reaching 35, for example), will be very likely to violate RAP, simply because the NEW GIFT will not get to the NEW BENEFICIARY within the time allowed by RAP.

That was the problem with the provision in Alfred Hitchcock's will. The NEW gift would have been VOID under RAP because it might have vested more than 21 years after the lives in being at Hitchcock's death.[26]

So, to use the method of having the gift vested, with payment postponed, without causing RAP problems, you must NOT try to take the gift away from the first beneficiary if the first beneficiary dies before a certain age. Just let the remainder go into the first beneficiary's ESTATE—(and then by intestacy or by the provisions of any will the first beneficiary may have—giving the assets to a friend, spouse, charity—or the grandchildren's own issue).[27] The major point is that your client should NOT attempt to SHIFT the assets to a NEW beneficiary beyond the time allowed by RAP.

---

[24] For example, if Hitchcock had set up trusts "for each of my grandchildren, Peter, Paul, and Mary," then those children would be the <u>only</u> children included in the class—the class would be <u>closed</u>—and any grandchild born later would simply be excluded.

[25] The drafting was not as good as it should have been. But as indicated later, in Section C of this Chapter, the savings clause included in Hitchcock's will actually would have saved the gifts.

[26] In other words, the shifting executory interest might have shifted later the time allowed by RAP, and would thus have been held to have been void.

[27] The first beneficiary might NOT have left his or her estate to his or her own issue. It is quite common for a gift to be made to a person's spouse—who certainly does not constitute "issue." And in many states a spouse is an "heir" if a person dies intestate. A person may also choose to leave gifts to friends or charities, rather than relatives. So Hitchcock's attempted gift to a grandchild's "issue" is NOT the same as leaving it in the grandchild's ESTATE.

SAMPLE TWO—WILL OF NORMAN ROCKWELL

After providing that trust income was to be paid to the surviving spouse of each of Norman Rockwell's three sons, CLAUSE FIFTH Section (4) of the will of Norman Rockwell provided:

> Upon the death or remarriage, whichever first occurs, of the wife of a son of mine, … if issue of said son of mine shall then be living, the Trustee shall divide the original share into as many equal shares as there are children of my said son then surviving, or who being then deceased, leave issue then surviving, and shall pay over and distribute one of such shares to the then living issue of each then deceased child of my said son … and one of such shares to each then surviving child of my said son.

QUESTIONS:
WHAT IS WRONG WITH THIS PROVISION?
HOW COULD IT HAVE BEEN CORRECTED?

ANSWERS:

A.   WHAT IS WRONG WITH THE PROVISION?

The difficulty here is what is known as the "unborn widow"[28] problem! Norman Rockwell, or his lawyer, was trying to use the wife of one of the <u>sons</u> of the testator as a measuring life! This cannot be done, as written.   For example, there is no guarantee that the woman to whom Rockwell's <u>son</u>, Peter, might have been married at Peter's death would have been someone who was alive when <u>Norman Rockwell</u> died. If Peter, at Peter's death, were in fact married to Sally, who had not been alive when Norman Rockwell died, then Peter's widow, Sally, would not have been a "life in being" at Norman Rockwell's death, and thus could <u>not</u> have been used as a "measuring life." Therefore, all the gifts dependent on surviving <u>Sally</u> would be <u>void</u> under RAP, because they might have vested later than 21 years after the death of some life in being at the creation of the interest.[29] True, <u>Peter</u> could have been a good measuring life for his own children.[30] But that is <u>not</u> how the provision is written. Instead Peter's children take <u>only if they survive Sally</u>! And Sally might have turned out to be an "unborn widow!" Therefore, the gifts

---

[28] Leach, "Perpetuities in a Nutshell," 51 Harv. L. Rev. 638 (1938).

[29] Notice that <u>Sally's</u> gift is GOOD. <u>She</u> will be ascertained no later than the death of <u>Peter</u>, who would have been a good measuring life. It is generally the gifts AFTER the gift to the "unborn widow" that fail.

[30] All of Peter's children would have been born during Peter's life or within 9 months thereafter, so all of Peter's children would have been considered to have been lives in being by the time Peter died.

to Peter's issue who survive Sally would all have been void under RAP because of the "unborn widow" problem.

B.   HOW COULD THE PROVISION HAVE BEEN CORRECTED:

FIRST: Try to <u>avoid</u> using the terms "wife" or "widow," (or "husband," "widower" or "spouse") for anyone <u>other than</u> the person <u>writing the will</u>. (The surviving spouse of the <u>testator or testatrix will</u>, of necessity, be someone who was alive at the death of the testator or testatrix. That is <u>not</u> true, however, for the spouse of any person who <u>survived</u> the testator or testatrix.)[31]

So one possibility for avoiding the "unborn widow" problem is simply to <u>name</u> the potential widow—e.g., "if my son's wife, Nora, survives my son." This is dangerous, however, because of the possibility that Nora might die, (or divorce the son), and the son might later marry a woman named Anna. If Nora had been the one named in the will, then Anna would get nothing—no matter how long or happy the son's second marriage had been. It is unlikely that would have been the intent of the testator.

SECOND: Use the word, "wife" or "widow" to include anyone to whom the son might be married at his death, but simply do not make the gifts over, at the death of the widow, dependent on surviving the <u>widow</u>. Instead, make the gifts over payable to the son's issue, determined as of 21 years after the death of the <u>son, or</u> at the death of the widow, which ever comes <u>first</u>. That way, the provision will not violate RAP; will provide for anyone who may turn out to be the son's widow; and will <u>probably</u>[32] send the gift over to people who are actually alive at the widow's death.

THIRD: Keep the assets in a <u>trust</u> for a limited time, giving the income of the trust to the son's widow until 21 years after the <u>son's</u> death, (or until the widow dies, which ever comes <u>first</u>), and then simply terminate the trust.[33]

Upon termination of the trust, (21 years after the death of the <u>son</u>—who would be a <u>good</u> measuring life), give the long-living widow[34] a certain percentage of the remaining trust assets outright, and give the rest outright to the son's issue who are then surviving. This will make it possible to include anyone to whom the son was married at the time of his death, and will also

---

[31] Remember, it is the people who <u>survive the testator</u>—including the testator's sons and daughters—who may marry or re-marry <u>after</u> the death of the testator, and thus end up married to someone who had not yet been born when the <u>testator</u> died.

[32] The gift may, in fact, go into the estate of a person who is dead at the time for distribution—but this is fairly unlikely to happen. Yet if the son's widow lived for 25 years after the son's death, and then died, the assets might go into the estate of someone who was one of the son's "issue," but had died a mere 21 years after the son's death.

[33] By terminating the trust no later than 21 years after the death of the son, no gift would violate RAP.

[34] The son's widow, at this point, must have lived for 21 years after the son's death—which may mean that she is getting on in years, or that the son died when he was quite young, or that in fact the widow <u>did</u> turn out to be someone who was much younger than the son.

insure that the remaining assets of the trust will be distributed only to people who are alive at the time for distribution.

SUMMARY: If you use the word "wife," "widow," "husband," "widower," or "spouse" for anyone other than the testator or testatrix, BE SURE to do the special drafting required to avoid the "unborn widow" problem!

C.   SAVINGS CLAUSES

Just to be on the safe side, most people who draft wills and trusts include a Rule Against Perpetuities Savings clause. In fact, both Alfred Hitchcock and Norman Rockwell had such savings clauses included in their respective wills.[35] Drafting a good savings clause takes skill—if you do not want the savings clause itself to be thrown out by the courts.[36]

There are two places a RAP savings clause might normally be included—with the gift itself, or in a separate provision of the will. And there are two basic things a savings clause must do. First, it must cut off the "dead-hand" control within the time allowed by RAP. Second, it must then distribute the assets effectively.

As you read the following sample savings clauses, try to ascertain how effective each one is at meeting these two requirements. The first sample, from the will of Humphrey Bogart, was contained with the gift itself. The next two samples, from Elvis Presley and Alfred Hitchcock, were contained in separate provisions of their respective wills.

SAMPLE THREE—SAVINGS CLAUSE FROM HUMPHREY BOGART

Article SEVENTH, Section (e) of Humphrey Bogart's will states:

> ...said trust shall continue and the net income thereof shall be paid, in quarterly installments, to my sister, FRANCES BOGART ROSE, so long as she shall live, and thereafter to her issue, living from time to time, per stirpes. This trust shall terminate upon the decease of the <u>last survivor of my sister FRANCES and all her issue surviving at the time of my decease, and thereupon the principal and any</u>

---

[35] And in fact, both savings clauses would have worked, to reform the gifts sufficiently to make them good.

[36] In <u>Hagemann v. National Bank & Trust Co.</u>, 237 S.E.2d 388 (1977), the Virginia Supreme Court simply <u>refused to implement a RAP savings clause</u>! The court said, with feeling, that it was clear the testatrix had <u>intended</u> to include provisions that violated RAP, and stated that the court was not about to help her do so. In addition, the court was angered by the fact that the testatrix seemed to be trying to incorporate in the savings clause the very provisions that had violated RAP in the first place. The court noted that the savings clause was almost a verbatim copy of a savings clause found in a standard form book!

undistributed income thereof shall go and be distributed to THE HUMPHREY BOGART FOUNDATION. [Emphasis added.]

Article EIGHTH of the will provided that THE HUMPHREY BOGART FOUNDATION was to "have as its primary purpose the making of grants for the aid of medical research, with special reference to the field of cancer."

QUESTIONS:

> HAS THE SAVINGS CLAUSE TERMINATED THE TRUST WITHIN THE TIME ALLOWED BY RAP?
> DOES IT PROVIDE FOR AN EFFECTIVE DISTRIBUTION?

ANSWERS:

The answer is YES, on both counts. The trust is terminated in time, because Bogart has specified termination at the death of "the last survivor of my sister FRANCES and all her issue surviving at the time of my decease." Thus Bogart made a good collection of measuring lives—members of a closed class, all of whom were alive at the death of the testator.

Bogart might have extended the term of the trust for an additional 21 years. Instead, he made an outright gift to the Foundation.

The gift to the Foundation clearly meets the second requirement—effectively getting the assets to the Foundation within the time allowed by RAP.[37]

Was the savings clause needed in Humphrey Bogart's will? Definitely! Had he simply provided that the income was to go to the issue of FRANCES, "living from time to time," the trust would have had no ascertainable ending, and would definitely have violated RAP.

SAMPLE FOUR: SAVINGS CLAUSE FROM ELVIS PRESLEY

ITEM XIV(a) of the will of Elvis Presley provides:

---

[37] Actually, there MIGHT have been problems with the gift to the Foundation, under the theory of "administrative contingencies." Article EIGHTH of Bogart's will provided, "If the circumstances shall ever be such that THE HUMPHREY BOGART FOUNDATION shall become entitled to receive any property pursuant to the provisions of either Clause SIXTH or Clause SEVENTH hereof, or both such Clauses, then I direct my trustees to cause to be formed a non-profit corporation bearing that name to receive such property." [Emphasis added.] IF the Humphrey Bogart Foundation was not in fact in existence at the death of the testator, and if it took the trustee more than 21 years after the death of all the lives in being to get the Foundation formed, then the gift would violate RAP because of the "administrative contingencies" aspect of RAP. In California, where Bogart lived at the time of his death, the courts have held that this sort of "administrative contingency" will not cause a violation of RAP—but that a reasonable time will be implied, instead. Nevertheless, in your own drafting, BE SURE THE CHARITY TO WHICH THE GIFT IS MADE WILL BE IN EXISTENCE AT THE TIME THE GIFT IS TO VEST—OR DIRECT THAT CY PRES IS TO BE APPLIED.

Having in mind the rule against perpetuities, [Yes—this is from Elvis!], I direct that (notwithstanding anything contained to the contrary in this last will and testament) each trust created under this will (except such trusts as have heretofore vested in compliance with such rule or law) shall end, unless sooner terminated under other provisions of this will, twenty-one (21) years after the death of the last survivor of such of the beneficiaries hereunder as are living at the time of my death; and thereupon that the property held in trust shall be distributed free of all trust to the persons then entitled to receive the income and/or principal therefrom, in the proportion in which they are then entitled to receive such income.

QUESTIONS:

HAS THIS PROVISION TERMINATED THE TRUST WITHIN THE TIME ALLOWED BY RAP?
DOES IT PROVIDE FOR AN EFFECTIVE DISTRIBUTION?

ANSWERS:

YES and NO! The provision does terminate the trust in time—again using a collection of measuring lives described as "the beneficiaries… [of the trust]… living at the time of my death." This would be a closed class of lives in being at the creation of the interest, so they would be good measuring lives. And Elvis has appropriately used the 21 years available AFTER the death of all the people used as measuring lives.

But the distribution is NOT EFFECTIVE. As you may recall from Chapter 4, part B, the trust established by Elvis Presley in his will was a discretionary trust. The trustee was authorized, "to accumulate the net income or to pay or apply… the net income and… [any] portion of the principal at any time and from time to time" to various beneficiaries as the trustee might determine. Elvis stated that, "Any decision of the Trustee as to whether or not distribution shall be made, and also as to the amount of such distribution, to any of the persons described hereunder shall be final and conclusive and not subject to question by any legatee or beneficiary hereunder."

So could any beneficiary, ever, claim to be "entitled" to receive income from Elvis's trust? No! By neglecting to realize that the gift made at the end of a savings clause is a new gift, not just a continuation of the prior trust, the drafter of Elvis's will failed to meet the second requirement of a savings clause—distributing the assets effectively!

This may demonstrate that before you can draft an effective <u>savings clause</u>, you must <u>first understand RAP</u>!

As you analyze the next savings clause, from the will of Alfred Hitchcock, try to determine if the great mystery writer, (or his lawyer), was able to understand the complexities of RAP.

SAMPLE FIVE: SAVINGS CLAUSE FROM ALFRED HITCHCOCK

Article V, Section 6(i) of the will of Alfred Hitchcock provides:

> Unless sooner terminated in the manner hereinbefore provided, each of the separate trusts provided for in this Paragraph V, [for Hitchcock's grandchildren], shall cease and terminate twenty-one (21) years after the death of myself, my wife, ALMA REVILLE HITCHCOCK, my daughter, PATRICIA HITCHCOCK O'CONNELL, and all of the children of my said daughter who are living at the time of my death. Upon such termination, the entire principal of each of the trusts, together with any accumulated income, shall be distributed to the persons for whom said estate is then held in trust under the provisions and in the same proportions hereinabove provided, and if there be no such persons then living, then to the UNIVERSITY OF CLAIFORNIA AT LOS ANGELES MEDICAL CENTER.

QUESTIONS:

> HAS THIS PROVISION TERMINATED THE TRUST WITHIN THE TIME ALLOWED BY RAP?
> DOES IT PROVIDE FOR AN EFFECTIVE DISTRIBUTION?

ANSWERS:

The answer is YES, on both counts. Although this looks very much like Elvis's ineffective savings clause, this one works—although it could have been more clearly drafted. The difference between the ultimate effectiveness of the savings clauses used by Presley and Hitchcock is caused by the differences in the ORIGINAL TRUST PROVISIONS of each will.

In Elvis's will, a discretionary trust was established, and no beneficiary ever was "entitled" to anything. In Hitchcock's will, on the other hand, although the trustee had some discretion over payment of income prior to the time a grandchild reached 21, after that time the trustee's discretion became quite limited, and the grandchildren did become "entitled" to various amounts of income and principal at certain clearly specified times, in certain specified amounts.[38] Basically, the assets of each of Hitchcock's trusts were vested in a specific grandchild, with payment postponed, (and subject to a divesting condition which violated RAP, as discussed in Section B of this chapter.)

Notice that both Elvis and Hitchcock <u>needed</u> RAP savings clauses in their wills. But the clause which worked for Hitchcock would <u>not</u> have worked for Elvis.

Remember: STANDARD RAP SAVINGS CLAUSES CANNOT BE BLINDLY COPIED FROM ONE DOCUMENT INTO ANOTHER!

Why did the savings clause work for Hitchcock? First, Hitchcock chose an appropriate group of measuring lives, (his wife, daughter and grandchildren living at his death), and then terminated the trust 21 years after the last to die of those people who had been selected as measuring lives. So far, the Hitchcock and Elvis clauses are very much alike.

The next aspect of the savings clauses is the distinguishing factor between them. Hitchcock distributed the assets effectively, because the prior <u>trust</u> provisions described descendants who would have been clearly identifiable, and "entitled" to the proceeds at the time selected for distribution. The trust provisions, read with the savings clause, would have specified which descendants were "entitled" to get the assets, in what percentages.

And what if there had not been any descendants living at the time for distribution under Hitchcock's savings clause? That aspect of the final distribution is also covered effectively—using the same method as that used by Humphrey Bogart—by making a final gift to a charity.

So Hitchcock's RAP savings clause works.

But how could it have been better drafted? First it is nearly always better simply to make a <u>new</u> gift in the savings clause—to specify directly who is to take the ultimate distribution—(e.g., "my issue living at the time of termination of the trust, by representation")—rather than trying to use the prior trust provisions. Openly making a new gift will help force the drafter to recognize that by the time the savings clause comes into effect, the interests simply must vest—and the testator must let go of all remaining control, and the provisions of the prior trust <u>cannot continue</u>! So the

---

[38] Hitchcock's will in Article V, Sec. 6(b) provides, "Upon each of said... [grandchildren] attaining the age of twenty-one (21) years, respectively, the Trustees shall thereafter pay currently to such child <u>all</u> of the net income from his or her trust until such child shall attain the age of thirty-five (35) years or shall die, whichever event shall first occur." [Emphasis added.] Article V, Sec. 6(c) then goes on to provide, "When any of such... [grandchildren] shall attain the age of twenty-five (25) years, respectively, the Trustees shall immediately deliver to such [grand]child one-third (1/3) of the then balance of the principal (and accumulated income) of his or her trust." Sections (d) and (e) continue that when a grandchild "shall attain the age of thirty... the Trustees shall immediately deliver to such [grand]child one-half ... of the then balance... [and when the grandchild reaches 35]... the Trustees shall immediately deliver to such [grand]child all of the remaining balance of the principal (and accumulated income) of his or her trust." Not much discretion is left for the Trustees under these provisions!

first way to have improved Hitchcock's savings clause would have been to make a clear, new gift to the intended beneficiaries.

The second way in which Hitchcock's savings clause could have been better drafted is more significant. With regard to the final gift to the UCLA Medical Center, consideration should have been given to the doctrine of "cy pres," also called "equitable approximation." What if the Medical Center, by the time for distribution, had been closed or renamed or combined with some other medical center?

Whenever a gift is made to a charity, it is a good idea to specify what happens if that charity no longer exists at the time for distribution. Should the court apply "cy pres" to give the assets to another, similar charity? (Another part of UCLA? Or another medical center?) Or does the testator want to specify his own list of charities? And then perhaps direct that cy pres be applied when the testator's own list of charities is exhausted?

The issue should be discussed with your client, and included in the final provisions of any clause you draft that includes a gift to charity.

Now that you have had a short refresher on the Rule Against Perpetuities, and have observed the importance—and some of the complexities—of a Rule Against Perpetuities savings clause, you may want to try your hand at the brief drafting exercise which follows.

D.   DRAFTING EXERCISE 11—RULE AGAINST PERPETUITIES SAVINGS CLAUSE

The senior partner in your firm has just drafted a complex will for a major client. The senior partner feels that she has done an appropriately expert job on the will. But ever since law school, the senior partner has been unable to shake a persistent uneasiness about the Rule Against Perpetuities, (RAP). Therefore, she has asked you to draft an effective RAP savings clause to be included at the end of the will.

You have determined that it is probably the better part of valor just to do as you are told, rather than offer to check the will for any RAP violations. You must, however, ask the senior partner at least two questions about the contents of the will. First, are there any discretionary trusts included in the will? Second, to whom should the assets be given if any gifts, as drafted, somehow turn out to violate RAP? If the senior partner says that any charity is to be an ultimate beneficiary, then you must trouble the senior partner with one more question. Is the doctrine of "cy pres" to be applied with regard to the gift to the charity—and if not, to whom should a failed charitable gift be given?

For drafting purposes, you may now make up any answers you like to the questions you would have asked the senior partner.

As you begin this drafting, you may want to look at the Pointers for Drafting which follow.

E.   POINTERS FOR DRAFTING

1.   As you begin drafting a RAP savings clause, remember that there are two things you must do. You must terminate all trusts in time, and you must be sure that all assets are finally distributed within the time allowed by RAP.

2.   To be sure that all trusts terminate in time, specify an appropriate group of measuring lives. Remember that the persons to be used as measuring lives must have been alive at the death of the testator, and must have been members of a closed class at that time.[39] They must also be people who can be ascertained and followed with reasonable expenditure of time and money. Usually, the selected lives in being will just be the beneficiaries named in the will who survived the testator, or all the testator's issue alive at the death of the testator, or a combination of both these groups.

3.   After you have defined the measuring lives, indicate whether the trusts are to terminate on the death of the last to die of the persons selected as measuring lives—or 21 years after the death of that last measuring life. (It is, of course, permissible to use any period of time shorter than 21 years.)

4.   Make a new gift, specifying to whom the assets are to be distributed upon termination of the trusts. Try to word this gift in such a way that the assets will only go to persons alive at the time for distribution. BE SURE that if you give the assets to the testator's "heirs" you specify whether those heirs are to be determined as of the date of death of the testator, (the usual meaning of "heirs," and a bad idea in a savings clause), or are to be determined as if the testator had died at the time for distribution, (a much better idea, in order to avoid running the assets through the estates of people who have already died).

5.   If a gift to a charity is involved, specify whether the doctrine of "cy pres" is to be applied by the court, if the intended charity is no longer in existence at the time of the termination of the trust. If the court is to apply "cy pres" then perhaps your client would like to give some guidance as to which aspects of the client's general charitable purpose are most important. Is the testator primarily concerned with helping abused children? Or helping

---

[39] See Section II. B. of this chapter for description of a closed class

families in general within the state where the client lives? Or helping children who are under a certain age? Or is the client simply willing to leave decisions of that nature to a court at some future date?

6.   If a charitable gift is involved, would your client like to make a list of specific charities to receive the assets if a prior charity is no longer in existence? At some point, would your client rather have the assets go to friends or family, rather than to a charity?

7.   Remember that when funds are given for research on particular medical problems, those specified problems may ultimately be solved. Polio, for example, was ultimately essentially eradicated—even though we seem not to have been as successful with many other medical problems.

8.   If possible, make your RAP savings clause so self-contained that it can stand alone, and will not be endangered if other parts of the will are later changed by codicil—and no one then remembers to check on what effect, if any, the new changes made by the codicil will have on the existing RAP savings clause.

F.   PRACTICE QUESTIONS FOR THE RULE AGAINST PERPETUITIES

Remember: the various modifications of RAP, such as "cy pres,"[40] "wait and see,"[41] and USRAP, (Uniform Statutory Rule Against Perpetuities)[42] simply allow a court either to: (1) reform a gift that violates common law RAP;[43] or (2) wait until the death of the lives in being plus 21 years,[44] or wait a total of 90 or 1,000 years,[45] to see if the gift does vest too remotely— and then possibly reform the gift.[46]

So if you want to avoid subsequent litigation, simply draft provisions that do not violate RAP! The following questions are intended to help you learn how to draft provisions that will be effective <u>without court intervention</u>—that is, without relying on "cy pres," "wait and see," or USRAP.

---

[40] "Cy pres" allows a court to modify a provision that violates RAP by cutting down the number of years specified—from 25 to 21, for example, so that the provision no longer violates RAP.

[41] This allows courts to wait until expiration of the time allowed by RAP, and consider any interest that has in fact vested by that time to be good.

[42] This allows a ninety year period for "wait and see," followed by reformation, if necessary. In some jurisdictions this has now expanded to 1,000 years!

[43] This is the solution under "cy pres."

[44] "Wait and see."

[45] USRAP.

[46] Id.

Therefore, applying the common law Rule Against Perpetuities (RAP) for each of the following provisions answer the following questions:

(1)   When was the interest created?   (Death of the testator, creation of the power of appointment, exercise of the power of appointment, creation of the trust, etc.);[47]

(2)   Who should be used as the measuring life or lives? and;

(3)   Does any attempted gift violate RAP?

Then, if a gift violates RAP as written, explain how the attempted gift might have been better drafted so that it would not have violated the Common Law Rule Against Perpetuities. Answers and explanations for all of these questions follow the questions.

PRACTICE QUESTIONS:

1.   In her will T devised land, "to C for life, then to such of C's children as shall survive C." At her death T was survived by her only child, C, and by C's two children, who were ages 10 and 12.

2.   In his will T gave property, "to my daughter, D, for life, then to such of my grandchildren as reach 21." At his death T was survived by T's four children, A, B, C, and D, and by two grandchildren, X and Y, ages 10 and 12.

3.   In her will T gave property, "to my son, S for life, then to such of my grandchildren as reach the age of 25." At her death, all of T's four children had already died, and T was survived by two grandchildren, X and Y, ages one and two.

4.   In his will T bequeathed a valuable painting, "to my son, B, for life, then to my first grandchild to graduate from law school." At his death T was survived by three children, A, B, and C, and by two grandchildren, X and Y, ages two and three respectively.

5.   S created a revocable living trust in 1990, giving herself the right to income for life, and directing the trustee on the death of S "to pay the income, annually, to my daughter, D, for life, and then to distribute the assets to those of my children or grandchildren who survive D, at whatever time and in whatever share or shares D may appoint by her will." S retained the power to revoke or amend the trust until she died, but never changed any of

---

[47] Remember, an interest is considered to have been created, for RAP purposes, when the document creating the interest becomes irrevocable.

the provisions of the trust. At her death in 1995, S was survived by her children, D and E, and by D's two children, X and Y, who were then ages one and two. D died in 1996, and in her will appointed the assets, "to such of my children as shall reach the age of 25." When D died in 1996 she was survived by her brother, E, and by D's two children, X and Y, who were then ages two and three.

6.   In 1990 S created an irrevocable trust, directing that the trustee should "pay the income to me for life, then pay the income in equal shares to all of my children, for their lives, then terminate the trust and distribute the assets equally to those of my grandchildren who shall be alive at the time of termination of the trust." When the trust was established in 1990 S had two children, A and B, and three grandchildren, X, Y, and Z, ages four, six, and eight respectively. At S's death in 1996 he was survived by his two children, A and B, and by the same three grandchildren, X, Y, and Z—each of whom was six years older than he or she had been when the trust was established.

ANSWERS:

Answer to Question 1:

(1)   The interest was created when T died, and her will became effective.

(2)   C should be used as the measuring life. Since C was still alive at T's death, C might have had or adopted more children, so C's children were not a closed class, and thus could not be their own measuring lives. So looking for the relevant parent of C's children, we find, not surprisingly, that C is the relevant parent of C's children. C was a closed class at T's death. There was only one person named C. C was a life in being at the death of the testator, and is therefore the measuring life for the gift to C's children.

(3)   No gift violates RAP, no matter how young any of C's children may be, because we will know at C's death exactly which of C's children shall have survived C.
        Therefore, the gift is good under RAP. No need to re-draft the provision.

Answer to Question 2:

(1)   The interest was created when T's will went into effect, at T's death.

(2)   The measuring lives will be <u>all four</u> of T's children who were living at T's death, even though D is the only one of T's children mentioned in the gift. Because T is survived by

at least one child, T's grandchildren would not yet be a closed class, since more grandchildren could be born or adopted after T dies. So we must use the relevant PARENTS of the beneficiaries as the measuring lives. <u>All four</u> of T's children are potential parents of T's grandchildren. So <u>all four</u> of T's children who survive T will be used as measuring lives.

(3)   No gift violates RAP. If all four of T's children were hit by a truck, (and died), the day after T's death, then all of T's grandchildren would still be sure to reach 21, if they ever did, within 21 years after their respective parents had died.

So no gift violates RAP – and it really doesn't matter what ages the existing grandchildren were at the time of T's death. No need to re-draft the provision.

Answer to Question 3:

(1)   The interests were created when T's will went into effect – at T's death.

(2)   The grandchildren can be their own measuring lives! The two existing grandchildren, X and Y, are members of a <u>closed class</u>, because <u>all</u>, of the potential <u>parents</u> of T's grandchildren, (T's children), had already died <u>before T died</u>. So there can be <u>no more grandchildren</u>, and the two existing grandchildren were lives in being at the creation of the interest, and members of a closed class. Therefore, X and Y will be their own measuring lives.

(3)   No interest violates RAP. It may take that one year old grandchild, X, more than 21 years from the death of T to reach the age of 25. But because X is his or her own measuring life (as a living member of a closed class at the creation of the interest), then X has his or her whole life to try to make it to 25. If X makes it to 25, fine. If X dies before reaching 25 the gift to X will fail. But it did not violate RAP, because we will know, for sure, whether the gift has vested or failed within the life of X – (one of the measuring lives). The same analysis, of course, applies to the gift made to the two year old, Y, which is also good under RAP.

Redrafting: As it happens, all of the gifts are good. However, that could not have been known when the will was <u>drafted</u>. So the will should have been <u>drafted</u> using the age of

21 for the grandchildren, instead of the age of 25 – just in case at least one of T's children did turn out to survive T.[48]

Answer to Question 4:

(1)   The interest is created when T dies, and his will becomes effective.

(2)   All three of T's children, A, B, and C, will be the measuring lives. The existing grandchildren cannot be their own measuring lives, because they are not members of a closed class, because their parents are still alive and might have or adopt more people who would be considered grandchildren of T. So we must use the parents of the beneficiaries – all of T's children – as the measuring lives. If all three of T's children were hit by a truck, (and died), the day after T's death, would we be sure that whichever grandchild turned out to be the first one to struggle through law school successfully would do so within 21 years after the unfortunate deaths of A, B, and C? No. And the ages of specific grandchildren are irrelevant. So the gift intended for the first brave grandchild to graduate from law school fails. UNLESS one of the grandchildren had been considerably older at the death of T, and had ALREADY happily graduated from law school at the death of T! If that were the case, then we would know, at the death of T, who would be entitled to the gift. And the foresighted grandchild, who had ALREADY graduated from law school at the death of T, would be entitled to the painting.

That would NOT work, however, if the most law school-prone grandchild, at the death of T, still had even one semester to go before graduating from law school. All sorts of things can happen in that final semester. If the grandchild who had almost become a law school graduate, at the last minute, decided to go live on a desert island instead, it might be more than 21 years before any other grandchild would successfully complete law school. So the gift would fail, (no matter what the ages and academic status of the existing grandchildren), if no grandchild had ALREADY graduated from law school prior to the death of T.

How could the gift have been better drafted? If T did not expect any more grandchildren to be born or adopted, he could have named his existing grandchildren, (X and Y), thus making them into a closed class, who could serve as their own measuring lives. Then if one of the grandchildren named in the will, X, for example, at age 84, finally graduated

---

[48]   Using 21 instead of 25 would have allowed any child of T who survived T to be used effectively as a measuring life because all of the gifts to the grandchildren would be sure to vest, if at all, within 21 year after the death of the last of T's children alive at T's death.

from law school, and was the first grandchild to do so, then he or she would win the painting.

Or T might have provided that the offer of the painting, (so to speak) would stay open only for 21 years after the death of the last to die of all of T's issue alive at T's death.[49] That would create a closed class of all three of T's children, plus T's two existing grandchildren. If you added 21 years after the death of the last to die of those five people you might have a very long time for some grandchild, (including a grandchild born after the death of T), to complete law school.[50]

Answer to Question 5:

(1)   This is harder. Because this was a <u>revocable</u> trust, RAP did NOT begin to run until the <u>death of the settler</u>, S, in 1995.[51] So the interests are considered to have been created at the <u>death</u> of S, in 1995, even though the trust was first established in 1990. Because the donee of the power of appointment, D, cannot appoint to herself, (because she will not "survive" herself), and because she is only permitted to appoint by will, this is a special, testamentary power of appointment.[52] Therefore, RAP begins to run when the <u>power is created</u> – when the document creating the power becomes irrevocable – which is in <u>1995</u>, (when the settlor dies, and can therefore no longer revoke the trust).[53]

(2)   The measuring lives <u>appear</u> to be both of S's children, D and E.[54] (As it turns out, E will NOT be a measuring life.) Since the grandchildren appeared not to be a closed class when S's revocable trust became irrevocable, (at S's death), then we would, at first, think we should use the parents of the grandchildren as the measuring lives. So D and E would <u>appear</u> to be the measuring lives – as of S's death, and it would <u>appear</u> that the gift would violate RAP.

---

[49]   For example, T might have said that the painting should be given "to the first of my grandchildren to graduate from law school prior to 21 years after the last to die of my issue alive at my death."

[50]   Notice that it would not matter which of the grandchildren happened to win the painting. RAP is only concerned with making sure that the gift vests, if at all, with SOMEONE during the time allowed by RAP. It is the <u>delay in vesting</u> that is of concern with RAP – not who actually gets the painting.

[51]   Remember, RAP only starts when the document that creates the interest becomes irrevocable – when the donor actually lets go of an interest in the property.

[52]   It is also an "exclusive" power of appointment, because D can <u>exclude</u> one or more objects of the power – as she has, by leaving her brother out entirely.

[53]   ONLY when the settlor died did she finally give up the power to get the property back at any time she liked. So it was at the death of the settlor that RAP actually began to run.

[54]   Remember, a measuring life need not be mentioned in the document, or get any gift under the terms of the document. The fact that E might produce grandchildren of the settlor is sufficient to make E appear to be a measuring life for the children E might have.

(3)   HOWEVER, the attempted gift to <u>D's children</u> who reach 25 is VALID. Because this gift is created by a power of appointment, we may apply the Second Look Doctrine.[55] That is NOT a modification of the common law Rule Against Perpetuities, but is simply a bit of common sense which has been around for a long time. At the death of S, the <u>donor</u> of the power of appointment, we had no idea how the power might be exercised. The donor, S, had in effect given the <u>donee</u>, D, the power to fill in a blank in the document of the donor.[56] But <u>until that blank was filled in,</u> we could not tell whether the gift that would ultimately be made would violate RAP or not. So we simply take a SECOND LOOK at the facts, as they exist at the time of the EXERCISE OF THE POWER, and apply RAP in light of the facts EXISTING AT THE TIME OF THE EXERCISE of the power. RAP started to <u>run</u> when the donor <u>created</u> the power. But we may look at the facts that exist at the time the power is <u>exercised,</u> to see if the gifts will in fact vest or fail within the time allowed by RAP.[57]

In this case, the Second Look doctrine helps tremendously. If S had said in her <u>own</u> will that the assets should ultimately go to such of D's children as reached the age of 25, the gift would have been void, because D might have had another child after S's death, who might have reached 25, but not within 21 years after the death of the measuring life, D.

Using the <u>Second Look doctrine</u>, however, we can take account of the facts that have actually occurred between the time of S's death and the time of the exercise of the power. It turns out that in fact D has NOT had any more children after S's death. (And D is not about to have any more children now that she has died)[58] So in fact, D's two cute little kids, X and Y, were LIVES IN BEING, and MEMBERS OF A CLOSED CLASS,[59] when S's document became irrevocable at S's death. So X and Y actually <u>can</u> serve as their <u>own</u> measuring lives. X and Y may or may not make it to 25 – but we will know whether or not each reaches 25 within the lives of D's two children,[60] who turned out, using the Second Look doctrine, to have been members of a closed class at the creation of the interest.

---

[55]   Basically, the Second Look doctrine allows us to <u>look at the facts as they exist</u> at the time of the <u>exercise</u> of a <u>power of appointment,</u> instead of <u>imagining,</u> at the time the power is created, what <u>might</u> happen between the time of the creation of the power and the time of the exercise of the power.

[56]   Thus, exercise of a power of appointment makes the ultimate gift the result of something of a two-step process. First, the donor creates the power. Second, the donee exercises the power. And the ultimate gift is not made until <u>both</u> steps – creation and exercise – have been completed.

[57]   This causes no delay in ascertaining when the gifts will actually vest or fail. Because we had to wait, anyway, until the power was exercised, to see what the gift would be, it causes NO problem to take a Second Look, at the time the power is exercised, to see what the facts actually are at that time. The Second Look doctrine only applies to the time between creation and exercise of the power. It does NOT allow delaying the application of RAP for any additional time.

[58]   If D were a man, instead, and D's wife were pregnant with D's child when D died, the common law RAP would consider D's posthumously born child to have been a life in being at D's death – if the child were born alive. Again, most states simply disregard the possibility of a man being assisted by a sperm bank to have a child ten years after the man had actually died.

[59]   They were in a closed class, because in fact D had no more children before her death. We didn't know that the class was closed <u>until</u> D's death. But then, applying the Second Look doctrine, we can see that X and Y <u>can be their own measuring lives</u>.

[60]   X may die at age 24, and Y may die at age 18. Either event will have happened with in the life of X or Y.

So no need to redraft this provision. (And <u>D's</u> attorney, at the time he or she drafted D's will exercising the power, could have been certain that the provisions, as drafted, would work, IF D's attorney could have relied on D's statement, at that time, that she would not have or adopt any more children.) Nevertheless, it would have been better form for D's attorney, when exercising the power, to have referred to D's children by name and to have indicated that both of D's children had been alive when D died.

Answer to Question 6:

(1)   Because this trust was <u>irrevocable</u> when it was created in <u>1990,</u> the interests are considered to have been created in <u>1990</u>, and that is the time at which RAP began to run.[61] Note that the SETTLOR of the trust, S, was STILL ALIVE when RAP began to run.

(2)   Only the SETTLOR is a good MEASURING LIFE for this provision! Because the settlor was still alive when RAP began to run in 1990 the settlor might still have had or adopted more children. Thus the settlor's children, A and B, who were alive at the creation of the interest, could NOT be used as measuring lives, because they were NOT members of a closed class at the creation of the interest – in 1990. So the only good measuring life would have been the parent of the beneficiaries – <u>S</u>!

Note that this time we <u>cannot</u> use the Second Look doctrine, because <u>no power of appointment is involved</u>. The Second Look doctrine is ONLY available when gifts are made by exercise of a <u>power of appointment</u> – by the use of a two-step process, so to speak.[62]

(3)   The attempted gifts to S's grandchildren are VOID, because they violate RAP. The gifts to S's own children would vest at the death of S, the measuring life, because by the time of S's death all of his own children would have been born. So the gifts to S's <u>children</u> would comply with RAP (as long as there were no attempts to reallocate the income to grandchildren after one of S's children died).[63] But the attempted gifts to the settlor's own grandchildren, are VOID as a violation of RAP – primarily because these gifts to

---

[61] Remember, RAP begins to run when the document creating the interest becomes irrevocable. This document was irrevocable from the time it was written, so the interests are deemed to have been created when the trust was created because it was an irrevocable trust.

[62] With gifts made by a power of appointment the first step is creation of the power. The second step is exercise of the power. No gift is actually made until both steps have been taken. So there is no problem with looking at the facts as they exist when the second step is taken – when the power is exercised.

[63] Attempting to shift income away from a child who died would cause the same RAP problems discussed in Section B.I. of this chapter with regard to the will of Alfred Hitchcock.

grandchildren were made in an IRREVOCABLE DEED,[64] not a WILL, and therefore RAP started to run while the SETTLOR WAS STILL ALIVE.

Remember: The GRANTOR is the only SURE measuring life for a provision created by a DEED![65] That is because with a deed, the grantor is still alive, and thus might still have or adopt more children. So the grantor's <u>children</u> are <u>not</u> a closed class, and <u>cannot</u> be used as measuring lives. That leaves only the parent of the children – the grantor himself or herself.

How could this gift have been redrafted? If the settlor, in 1990, really wasn't intending to have or adopt any more children, then he or she could just have <u>named</u> the then existing children, A and B, and have provided that the ultimate gift should go to whatever <u>children of A and B</u> were alive at the termination of the trust, when A and B died. Then everything would have worked out fine – by making A and B into a closed class of people who <u>could</u> be used as measuring lives.

SUMMARY:

Clearly, it is your responsibility, as the attorney for a settlor or testator, to notice any potential RAP problems, ask the necessary questions, and then do the appropriate drafting to make sure that the client's intended gifts are effective under the common law Rule Against Perpetuities – without the need to rely on any future court for reformation.

By careful drafting, and recognizing that measuring lives must be a <u>closed class</u> of people, <u>alive at the creation of the interest</u>, you should be able to accomplish nearly all of the goals of your clients – <u>without</u> drafting anything that violates the Rule Against Perpetuities!

---

[64] Because the deed is irrevocable, as most deeds are, RAP starts to run just as soon as the deed goes into effect.
[65] Because the grantor is still alive, he or she may still have or adopt more children. Therefore, the grantor's existing children are <u>not a closed class</u>, and <u>cannot</u> be used as measuring lives for anyone. An easy way around this, of course, is just to NAME the grantor's existing children, thus <u>closing</u> the class, and making the existing children into good measuring lives. Then the final gift should go only to people who are alive at the death of the last to die of all the <u>named</u> children.

CHAPTER 9.   PROTECTION OF THE SURVIVING SPOUSE— THE AUGMENTED ESTATE—UPC II

A.   STATUTORY PROTECTION FOR A SURVIVING SPOUSE

In virtually every part of the United States, there is some statutory protection for a surviving spouse. This is based on a strong social policy that a person should be obligated to provide some support for a surviving spouse before making gifts to others. At common law, this usually took the form of dower or courtesy rights in land. Today the protection is much more likely to be in the form of a statutory right to a certain fraction of the decedent's assets—both real and personal

In community property states,[1] because each spouse is automatically entitled to one-half of the earnings of the other spouse, throughout the marriage, no additional protection is needed at the death of a spouse EXCEPT when the couple has recently moved from a non-community property state to a community property state—for retirement, for example. This issue will be discussed later.

For now, some illustrations and examples may help to clarify the problems and help you to appreciate the various patterns for statutory solutions. For purposes of illustration, we will assume, each time, that the husband died first, and that the wife therefore was entitled to a statutory share of the husband's estate—no matter what the husband may have provided in his will. Remember, throughout this chapter, that in most cases the law applies in exactly the same way to both husband and wife—no matter who happens to die first. It simply makes it easier to understand the various problems and solutions if we avoid switching back and forth unnecessarily between husband and wife.

So, assuming that the husband dies first, what might he have done with his property, under the terms of his will? Legally, a testator might have devised his property to anyone he liked. So let us assume that the husband, being annoyed with his wife, decided to write a will leaving ALL of the husband's property to his brother, Bob, and nothing to the husband's own beloved wife.

What could the wife do in such a situation? In all likelihood, she could elect under the applicable statutory provisions to "take against the will," and take her statutory share—usually one-third or one-half of the property the husband could otherwise have given away by will. So

---

[1] The nine community property states are: Arizona, California, Idaho, Louisiana, Nevada, New Mexico, Texas, Washington, and Wisconsin. In addition, Alaska statutes authorize residents or non-residents to establish Alaska community property trusts, which may include <u>land</u> not situated in Alaska! Alaska Statutes, 34.77.100

the wife, in this situation, might have a right to an elective share of one-third of the husband's probate estate—no matter what the husband's will said.

So, angry husbands, (and wives), over the years, have found various "loopholes," which they considered to be clever ways of making sure that there really wouldn't be much property left in the relevant probate estate.

The husband in our illustration, for example, knowing that he had a terminal illness, might simply GIVE brother Bob all of the husband's assets, three days before the husband died. In that case, the gift would normally be considered to be completed inter vivos gift—and there simply wouldn't be anything in the probate estate against which the wife could elect. (So sorry, my dear.)

Or, if the husband were not sure he was going to die fairly soon, and didn't actually want to part with all ownership of his assets, he might simply put all of his assets into an inter vivos trust. The husband might retain the right to income, and then direct that all assets in the trust at the husband's death should go to his brother, Bob.

In addition, the husband might think that if he made the inter vivos trust an irrevocable trust, then it would be quite clear that there <u>really</u> wouldn't be <u>any assets</u> left in the husband's probate estate when he died. (Sorry again, my dear.)

The inter vivos trust, of course, could be designed to pay <u>all</u> income from the trust to the husband for his life, and he might also be a <u>trustee</u> of the trust—just to be sure that the assets were properly invested. But again, since there would appear to be no assets in the probate estate at husband's death, the surviving wife who had a statutory right to one-third of the probate estate might end up without being able to get a cent from the estate of her dearly departed husband.

If the husband, during the marriage, had kept all of the property in his own name, then the surviving wife might be in very bad shape indeed, at his death, if he had decided to use one of the loopholes described above.

Using methods like these to leave the surviving spouse without a cent seemed to be strongly contrary to public policy—for two reasons. First, since the husband and wife were considered to be a "team" during the marriage, there was no reason why the "team" assets should not have been shared between team members when one of them died. Second, there seemed to be no reason why the public, (via welfare, and the like) should possibly have to provide support for the wife of a man who could perfectly well have arranged to provide support for his own wife.

So state legislatures in non-community property states have gradually been strengthening statutory rights of election, with the goal of making fewer and fewer loopholes available.

In COMMUNITY PROPERTY states, because all of the earnings of both spouses automatically are divided equally between the spouses as the earnings come in, there is no need for special protection of the surviving spouse IF the husband and wife remain domiciled in a community property state for the full duration of the marriage.

However, if a husband and wife start off the marriage living in Maine, for example, which is a non-community property state, and only the husband works outside the home, (while the wife is doing a tremendous amount of work raising the five children, running all the local charities, etc.), and then the couple moves to Arizona to retire, the wife might be in very bad circumstances if her husband did not voluntarily provide for her. Arizona, as a community property state, does not provide for an elective share for the surviving spouse. And the elective share that would have been available, had the couple stayed in Maine, would no longer be available if the husband died domiciled in Arizona!

This is a particularly significant problem, because many of the community property states are "sunbelt" states,[2] to which many people from more northern states may move when they retire.

To date, several of the community property states[3] have recognized this problem, and have provided statutory solutions that are quite similar to the statutory protections provided by non-community property states and similar to the pattern set forth in the Uniform Probate Code's Augmented Estate.

B.   THE AUGMENTED ESTATE

So what is the Uniform Probate Code's Augmented Estate and how does it work?

First, there are three versions of the Augmented Estate. The first version, found in the earliest version of the Uniform Probate Code, was adopted by several states during the years after 1969. The second version, contained in the 1993 revision of the Uniform Probate Code, has been adopted by a number of states since its promulgation in 1993. The third version is contained in the 2008 amendments to the Uniform Probate Code.

---

[2] For example, Arizona, California, Nevada, and New Mexico are all frequent destinations for retired people. Louisiana and Texas, of course, would also be attractive to elderly people who had seen enough winters in Maine.

[3] California Probate Code, Sections 66 and 101 to 103. Idaho Code Sections 15-2-201 to 208. New Mexico statutes, Sec. 40-3-8. Washington statutes, Sections 26.16.220, 230, 240, 250. See also: Louisiana Civil Code, Book IV, Title III, Art. 3526.

Because the elective share provisions in the Uniform Probate Code (UPC) are considerably more complex than virtually any elective share statute that preceded it, and do an interesting job in trying to plug some of the loopholes that had been discovered under prior legislation, we will spend some time learning to understand the 2008 version of UPC, hereafter just called Augmented Estate. An understanding of the UPC Augmented Estate will make any other scheme of statutory protection seem quite clear and simple by comparison.

C.   TRANSLATING THE AUGMENTED ESTATE

The full text of the 2008 Augmented Estate provisions of Uniform Probate Code are included in part F of this chapter. Go ahead and read them, if you like. But you will probably find, after the end of a few pages, that you feel you have absolutely no idea what is going on—and would never have a ghost of a chance of explaining the statute to a client!

Yet every will or estate plan must be drafted with recognition of the fact that if a surviving spouse is not adequately provided for, he or she may elect to take against the will, and thus wreck havoc with the entire will or estate plan. So it is necessary for you, and your clients, to have a basic idea of the elective share that may be available to the surviving spouse.

Because you cannot accurately predict where your client will be domiciled when he or she dies, or what the particular statutory provisions will be in that jurisdiction at that time, you should, at a minimum, understand the most recent Uniform Act on the subject.

Therefore, as a means of translating the Augmented Estate—both for lawyers and for clients—I have made up a set of formulas, which seem to have proved quite helpful, to both students and practitioners, in a jurisdiction that was one of the earliest states to adopt a version of the UPC augmented estate.[4]

D.   HELPFUL FORMULAS FOR CALCULATING AUGMENTED ESTATE

These formulas, although they appear complex at first, actually will help you to see the overall pattern of the augmented estate, thus helping both you and your client to design successful wills and estate plans.[5] Again, particular statutes will vary from one jurisdiction to another. Yet if you can understand the current UPC, you can understand anything! And a basic understanding of the applicable Uniform Act is probably appropriate for any field of law.

---

[4] Colorado adopted the first version of UPC Augmented Estate provisions in 1994 and they became effective in Colorado on July 1, 1995.

[5] After years on a law school Admissions Committee, it seemed clear to me that many people who are attracted to law school are very weak in math skills. As one such person, I have kept the numbers as simple as possible—numbers everyone could have worked with in second grade. So, have courage!

To see how the formulas work, first think of the augmented estate as a big box, composed of five smaller boxes, into which will be put nearly ALL of the assets of BOTH the husband and wife. As illustrated below, the big box represents the entire augmented estate.

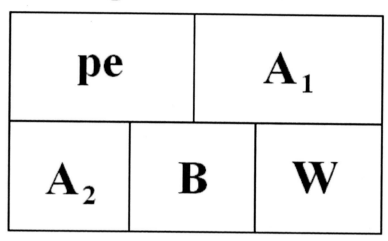

As you will see, the surviving spouse is allowed to take her elective share first from the two boxes on the top row, and only when they are empty can she dip into the lower row. So it is important to know which assets are considered to go into which boxes.

Because everything contained in all five boxes is what is meant by the augmented estate, then the first formula simply states that the augmented estate, (designated as AE in the formulas), equals the sum of what is in all of the boxes.

So the FIRST FORMULA is simply:

$$AE = pe + A_1 + A_2 + B + W$$

(That is consistent with the definition in Section 2-203, as you will see later.)

Now it is important to find out just what is meant by each of the terms, "pe," "A_1," "A_2," "B," and "W." As we discuss each of these terms you should refer back to the statute, in part F, to see how the statute defines the contents of each box.

The symbol "pe," (See Section 2-204), is used to describe the assets in the net PROBATE ESTATE of the deceased spouse—the property that the deceased spouse <u>could</u> have devised by his or her will.

The symbol "A_1," (See Section 2-205(1)), is used to describe property given AWAY by the decedent to someone other than the surviving spouse by means of joint tenancy, exercise of a power of appointment, etc.

AND

Property given AWAY by the decedent at any time during the marriage, with other types of "strings attached,"[6] (See Section 2-205(2));

The symbol "A_2," (See Section 2-205(3)), is used to refer to property which had been given away "with strings attached," but for which the "strings" were CUT within TWO years before decedent's death, (See Sections 2-205(3)(A) and (B));

AND

Outright gifts made within TWO years of date of death, to the extent the gifts exceeded $12,000 to any one donee in either of the two years immediately preceding decedent's death (see Section 2-205(3)(C)).[7]

In other words, the property in the A_2 box is basically property for which the "attaching strings" had been cut within two years of death; plus outright gifts over $12,000 made to any one done in either of the TWO years before death.

Combined, the A_1 and A_2 property will thus pick up most of the property that previously had been kept out of the probate estate by use of the various loopholes.

The next two boxes in the augmented estate are relatively new concepts—designed to "equalize" things between the spouses—by giving the decedent "credit" for property he, (or she), has already given to the surviving spouse—and by bringing in the property belonging to the SURVIVING SPOUSE—so that the COMBINED assets of the couple are divided—not just the assets of whichever spouse happens to die first.

The symbol "B" is used to describe property that basically was given by the decedent to the surviving spouse—outside the will. (See Section 2-206.) This would include, for example, the decedent's share of joint tenancy property, which would pass to the surviving spouse at death, but would not have been part of the probate estate.

---

[6] The statutory sections, of course, give the actual definition for the property included. By "strings attached" I just mean that the donor has retained some sort of right to the property—for example the right to income, or the right to possession.

[7] States which enact the 2008 version of the UPC, instead of providing a specific number, such as $12,000, may instead say "the amount excludable from taxable gifts under 26 U.S.C. Sec 2503(b) on the date next preceding the date of the decedent's death." UPC 2-205(3). This will allow the exclusion under the augmented estate to stay consistent with the federal gift tax exclusion.

The symbol "W" is used to describe the property that already belonged to the WIDOW or WIDOWER—i.e. the property already belonging to the surviving spouse (plus anything that passed to the surviving spouse because of the decedent's death which has not been included elsewhere). (See Section 2-207.)

One of the interesting things about the W property is that under 2-207(a)(2), property that the surviving spouse gave away during the marriage with strings attached, or within two years of decedent's death, for example, is brought back into the augmented estate as W property. Again, this tends to "equalize" things.

For example, if a wife, knowing that her husband had a terminal illness, sweetly gave away most of the property she already owned, (retaining only the income and the use for life, of course), thus intending to make the W part of the augmented estate very small, Section 2-207(a)(2) would bring the wife's gifts back into the augmented estate—just as it would have brought back similar gifts made by the husband.

This part of the definition of W property is designed to prevent the presumptive surviving spouse, at the last minute, from trying to "empty" the W box so that she would be able to take more from the A_1 box, for example. As you will see from the following formulas, the more the surviving spouse already owns of the COMBINED assets of the team, the less she will be able to take from her husband's property. But the goal of the statute is to prevent either spouse from unfairly manipulating the contents of various boxes.

To summarize, then, by using the First Formula, AE $=$ pe $+$ A_1 $+$ A_2 $+$ B $+$ W, we have now been able to figure out what is included in the augmented estate.

Now how should we go about figuring out how much, if any, the surviving spouse can take from the augmented estate as her elective share? And from which box or boxes should she take the additional amount necessary?

Remember that anything the surviving spouse takes by means of election was previously devised—or given—to some other person or institution! So it makes a great deal of difference, to a number of people, which assets the surviving spouse takes away from other donees in order to end up with the proper amount for her elective share.

Section 2-203 of the statute provides a sliding scale for how much of the combined property of the husband and wife is subject to the provisions of the elective share – depending on how long the husband and wife have been married. For example, if the marriage had been in existence for less than one year, only 3% of the total property owned by the husband and wife would be subject to the elective share. If the couple had been married for ten years, but less than eleven years, then 60% of the total property owned by the husband and wife would be subject to the elective share.

Once a couple has been married for fifteen years, then the total amount of property held by both spouses, 100%, will be subject to the elective share. The reason for this sliding scale is a policy decision that the surviving spouse of a fifteen year marriage should be entitled to a larger share than the surviving spouse of a marriage that was in existence for only six months, for example.

Remember, if there has been a divorce prior to the death of one of the parties, then the surviving EX-spouse would have no right to any elective share. The elective share is only for someone who was still married to the decedent at his, (or her), death.

This portion of the augmented estate, (3%, 60%, 100%) is called the "marital property portion of the augmented estate". [See 2-203(b).] Under 2-202(a) the surviving spouse has a right to take one-half of the "marital property portion of the augmented estate."

So, in practice, you would add up everything included in all five boxes of the augmented estate, $(pe + A_1 + A_2 + B + W)$, and then multiply that number by the applicable percentage.

For example, if the marriage had existed for 10 years, but less than 11 years, then if the total in all five boxes added up to 100 (million dollars), then you would multiply 100 times 60%, and come out to the conclusion that the "marital property portion of the augmented estate" is equal to 60 (million dollars).

The surviving spouse, under 2-202(a) would be entitled to one-half (50%) of this amount. So the surviving spouse would be entitled to one-half of 60 (million dollars), or 30 (million dollars).

In order to keep the math easy, I will try to use illustrations with numbers no larger than two digit numbers. In order to make it seem important, you may assume that that the number 2 means 2 million dollars, 30 means 30 million dollars, and so forth.

So, if all the items included in all five boxes, $pe + A_1 + A_2 + B + W$, added up to $100 million, and the marriage had been in existence for ten years, but less than eleven years, then the "marital property portion of the augmented estate" would be $60 million, (100 times 60%), and the surviving spouse would be entitled to half of the $60 million, which would be $30 million.

Now we have to figure out how the surviving spouse should go about getting that $30 million. How much can she take from each of the "boxes" in the augmented estate?

First, Section 2-209 provides that you must take into consideration how much of the $30 million the surviving spouse already has. This includes the property the surviving spouse has already gotten from the deceased spouse – by gifts in the will, by intestate succession, or by other means, such as being named the beneficiary of life insurance on the life of the deceased spouse. It also includes some percentage of the property the surviving spouse owned in her own right – the property in the W box.

To figure this out, it helps to use the SECOND FORMULA,

$$C = D + B + PW$$

In this formula:

C   equals what the surviving spouse is CONSIDERED to have before she takes anything by election[8]

D   equals what the surviving spouse got by DESCENT or DEVISE (This property which would have come out of the probate estate – by descent if the husband died without a will, or by devise if the husband devised something to his wife by his will.)

B   equals the same thing it did before – which was basically property the decedent had given his wife outside the probate estate – such a making his wife the beneficiary of his life insurance, and the like.

PW   stands for the statutory percentage (P) times the property that is in the W box [See 2-209(a) (2).][9]

So, in the example used above, since the "marital property portion of the augmented estate is 60% of the actual amount in the augmented estate, (because the marriage lasted for ten years but

---

[8] U.P.C. Section 2-209

[9] 2-207 is the W box. The statute then goes on to provide, at UPC 2-209(b), that, "The marital property portion under subsection (a) (2), [the amount included in W], is computed by multiplying the value of the amounts included in the augmented estate under Section 2-207 by the percentage of the augmented estate set forth in the schedule in Section 2-203(b) appropriate to the length of time the spouse and the decedent were married to each other."

less than eleven years), then only 60% of the property in the W "box" is included in calculation of what the surviving spouse is CONSIDERED to have before she elects.

That's why you need this SECOND FORMULA. In any marriage that has continued for less than fifteen years, what the surviving spouse is CONSIDERED to have is actually less than what she really has. So be sure to use this formula when calculating the surviving spouse's share of the augmented estate.

Then, by filling in the numbers in the second formula, you can figure out how much the surviving spouse is <u>considered</u> to have already, and then compare that number with the amount of the elective share to which she is entitled.

For example, if the entire augmented estate were worth $100 million, and the couple had been married for ten years, then the marital property portion of the augmented estate would be $100 million times 60%, which is $60 million. Then the surviving spouse would be entitled to half of that amount, or $30 million. If, after applying the second formula we found that the surviving spouse was <u>considered</u> to have $35 million already, (because most of the property had been in the B and W boxes), then she would NOT be entitled to elect – because she would already have more than half of the marital property portion.

The surviving spouse would not be required to give anything back. She just would not be entitled to take back any of the gifts which her husband had attempted to make to others – either by will, or by the various gifts included in the A_1 and A_2 boxes. It should be the goal of any estate plan to make things come out this way – so that the provisions of the will, and the various inter vivos gifts made will be effective, and money will not have to be spent on litigation to determine the elective share of the surviving spouse.

However, in the example above, if after using the second formula we ascertain that the surviving spouse is <u>considered</u> to have "only" $20 million of the $30 million to which she is entitled, then we would have to go ahead and figure out where she should get the additional $10 million to which she is entitled.

Section 2-209(c) and (d) provide remarkably convoluted instructions on how to go about getting the additional $10 million for the surviving spouse. Basically, those sections provide that the surviving spouse is first to take the same fraction of EVERY item in boxes pe and A_1 – to give her the additional $10 million she needs. Only if she cannot get the $10 million from the two top boxes will she be authorized to go after property that is in the A_2 "box."

In essence, Section 2-209(c) can be boiled down to the third formula, which is:

THIRD FORMULA:

$$T_1 = x \, (pe - D + A_1) = g$$

(to be explained later), and

Section 2-209(d) can be boiled down to the fourth formula, which is:

FOURTH FORMULA:

$$T_2 = y \, (A_2) = PAE - (C + T_1)$$

Now to try to explain the purpose for these last two formulas in plain English. The Third Formula, which starts with T_1, indicates how much the surviving spouse can TAKE, on her first take, TAKE ONE, from the top row of boxes.[10]

The Fourth Formula, which starts with T_2, indicates how much the surviving spouse can take on her second take, TAKE TWO, from the A_2 box on the bottom row, IF she was not able to get enough by means of her take one.[11]

As you will see, eventually, using the same example discussed above, if the surviving spouse were able to get the additional $10 million to which she is entitled just by taking property from the top row of boxes, she would stop there, and only the TAKE ONE formula would be necessary.

But if, for example, the surviving spouse could get "only" $8 million from the top row of boxes, then she would still need $2 million more—and would be entitled to use the TAKE TWO formula, to take the additional property from the A_2 box.

Notice that the surviving spouse will never "take" anything from the B box or from the W box because that is all property that the surviving spouse already owns.

Now comes the fun part. Because Sections 2-209(c) and (d) both say that the amount taken by the surviving spouse out of the various boxes must be "apportioned" so that the liability of all donees is "in proportion to the value of their interests therein," the statute means that the same fraction must be taken away from each gift in any particular box. In other words, if the surviving

---

[10] See Section 2-209(c)

[11] See Section 2-209(d)

spouse is entitled to take $2 million from the A_2 box, she cannot just go after the easiest $2 million to find. She must take an <u>equal fraction</u> from <u>every</u> asset in the A_2 box, until she ends up with a total of $2 million.

Therefore, we need the Third and Fourth Formulas to help us figure out what FRACTION the surviving spouse is entitled to take from EVERY asset in the relevant box or boxes.

Since that FRACTION is unknown, we use "x" to represent the unknown fraction in the Third Formula; and "y" to represent the unknown fraction in the Fourth Formula. Then we simply solve for "x" or "y."

In applying the Third Formula, to ascertain what fractions the surviving spouse can take, as TAKE ONE, from all of the assets in boxes "pe" and "A_1"; do the following:

FIRST, figure out the amount of the augmented estate to which the surviving spouse is entitled— for example, $30 million from an augmented estate of $100 million, if the marriage had lasted for 10 years.[12]

SECOND, figure out how much of that $30 million the surviving spouse is already considered to have, (by using the Second Formula, $C = D + B + PW$).

THIRD, subtract what the surviving spouse already is Considered to have from the elective share to which the surviving spouse is entitled—$20 million subtracted from $30 million, in our example. Then you will know that the surviving spouse already is considered to have $20 million of the $30 million to which she is entitled. So she needs $10 million more.

Then, apply the Third Formula, to see what FRACTION the surviving spouse is entitled to take, as TAKE ONE, from every asset remaining in the pe and A_1 boxes, in order to get the additional $10 million which will bring her up to a total of $30 million.

Remember that the surviving spouse will never take property away from herself—and the surviving spouse may already have gotten something from the probate estate by Descent or Devise, (the "D" property).

---

[12] The surviving spouse is entitled to one-half of the marital-property portion of the augmented estate. In this case, based on the percentages given at the beginning of the augmented estate statute (Sec. 2-203(b)), the marital-property portion is 60 percent of the total value of the augmented estate, because the couple had been married for 10 years. So in our example, the marital property portion is $60 million and the surviving spouse is entitled to one-half of that, which is $30 million.

So the T_1 formula starts out by saying that the surviving spouse is entitled to take some fraction, ("x"), of all of the property <u>left</u> in the "pe" box, (pe minus the D property which she got by descent or devise), plus that same fractional amount of <u>all</u> of the assets in the A_1 box.

When she has taken the proper fractional share of what is left in "pe" plus the same fractional share of everything in "A_1," then the surviving spouse should end up with the amount which it is necessary for her to GET, (represented by "g" in the formula), in order to have her proper share of the augmented estate.

We will put some numbers in the formulas in the next section, so that you can see how things actually work. For now, just try to understand the basic concept, that the Third and Fourth Formulas allow you to solve for "x" and "y," respectively, so that you know what fraction to take from each item remaining in the various boxes.

Notice that if, on TAKE ONE, the <u>fraction</u> comes out to be the number "<u>one</u>" then that means that you can take 100 percent—in other words EVERYTHING that is left in both the "pe" and the "A_1" boxes.

If the fraction for the Third Formula comes out to be GREATER than the number one, that means you will need to take everything which remains in the top two boxes, and then go on to TAKE TWO, using the Fourth Formula, to take the necessary additional assets from box A_2.

Now, for some actual numbers, in Section E of this chapter.

E.   SAMPLE PROBLEMS FOR CALCULATING THE AUGMENTED ESTATE—WITH ANSWERS!

To see how the formulas described in Section B actually work—and thus to solidify your understanding of the basics of the augmented estate—try working your way through the following problems.

To keep things easy, so that you can do all of the necessary math in your head, I have used primarily one or two digit numbers.

To make this seem important, you may want to pretend that the numbers actually represent millions of dollars. In other words, when I use the number 5, you can pretend that it actually means 5 million dollars. In any case, it is understanding the <u>relationship</u> between the numbers which is important.

In real life you would have a calculator, or a paralegal, or a recent graduate of some law school, to do all of the necessary math. So here goes.

PROBLEM ONE:

Assume that:

Net probate estate	= 50 (million dollars),	so pe = 50
Everything in box A_1	= 20 (million dollars),	so A_1 = 20
Everything in box A_2	= 15 (million dollars),	so A_2 = 15
Everything in box B	= 5 (million dollars),	so B = 5
Everything in box W	= 10 (million dollars),	so W = <u>10</u>
		TOTAL = 100

So the total Augmented Estate equals 100 (million dollars).

FIRST FORMULA: (To figure out how much is in the augmented estate)

$$AE = pe + A_1 + A_2 + B + W$$

$AE = 50 + 20 + 15 + 5 + 10 = \underline{100}$ (or $100 million)
Now, how much of the $100 million is the surviving spouse entitled to take as her elective share?

If the couple had been married for 10 years, then the marital property portion of the augmented estate would be $60 million,[13] and the surviving spouse would be entitled to one-half of that, which is $30 million[14] (or 30, in our example).

Now, assume that the decedent gave his (or her) spouse $10 million by will.
So the "D" property is $10 million, and

$$D = 10$$

SECOND FORMULA: (To figure out what the surviving spouse is CONSIDERED to have already)

$$C = D + B + PW$$

_____

[13] Section 2-203
[14] Section 2-202(c)

[Remember PW is the percentage from 2-203, times the amount of property in the W box.]

Filling in the numbers from above,

$$C = D + B + PW$$
$$C = 10 + 5 + [(6 / 10) \text{ x } 10]$$
$$= 10 + 5 + 6 = \underline{21}$$

Since the surviving spouse is entitled to $30 million, and is CONSIDERED to have "only" $21 million, she has a right to elect, to take her statutory share of the augmented estate. Subtracting $21 million (what she is already CONSIDERED to have) from $30 million, (the amount to which she is entitled), we find that the surviving spouse is entitled to an additional $9 million.

We now need to find out what fraction she should take—from all assets remaining in the "pe" box, and from everything in the A_1 box—in order to obtain the additional $9 million to which she is entitled. So we use the Third Formula.

Using the same numbers we have used above, we simply put them into the Third Formula—and solve for "x"—to find out what <u>fraction</u> of the items remaining in pe and A_1, should be taken by the surviving spouse to end up with an additional $9 million.

THIRD FORMULA—TAKE ONE

$$T_1 \quad = \quad x(pe - D + A_1) \quad = 9$$

$$T_1 \quad = \quad x(50 - 10 + 20) \quad = 9$$

$$x(40 + 20) \quad = 9$$

$$60x \quad = 9$$

$$x \quad = 9 / 60$$

$$\boxed{x \quad = 3 / 20}$$

Since x ends up equal to 3/20, we know that the surviving spouse should take 3/20 of everything left in "pe," plus 3/20 of everything in A_1, in order to end up with the additional 9.

Let's see if that works.

$$3/20 \quad \times \quad 40^* \quad = \quad 120/20 \quad = \quad \underline{6} \quad (^*\text{What's left in pe})$$

$$3/20 \quad \times \quad 20^{**} \quad = \quad 60/20 \quad = \quad \underline{3} \quad (^{**}\text{Everything in } A_1)$$

$$6 \quad + \quad 3 \quad = \quad \underline{9}$$
$$(\text{from pe}) \quad (\text{from } A_1)$$

Good! We have now illustrated that if the surviving spouse takes 3/20 of everything left in "pe," plus 3/20 of everything in A_1, she will end up with her proper statutory share of $9 million.[15]

It was not necessary in this problem to go to TAKE TWO, because there were sufficient assets in the "top" row of boxes to make up the appropriate share for the surviving spouse.

But what if the numbers had been different? Problem Two illustrates what happens when it is necessary to use both TAKE ONE and TAKE TWO.

PROBLEM TWO: [Using an entirely different set of numbers]

Assume that:

pe = 4; A_1 = 6; A_2 = 75;
B = 5;   W = 10;   D = 1

FIRST FORMULA:

$$AE = pe + A_1 + A_2 + B + W$$

$$AE = 4 + 6 + 75 + 5 + 10 = \underline{100}$$

If the parties had been married for ten years, the marital property portion would be 60 percent, and the surviving spouse would be entitled to one-half of that, which would be $30 million.

---

[15] When the assets that the surviving spouse TOOK by election are added to the assets the surviving spouse actually had <u>prior</u> to election, she may well end up with <u>more</u> than the percentage specified in the statute. This is because NOT EVERYTHING the spouse actually owned, in the W box, was CONSIDERED to be included in "PW."

SECOND FORMULA:

$$C = D + B + PW$$

$$C = 1 + 5 + [(6/10) \times 10] = 1 + 5 + 6 = \underline{12}$$

So the surviving spouse is CONSIDERED to have $12 million, and needs $18 million more to make up her statutory share of $30 million.

So we first use the formula for TAKE ONE.

THIRD FORMULA:

$$T_1 \quad = \quad x(pe - D + A_1) \quad = 18$$

$$T_1 \quad = \quad x(4 - 1 + 6) \quad = 18$$

$$x(3 + 6) \quad = 18$$

$$9x \quad = 18$$

$$x \quad = 18/9$$

$$\boxed{x \quad = \quad 2}$$

Since "x," the fraction, comes out as 2, and is thus a number <u>greater than one,</u> you know that you really can't get sufficient assets out of the top two boxes to be able to make up the statutory share for the surviving spouse. So you take <u>everything</u> remaining in the top two boxes, (a total of $3 million from the "pe" box and a total of $6 million from the A_1 box), and end up with a total of $9 million from TAKE ONE.

The surviving spouse is still short by $9 million, so you must go to TAKE TWO, and take the remaining amount necessary from box A_2. Since the statute says that you must take an equal fraction from every asset in box A_2, you need to figure out what fraction of each asset in A_2 must be taken back to make up the statutory share for the surviving spouse. So you use the Fourth Formula.

FOURTH FORMULA—TAKE TWO:

$$T_2 \quad = \quad y(A_2) \quad = 9$$

$$T_2 \quad = \quad x(75) \quad = 9$$

$$75y \quad = 9$$

$$y \quad = 9/75$$

or

$$\boxed{y \quad = \quad 3/25}$$

Taking $3/25$ of 75 we get $3/25 \ \times \ 75 \ = \ 3 \ \times \ 3 \ = \ \underline{9}$

Good! The surviving spouse was entitled to $30 million. She was CONSIDERED to have $12 million, so she needed $18 million more. She was able to get an additional $9 million by TAKE ONE, and then the final $9 million needed by using TAKE TWO. So she ends up with the proper statutory share of $30 million.

But notice what havoc this might have wrecked with the decedent's estate plan! Not only has the surviving spouse taken <u>everything</u> that remained in the net probate estate—she has also TAKEN BACK various INTER VIVOS gifts made throughout the marriage!

Among the property thus TAKEN BACK by the surviving spouse may be the decedent's share of JOINT TENANCY property—which he held at his death as a joint tenant with his brother, Bob, for example!

It may come as quite a surprise to brother Bob that as surviving joint tenant he does NOT in fact now own all of the property held as a joint tenant!

As you see now, hopefully, this complex, convoluted augmented estate statute OVERRIDES both the law of inter vivos gifts and the law of joint tenancy in the jurisdictions where it is applicable! Clearly, it is ESSENTIAL that you understand the basics of the Augmented Estate!

Even if you do not practice in a jurisdiction that has adopted this version of the Augmented Estate, you may have clients whose rights as surviving joint tenants are <u>defeated</u> because of application of the Augmented Estate statute of some <u>other</u> jurisdiction! Remember, the U.P.C. 2-203(a) provides that these U.P.C. sections apply to <u>all</u> land in which the decedent has (or had) an interest, no matter where the land is located. So the U.P.C. says that it applies to land—even land situated in a state which has <u>not</u> adopted the U.P.C.!

By far the best solution, of course, is simply to provide the surviving spouse with enough property so that she (or he) will not be entitled to elect under the provisions for the augmented estate.

CHAPTER 10.   **INSURING THAT TESTATOR GETS HIS OR HER WAY**

INTRODUCTION

Even though you have done an excellent job of drafting a will or trust for your client, designed to distribute the property in just the way the client wishes, not everyone may be happy with the result. A surviving spouse may feel that he or she should have been given more property, or more control over the property given. Children may feel angry that they did not receive larger portions of the estate. And charities or institutions may be concerned that they did not receive as large a share as expected or were cut out entirely by the latest version of the will.

In nearly all states, a surviving spouse has some sort of right of election—to take the amount of property specified by the statute, no mater what any particular will or trust may say. The Augmented Estate discussed in Chapter 9, illustrates one such statute.

However, with very few exceptions, (as discussed in Chapter 1, footnote 7); no one <u>other</u> than the surviving spouse has any right to take against a will. So the line of attack for people and institutions <u>other</u> than the surviving spouse is to attack the validity of the will itself.

The easiest way to have a will declared invalid is to demonstrate that the testator lacked testamentary capacity when the will was signed, (as discussed in Chapter 2).

To try to discourage attack on the validity of the will by disappointed friends, relatives or institutions, several techniques are available. One such technique is to include a "no contest" clause in the will. Samples of such clauses follow.

A.   NO CONTEST CLAUSES.

SAMPLE ONE—WILL OF JOHN LENNON:

In paragraph EIGHTH of his four page will John Lennon included the following no-contest clause:

> If any legatee or beneficiary under this will or the trust agreement between myself as Grantor and YOKO ONO LENNON and ELI GARBER as Trustees, dated November 12, 1979 shall interpose objections to the probate of this Will, or institute or prosecute or be in any way interested or instrumental in the institution

or prosecution of any actions or proceeding for the purpose of setting aside or invalidating this Will, then and in each such case, I direct that such legatee or beneficiary shall receive nothing whatsoever under this Will or the aforementioned Trust.

That would seem to cover the bases. But the no-contest clause in Henry Fonda's will is even stronger.

SAMPLE TWO—WILL OF HENRY FONDA:

In Article NINTH of his two page will, Henry Fonda states:

> Except as otherwise provided herein, I have intentionally and with full knowledge omitted to provide for my heirs, including any persons who may claim to be my issue. If any beneficiary under this Will, or any legal heir of mine, or any person claiming under any of them, shall contest this Will or attack or seek to impair or invalidate this Will or any part or provision hereof, or conspire with or voluntarily assist anyone attempting to do any of those things, in that event I specifically disinherit each such person and all legacies, bequests, devises and interests given under this Will to that person shall lapse and be forfeited, and shall be disposed of as if such person (together with anyone claiming through such person under any anti-lapse law) had predeceased me without issue.

Now that really makes the intent of Fonda, (or his lawyer), clear! Yet both the Lennon and the Fonda no-contest clauses might have been strengthened.

Both Lennon and Fonda were right, that no one has an obligation to leave anything to anyone—except the surviving spouse. It is just as effective to leave someone "nothing" as to leave someone "one dollar." So both Lennon and Fonda were right on that point.

And both Lennon and Fonda were right on the first step of writing a no-contest clause—making their intentions clear.

However, there is a second step available which both Lennon and Fonda omitted. The second step, if your client is really serious about a no-contest clause, is to give the property to someone else. In other words, for the second step, you should say that whatever would otherwise have gone to the person who contests the will, (or his or her relatives), shall instead go to some other named person or institution, as the alternate beneficiary.

You could make as the alternate beneficiary a "mortal enemy" of the person or institution that might be expected to contest the will—or you could just name a charity as the alternate beneficiary. In any case, by saying that the property that would otherwise have gone to the person who contests the will, shall instead go to an alternate beneficiary, you have given the alternate beneficiary good motivation for watching for any possible contest.[1] The alternate beneficiary, in effect, steps into the role of "enforcer" of the no-contest clause.

Of course one big advantage of having a charity named as the "enforcer" is that charities generally do not "die," and if one charity does go out of existence, courts have full power to apply the doctrine of cy pres to substitute another charity for the original charity.

So, to write a really good no-contest clause, use both steps that are available. First, specify the actions which will cause the gift to be taken away from the primary beneficiary. Then give the gift to the alternate beneficiary, who will thereby be motivated to act as an "enforcer" for the no-contest clause.

And of course be especially careful about execution of the will—as discussed in Chapter 2.

You should also warn your client that there is wide variation among jurisdictions as to how willing a court may be to uphold the provisions of a no-contest clause. Some courts hold that if there was <u>probable cause</u> for the will contest, then the no-contest clause will not be enforced—even if the will contest fails.

But of course, if the will contest <u>succeeds</u>, then the no-contest clause fails along with all of the rest of the will!

B.   FORCED ELECTION—ESPECIALLY IN A COMMUNMITY PROPERTY STATE

A second way of trying to insure that the testator will get his or her way is to try to "bribe" other people. In essence, by using this technique a client in his or her will may say to a spouse, for example, "I will give you this thing, which you really want, if you do, or refrain from doing, the following." By use of this technique, the spouse, (or other beneficiary), may be forced to elect between doing what the spouse would like to do, and receiving the property offered under the will.

---

[1] Sometimes, disappointed friends, relatives, or institutions may "team up" or decide who should contest the will. For example, a beneficiary who is not getting a very large gift under the will, might be persuaded to risk that gift, and bring the will contest if OTHER unhappy persons agreed to reimburse the person who brought the will contest. That way; only a small gift need be risked—while every member of the "team" might stand to benefit from the will contest.

This basic technique can be used in any jurisdiction, of course, but it is used quite frequently in community property states. As you may recall, in community property states the basic pattern of property ownership during a marriage is that the husband and wife each own one-half of all assets that came into the marriage during the marriage, no matter which spouse actually brought home which paycheck.

Thus, in a community property state, the husband, for example, might "own" very little property that he could give away outright by his will. To persuade his surviving spouse to let him give away both her share and his share of certain assets, (and for possible tax reasons which will not be discussed here), the husband might word his will in such a way as to "force" his wife to elect either (1) to let her husband give away her share of community property, or (2) to give up certain gifts offered by the husband's will.

Examples of forced elections in a community property state may help you to understand this concept.

SAMPLE THREE—WILL OF ALFRED HITCHCOCK

In section 1 of article II of his will, Alfred Hitchcock, of Los Angeles, California[2] stated:

> It is my intention hereby to dispose of all property of every kind and nature over which I have any power of testamentary disposition or appointment, including not only my share, but also, in the event that my wife, ALMA REVILLE HITCHCOCK, elects to take under this Will, my said wife's share of our community property.

SAMPLE FOUR—WILL OF HUMPHREY BOGART

Basically, Humphrey Bogart, (for some reason also a resident of Los Angeles), did essentially the same thing—with a few more details. The FIRST article of Humphrey Bogart's will provides:

> To the best of my knowledge all property (with the exception of our home) in which I have any interest or which stands in my name is community property of my wife and myself accumulated since the date of marriage. Our home although acquired with community funds is held by my wife and me as joint tenants and

---

[2] As you recall, the community property states are: Arizona, California, Idaho, Louisiana, Nevada, New Mexico, Texas, Washington, and Wisconsin.

therefore is not subject to disposition by this Will. It is my intention by this Will to dispose of all property over which I have any power of disposition or appointment, <u>including specifically my wife's interest in community property as well as my own.</u> <u>If my wife shall elect to take against this Will then I direct that the</u> <u>provisions of Clause SIXTH hereof[3] shall be of no force or effect</u> but that all other provisions of this Will shall be given full effect. I recommend to my wife that she elect to take under the provisions of this Will as it is my firm conviction that such will be to her best interests. [Emphasis added.]

In both of these samples, the two men involved provided trusts for their wives, funded with both the husband's and the wife's shares of the community property. By using the technique of forced election the husband's wills were able to put entire items of property, (not just the husband's one-half interest), into trusts—thus providing for unified management of the assets. That may well have been advantageous to everyone involved. But in effect, both Hitchcock and Bogart were giving away property they didn't own—by offering their wives something valuable in return.

As indicated above, although this technique of using a will to give away more than the testator owns is most frequently used in community property states, the same basic technique is also available in other states—not for tax purposes, but as a means of "bribing" a person to accept specific provisions of a will.

C.   DEPENDENT RELATIVE REVOCATION AND REVIVAL

One additional aspect of insuring that the testator gets his or her way on distribution of assets has to do with the doctrine of Dependent Relative Revocation and Revival. That doctrine was developed in order to take care of situations in which a court might find that a testator's revocation of a 2000 will, for example, was "dependent" on the testator's 2009 will being held to be effective. Under this doctrine, the 2000 will may be "revived" by the court—after the death of the testator—IF the court finds that the testator would have so intended.

Even though there is much writing on the subject, and occasional litigation, very few people actually draft wills that recognize the problem of Dependent Relative Revocation. One exception is found in the will of the Vermont philanthropist, John J. Flynn.

---

[3] This clause established a trust for Bogart's wife.

SAMPLE FIVE—WILL OF JOHN FLYNN:

The first paragraph of the will which Flynn signed on September 1, 1937, stated:

> BE IT KNOWN, That I, JOHN J. FLYNN, a resident of the city of Burlington, County of Chittenden, and State of Vermont being of sound and disposing mind and memory do hereby revoke any and all wills by me at any time heretofore made. But this revocation with respect to my will of August 16, 1932 with codicil of August 30, 1935 is conditioned upon the allowance of this instrument as my last will and testament. [Emphasis added.]

This makes it <u>clear</u> that the older will and codicil are <u>not</u> intended to be revoked <u>unless</u> the new will is held to be valid.

Sometimes, a clause like the one in Flynn's will would have been included because of the doctrine of "mortmain." Formerly, under the doctrine of mortmain, a testamentary gift to a charity might not have been upheld if the will had been signed within 90 days before the testator's death. The doctrine of mortmain was evidently one way of trying to avoid the possibility of the exercise of undue influence by a church or charity during a person's last illness.

Today, even though it is very unlikely that the doctrine of mortmain would be applied, it may still be a good idea to include a clause stating that an older will is not to be revoked UNLESS the new will is held to be effective.

Such a clause may be particularly important when a testator wants to be sure to preserve prior gifts to charities, or friends, or relatives, and is writing a new will that may be contested on the basis of undue influence or lack of testamentary capacity.

Including one short sentence, like that included by John Flynn, may be of great help in preserving gifts made by prior wills—in the event of a will contest.

Now, having studied a few special techniques available for helping to insure that the testator gets his or her own way, you may want to try your hand at the drafting exercise which follows.

D. DRAFTING EXERCISE 12—DRAFTING THE STRONGEST POSSIBLE NO-CONTEST CLAUSE

Your client has decided to make some testamentary gifts that are virtually certain to cause consternation among your client's friends and relatives. You are convinced, however, that your client has full testamentary capacity, and every right to make the intended gifts.

Since a will contest by various disappointed friends and relatives is highly likely, draft the strongest no-contest clause you are able to design.

You may make up any particular details you like for this situation—or just draft a basic no-contest clause.

As you begin your drafting, you may want to look at the Pointers for Drafting, which follow.

E. POINTERS FOR DRAFTING

As discussed in part A of this chapter, there are two basic steps for a no-contest clause. First, spell out the prohibited actions, which will cause gifts to be taken away from various persons or institutions. Second, give the forfeited property to some other person or institution.

While implementing these two steps, you may want to keep the following considerations in mind.

√1. What action by a friend, relative or institution will cause gifts to be forfeited? Filing suit? Threatening to file suit? Persuading some other person or institution to file suit?[4]

√2. How much of a forfeiture will be imposed; the whole gift? Or, the amount by which the gift would have exceeded the statutory share if the testator had died intestate?

√3. Will a contest by one family member cause gifts to other family members to fail? What happens if a daughter, for example, contests the will? Is she then treated as "having predeceased the testator?" Will that mean that the anti-lapse statute will apply, and the daughter's share will simply be given to her children instead? How can you draft around that problem?

---

[4] See footnote 1; regarding the possibility of "deals" being made between various unhappy people as to which one should bring the will contest—for the benefit of several of the unhappy people.

✓ 4.   What if ALL of the children contest the will, for example, thus causing ALL of their shares to be forfeited? Will the property then just go by intestacy—to the children in equal shares?

✓ 5.   Have you provided for an alternate gift—taking away the gift intended for someone who contests the will, and giving it instead to some other person or institution? Will the alternate beneficiary be likely to be a good "enforcer" of the no-contest clause?

✓ 6.   What if the intended "enforcer" simply strikes a deal with the various unhappy friends, relatives, and institutions, to avoid litigation, and all of them simply agree that the assets should be distributed in the way preferred by the parties to the agreement? Would the executor or personal representative of the will be allowed, or required, to go along with such an agreement?[5]

✓ 7.   Is there anything you could do to prevent the parties from redistributing the assets AFTER distribution by the estate? (Answer, "yes"—in theory—with a complex set of fees simple determinable and executory interests. Answer, "no"—for practical purposes).

✓ 8.   What happens if the "enforcer" dies before the testator? Have you provided for some sort of "back-up" for the alternate beneficiary—for an alternate "enforcer?"

✓ 9.   If you have used some charitable institution as the "enforcer," have you specifically directed that the doctrine of cy pres should be applied if the specified institution is no longer in existence? Have you considered having alternate "enforcers," to try to play them off against each other—such as the Sierra Club vs. a major Logging Rights organization?

✓ 10.   Is there any way you could combine use of a no-contest clause with the use of the Doctrine of Dependent Relative Revocation and Revival—so that unhappy children, for example, would have to persuade the court to strike down two or three wills before arriving at intestacy for their parent?

✓ 11.   Is there anything else you might do to try to strengthen the no-contest clause?

---

[5] See for example, C.R.S. 15-12-1101. "A compromise of any controversy as to …the construction, validity, or effect of any probated will, the rights or interests in the estate of the decedent, of any successor, or the administration of the estate, if approved in a formal proceeding in the court for that purpose, is binding on all the parties thereto including those unborn, unascertained, or who could not be located. An approved compromise is binding even though it may affect a trust or an inalienable interest."

CHAPTER 11.   PROTECTING THE WILL – AND THE CLIENT – DURABLE POWERS AND LIVING WILLS

INTRODUCTION

When a client comes in to discuss the drafting of a will, the attorney should also mention three other, related documents that are available.   These documents are: the Durable Power of Attorney for Financial Matters; the Durable Power of Attorney for Medical Matters; and the "Living Will," (also called a Medical Treatment Declaration).

Most estate planning lawyers today routinely offer their clients these documents.   And most clients are happy to have them.

As indicated in Chapter 3,[1] wills should be drafted with recognition of the possible existence and consequences of these additional three documents.   Without careful, coordinated drafting of these documents—unnecessary problems of ademption, abatement, and "survivorship" may arise.

Therefore, it is important for anyone drafting wills and trusts to have a basic familiarity with the following three documents. Some background may be helpful.

A.   DURABLE POWERS OF ATTORNEY

1.   WHAT ARE DURABLE POWERS?

Durable Powers of Attorney are used to allow your client, (called the principal), to delegate decision making authority to another person, (called the agent, or the attorney-in-fact), when the principal is no longer able to make his or her own decisions.

Durable Powers of Attorney are called "durable" because they are designed to be effective during the incapacity of the principal.   In fact, durable powers of attorney may be designed to "spring" into effect only when the principal becomes incapacitated.

---

[1] See especially section A of Chapter 3.

2.   WHY USE SEPARATE DURABLE POWERS FOR FINANCIAL AND
        MEDICAL MATTERS?

Although financial and medical powers could be combined in the same document, it is nearly
always better to use two documents. First, many clients entrust medical decisions to one person,
and financial decisions to another person. Frequently, this makes very good sense. The qualities
of concern and compassion which are valuable for medical matters may be quite different from
the qualities required for financial matters.

In addition, the financial power will be used at the bank, the stockbroker's and the real estate
office. The medical power will be used at the hospital or nursing home. There is no reason for
the bank to be concerned with medical matters, or for the hospital to be concerned with financial
matters.

Your client may well want to include specific instructions in the financial power as to properties
that are not to be sold, or financial advisors who are to be consulted if available. Similarly, in the
medical power, your client may want to include specific instructions on types of treatment and
care that would be deemed appropriate, and circumstances under which medical treatment should
be terminated and death allowed to come. Using separate documents will facilitate drafting the
specific instructions appropriate for your client.

3.   COORDINATION OF DURABLE POWERS WITH THE WILL

Among other things, it may be highly advisable to include a specific provision in a financial
power that the agent has the authority – and the obligation – to look at a copy of your client's
will, and then to AVOID selling any property that has been specifically devised in the will – if
possible.

Under Section 5-426 of the Uniform Probate Code a <u>Conservator</u>[2] already has the power to
examine the will while the principal is still alive, and the <u>duty</u> to try to act in a way that will
preserve the provisions of the will. Some state statutes also give the <u>agent</u> under a durable power
of attorney the right to examine the will of the principal while the principal is still alive.[3]
Especially because of the variation in state statutes, power to examine the principal's will should

---

[2] A Conservator is someone appointed by a court to handle financial matters for a person who can no longer handle his or her own financial matters.
[3] See Colorado, C.R.S. 15-14-608 Preservation of Estate Plan and Trusts, "The agent shall have access to and the right to copy, but not to hold, the principal's will, trusts, and other personal papers and records to the extent the agent deems necessary for purposes of exercising the agency powers."

be <u>specifically</u> included in a durable power of attorney for financial matters – unless your client directs otherwise.

If your client is not comfortable with letting the agent see the will prior to the client's death, that should also be specified in the durable power. In such a case, it would be especially important for the durable power to be carefully drafted to be consistent with the will. For example, the agent should be directed <u>not to sell</u> specific items – e.g., the items that have been specifically devised in the will.

Clearly, it is important to take time to coordinate durable powers with any will or trust you have previously drafted for your client.

Section 2-606(b) of the Uniform Probate Code provides that, "If specifically devised property is sold ... by a conservator or by an agent acting within the authority of a durable power of attorney ... the specific devisee has the right to a general pecuniary devise equal to the net sale price...." However, Payment of cash might be small consolation, indeed, to the devisee of great-grandmother's patchwork quilt – which had been sold at a garage sale by an agent who simply did not appreciate the significance of the quilt.

4.   PRESENT OR "SPRINGING" POWERS?

Durable powers of attorney may be drafted as either present powers or "springing" powers. A present power goes into effect when signed. A "springing" power only becomes effective when the principal becomes incapacitated. "Springing" powers generally seem to be more attractive to clients. They are also considerably more difficult to draft.

For example, if the power of attorney is to become effective only when the principal becomes incapacitated, who should make that decision on incapacity? It is not at all unusual for elderly parents and their children to have quite different ideas about the mental capacity of the elderly parents. All of us do "spacey" things every so often. Such conduct by the elderly, however, generally triggers more concern in their friends and relatives than would the same conduct by a younger person.

5.   SPRINGING POWERS – WHO DECIDES?

So who should decide when a Durable Power of Attorney goes into effect? It may be feasible to have an outsider, such as a doctor, make that decision. And there is no reason for an elderly person not to state his or her preference as to <u>which</u> doctor is to make the decision, AS LONG

AS APPROPRIATE BACK-UP IS PROVIDED. It is your responsibility as a lawyer to remind your client that his or her favorite doctor may have moved to another part of the country, may have died, or may otherwise be unavailable when it is time for the power to go into effect. It would be a serious mistake to have implementation of a durable power dependent on the certification of any one named person. So you should be sure to list one or more persons as "back-ups."

But that does not solve the most difficult problem. The most difficult problem in drafting a springing power is to decide how to make it clear, on the face of the power itself, that the person who signed the certification that the power should go into effect really was then entitled to be acting as "back-up" in that fashion. It might be, for example, that your client's favorite doctor really was available, but simply did not agree with the client's children that the springing power should go into effect.

So the favorite doctor would refuse to sign. Then the children might have better luck with one of the "back-up" doctors named. Yet legally, the power should not be in effect, because the favorite doctor was available, and simply refused to sign. But how is the banker, or stockbroker to know all of that? If a banker or stockbroker is expected to rely on a springing power, it should be clear on the face of the power that it has been validly put into effect.

A convenient wording to use in durable powers, borrowed from wills, is to say that if the specified first person named, "fails to qualify or ceases to act," then the named successor is to take over. But how do you prove to the banker or stockbroker that the first person named has failed to qualify or ceased to act?

If, in drafting the list of successors involved with a durable power, you specify that the unavailability of the first named person must be proved by attaching a death certificate for that person, you have some pretty clear proof, on which a banker or stockbroker could rely.

Proving <u>incapacity</u> of the first named person might be a great deal more difficult. But perhaps it would be sufficient to require that a doctor's certification be attached, stating that the first person named has become incompetent. Keep in mind that as a practical matter doctors may be extremely reluctant to sign any such certification.

As we discuss these problems of putting a durable power of attorney into effect, it is easy to realize why bankers and stockbrokers are sometimes very reluctant to recognize durable powers of attorney for financial matters under any circumstances – regardless of what state statutes may say as to the legality of such powers.

The same problems of implementation and recognition of springing powers will be present with medical durable powers as well. Yet the dangers of fraudulent attempts to put a medical power into effect may not be quite as great as they might have been with a financial power. In most cases, only real family and friends will be "hanging around" a person who is seriously ill, and without mental capacity to make decisions. And in any case, doctors are likely to give agents exercising medical durable powers fairly limited choices. So the danger of having an imposter make inappropriate medical decisions is probably considerably less than the danger of having an imposter try to drain a bank account.

In any case, when drafting either a financial power or a medical power, it is important to consider the interests not only of the principal but also of the banker, stockbroker, or medical provider who may be asked to rely on the power.

The easiest solution for implementation of a durable power is illustrated by the first sample in this chapter – just letting any two doctors sign the certification. But there may be practical difficulties with this. One difficulty might be in finding two doctors who are willing to take the time to sign a document that is not directly related to medical treatment.

Another difficulty, with medical powers, may arise if the doctors would simply prefer not to have their decisions questioned by a "meddling, emotionally distraught" friend or relative designated as the agent under the durable power. As long as the durable power is not implemented, the doctors may be free to make their own medical decisions – without having to try to explain everything to a friend or relative.

A solution some clients use is to state that the signatures of any three of five named people, (children, close friends, or the like), will be enough to cause the power to become effective. For the benefit of the banker, stockbroker, or doctor, you may want to provide space to have each of the signatures of the friends or relatives notarized.

In any case, the method used to cause a springing power to go into effect should be discussed with your client.

6.   WHAT IF THE AGENT NAMED IN THE POWER IS UNAVAILABLE?

This is basically the same problem as the problem of putting a springing power into effect. The solution is to name several successor agents, just as you normally would with successor trustees, and then to provide some means for letting the banker or health care provider be certain that the successor agent really is the one who is entitled to be acting.

7.   HOW CAN A DURABLE POWER BE REVOKED?

There are two basic ways in which a durable power can be revoked. State laws vary, of course, but normally, the first method of revocation is simply to allow a principal to revoke a durable power at any time – IF the principal then has the requisite mental capacity. The second method is revocation by a court appointed Conservator.[4]

A practical problem with either method, however, may be getting the durable power back from an unruly child who simply does not believe that the elderly parent is in fact capable of handling his or her own affairs. In that situation the unruly child may present to the bank a durable power which looks fine on its face, but that has in fact been revoked.

For this reason, and many others, it might be very helpful if a national registry of durable powers could be established, in which durable powers – and revocations – could be recorded, like land records, and accessible to anyone instantly by internet.

If the principal does not have the mental capacity to revoke a durable power, then the second method of revocation may be used. In most states a Conservator or Guardian, appointed by the court, will have authority to revoke a durable power. Normally, a Conservator or Guardian is given all of the powers the protected person would have had – which will INCLUDE THE POWER TO REVOKE THE DURABLE POWER OF ATTORNEY.

It is for this reason that a well drafted durable power of attorney will include a provision nominating as Conservator or Guardian the <u>same person</u> named as the agent in the durable power. Courts normally will appoint as Conservator or Guardian the person who has been nominated for that position by the protected person – while he or she had the capacity to make such choices. So if your client wants X to act as the agent under a durable power, the client should <u>also</u> name X as <u>Conservator or Guardian</u>. Of course, if it is the <u>agent</u> who has been acting improperly, the court will not appoint that person as Conservator or Guardian. But that decision will be made in open court, by an impartial judge.

Protecting the durable power in this way is especially important where there is likely to be controversy among family members – such as where the client's spouse or friend does not get

---

[4] On the request of family members, creditors, or Social Services, a court may appoint a Conservator or Guardian to take care of the assets or the person of an adult who is no longer capable of caring for himself or herself. Prior to general recognition of durable powers of attorney, this was the method generally used to protect mentally or physically incapacitated persons, and is still sometimes used today.

along with other members of the family, where the client's partner is disliked by the client's mother, and so forth. To avoid having an unhappy family member do an "end-run" around the durable power – by going to court and having himself or herself appointed as Conservator or Guardian, and then revoking the durable power – simply have the client, as part of the durable power, nominate the <u>agent</u> as the Conservator or Guardian, should one become necessary. That will probably avoid the expense and embarrassment[5] of a court proceeding to have a Conservator or Guardian appointed – (and will also avoid the <u>protections</u>[6] that are included with such a court proceeding).

8.   NOTIFY THE FAMILY

A financial power of attorney may be very dangerous in the wrong hands. It is sometimes referred to as a "license to steal." So it is probably a good idea to let other family members know who has been appointed as agent—so that the other family members may keep an eye on the agent.

With a medical power of attorney it is far more important to let family, friends and neighbors know who has been selected as the agent for medical matters. That way, everyone has a chance to adjust in advance to the fact that Sally, for example, will be the one to make any emergency medical decisions for Mom. Hopefully that will encourage Sally and Mom to have some serious discussions about medical matters in advance.

Hopefully that will also allow other family members and friends to adjust to the fact that Sally will be in charge.

It is a good idea to give <u>many</u> people copies of the medical power in advance. The agent, everyone listed as a potential successor agent, other family and close friends, the primary care physician, and the health care provider should all have copies.

In the medical power, list the name, current address, and all available phone numbers for each agent or successor agent. Then be sure to specify that these people are to act as agents—whether or not they are still living at the same address at the time the power is to be implemented.

---

[5] In a proceeding to have a Conservator appointed, it is necessary to prove that the person to be protected can no longer handle his or her own affairs. To prove, in open court, that a relative has become incompetent is an unfortunate situation for everyone involved. One of the major advantages of using a durable power, instead of having a conservator appointed, is avoiding the need for this public proof of incapacity.

[6] Court supervision DOES provide valuable protections for the protected person – at least in theory. The Judge usually will be an experienced and impartial person, who will have no personal conflicts of interest with any of the parties. Court supervision of the protected person's assets – available when a conservatorship is used – may also be a real advantage.

Remember, the medical power should make it as easy as possible for someone in the hospital emergency room to notify the appropriate agent.

SUMMARY:

Durable powers of attorney should be carefully drafted so that an agent acting under such a power does not inadvertently destroy important provisions of a trust or will. Trusts, wills and durable powers should be carefully coordinated to work in harmony to protect the assets and the person of a client.

Two sample forms for durable powers follow. Both provide interesting patterns, but also clearly indicate the need for individualized drafting of such powers. The first sample is for <u>Financial</u> matters, the second sample is for <u>Medical,</u> (or Health Care), matters. As you read through these two forms, try to figure out how you would <u>change them</u> to make them appropriate for an individual client.

9.   SAMPLE DURABLE POWER OF ATTORNEY FOR FINANCIAL MATTERS

Note: Use of the word "durable" is important to show that the power will not be revoked by disability. Some states require use of other specific words.

If powers are to be <u>limited</u>, specify that in the first paragraph— with details later.

Q: If the doctors involved do not like the person named as agent, might the doctors delay in signing the certification necessary to put this power into effect? What other options are available?

DURABLE POWER OF ATTORNEY
FINANCIAL MATTERS

I, _____, of Denver, Colorado, execute this General Durable Power of Attorney for Financial Matters, with the intention that each person named herein as my agent shall have the power to act in my place, as my agent, to the same extent as I could have acted for myself, with regard to all my financial matters.

ARTICLE 1. Designation of Agent

I appoint my friend, _____, now of Boulder, Colorado, as my agent, to act for me, in my name and in my place for all my financial matters. If _____ shall be unable to act, or shall fail to act or continue as such agent, I appoint _____ to be my agent for financial matters.

ARTICLE 2. Effective Date

This General Durable Power of Attorney shall become effective when two physicians certify on this document that I am no longer competent to make decisions about my financial affairs. This power of attorney shall not be revoked by mere passage of time, but shall remain in full force and effect until revoked by me.

Q: What are the advantages, and disadvantages to specific mention of various powers? How much detail should be included?

Note: The IRS seems to like to be mentioned by name on powers like this. If important for a particular client, specific Internal Revenue Code sections also seem helpful.

Q: Why is this important? To protect the durable power. Otherwise, a family member might have herself appointed by the court as Conservator – and then REVOKE the power of attorney. If the agent is the one nominated as Conservator that should prevent an "end-run" around the durable power.

ARTICLE 3. Powers

Any agent acting under this General Durable Power of Attorney for Financial Matters shall have all powers and authority permitted by law. The powers shall include, but are not limited to: payment and collection of debts; disposition of real and personal property as my agent may deem appropriate; power to act on any and all financial matters, including payment of rents; deposit and withdrawals from all accounts I may have at any financial institutions; and power to endorse all checks drawn to my order for deposit in any account I may have at any financial institution. My agent shall also have power to act in any matters involving the Internal Revenue Service or other state or local revenue agency, including preparation and filing of state, local and federal income taxes. My agent shall have full power to act in any financial matter to the full extent to which I might have acted myself, and shall be authorized to receive a Xerox copy of my will, so as to be able to act in accordance with the provisions of my will.

ARTICLE 4. Ratification and Photocopies.

I hereby ratify, confirm and hold valid all actions that my agent shall lawfully take pursuant to this power. A photocopy of this document shall have the same force and effect as the original document.

ARTICLE 5. Conservator

I direct that if a Conservator is appointed for me, that my Conservator be_____, or if he or she fails to qualify or ceases to act as my Conservator, then _____ shall be appointed as my Conservator.
EXECUTED this ____ day of January, 2009.

_____
Principal

Q: Should a notary be required for the doctor's signatures? Or is that asking the doctors to comply with too much red tape? If specific friends or family members are named to be the ones to decide when the power goes into effect, what happens if the people named die – or become incompetent?

STATE OF COLORADO   )
) ss.
COUNTY OF DENVER   )

The foregoing instrument was executed and acknowledged before me   this   _____   day   of   _____,   20___   by _____, the Principal.

Witness my hand and seal.

_____
                Notary Public

_____
_____
                Address

My Commission expires:

I, _____, a licensed physician, hereby certify that this General Durable Power of Attorney for Financial Matters should   become   effective   on   this   ____   day   of _____, 20____.

_____
          Licensed Physician

I, _____, a licensed physician, hereby certify that this General Durable Power of Attorney for Financial Matters should   become   effective   on   this   ____   day   of _____, 20____.

_____
          Licensed Physician

10. SAMPLE DURABLE POWER OF ATTORNEY FOR MEDICAL MATTERS

As you read the following sample Medical Power of Attorney from California, consider whether the form is readily comprehensible to a layman. How might you redraft this form to make it more comprehensible and more effective?

How would you draft a durable power of attorney for medical matters in a state that did not require use of a specific form? How much discretion should be given to the agent? How specifically should the principal indicate his or her wishes as to particular medical treatments? How could possible future changes in medical technology be taken into account?

I. Sample Durable Power of Attorney for Health Care – California Statutory Form

Q: Do these instructions seem clear to you? How helpful would they be to someone with a high school education? Could you draft a very clear, simple statement which might be more helpful?

Q: Might this power to override the agent lead to problems? Who decides whether the principal is capable of giving informed consent?

STATUTORY FORM DURABLE POWER OF ATTORNEY FOR HEALTH CARE
(California Civil Code Section 2500)

This is an important legal document which is authorized by the Keene Health Care Agent Act.

Before executing this document, you should know these important facts:

This document gives the person you designate as your agent (the attorney in fact) the power to make health care decisions for you. Your agent must act consistently with your desires as stated in this document or otherwise made known.

Except as you otherwise specify in this document, this document gives your agent the power to consent to your doctor not giving treatment or stopping treatment necessary to keep you alive.

Notwithstanding this document, you have the right to make medical and other health care decisions for yourself so long as you can give informed consent with respect to the particular decision. In addition, no treatment may be given to you over your objection at the time, and health care necessary to keep you alive may not be stopped or withheld if you object at the time.

This document gives your agent authority to consent, to refuse to consent or to withdraw consent to any care, treatment, service, or procedure to maintain, diagnose, or treat a physical or mental condition. This power is subject to any statement of your desires and any limitations that you

Q: Who would have standing, or motivation, to bring this matter to court on behalf of an elderly person?

Q: Are there any dangers involved with allowing an <u>oral</u> revocation of this document? What is to prevent a nurse, who does not agree with the choices being made by the agent, from simply declaring some morning that in a brief interval when the principal was lucid the principal revoked the agency?

Q: Is it important that the agent have access to all medical records? Why would the agent need to have authority to <u>disclose</u> the information? To <u>whom</u> should the agent be allowed to disclose the information?

include this document. You may state in this document any types of treatment that you do not desire. In addition, a court can take away the power of your agent to make health care decisions for you if your agent (1) authorizes anything that is illegal, (2) acts contrary to your known desires, or (3) where your desires are not known, does anything that is clearly contrary to your best interests.

The powers given by this document will exist for an indefinite period of time unless you limit their duration in this document.

You have the right to revoke the authority of your agent by notifying your agent or your treating doctor, hospital, or other health care provider orally or in writing of the revocation.

Your agent has the right to examine your medical records and to consent to their disclosure unless you limit this right in this document.

Unless you otherwise specify in this document, this document gives your agent the power after you die to (1) authorize an autopsy, (2) donate your body or parts thereof for transplant or therapeutic or educational or scientific purposes, and (3) direct the disposition of your remains. This document revokes any prior durable power of attorney for health care.

You should carefully read and follow the witnessing procedure described at the end of this form. This document will not be valid unless you comply with the witnessing procedure. If there is anything in this document that you do not understand, you should ask a lawyer to explain it to you.

Your agent may need this document immediately in case of an emergency that requires a decision concerning your health care. Either keep this DOCUMENT WHERE IT IS AVAILABLE TO YOUR AGENT AND ALTERNATE AGENTS OR GIVE EACH OF THEM AN EXECUTED COPY OF THIS DOCUMENT. YOU MAY ALSO WANT TO GIVE YOUR DOCTOR AN EXECUTED COPY OF THIS DOCUMENT.

DO NOT USE THIS FORM IF YOU ARE A CONSERVATEE UNDER THE LANTERMAN-PETRIS-SHORT ACT AND YOU WANT TO APPOINT YOUR CONSERVATOR AS YOUR AGENT. You can do that only if the appointment document includes a certificate of your attorney.

1. DESIGNATION OF HEALTH CARE AGENT. I,

_____

(Insert your name and address here)

do hereby designate and appoint _____

_____(Insert name, address, and telephone number of one individual only as your agent to make health care decisions for you. None of the following may be designated as your agent: (1) your treating health care provider, (2) a nonrelative employee of your treating health care provider, (3) an operator of a community care facility, (4) a nonrelative employee of an operator of a community care facility, (5) an operator of a residential care facility for

Q: How likely is it that any one for whom a conservator had been appointed would understand this paragraph?

Q: Might there be a good reason for not allowing a nursing home employee to be named as the agent?

the elderly, or (6) a nonrelative employee of an operator of a residential care facility for the elderly.)

as my attorney in fact (agent) to make health care decisions for me as authorized in this document. For the purposes of this document, "health care decision" means consent, refusal of consent, or withdrawal of consent to any care, treatment, service, or procedure to maintain, diagnose, or treat an individual's physical or mental condition.

2. CREATION OF DURABLE POWER OF ATTORNEY FOR HEALTH CARE. By this document I intend to create a durable power of attorney for health care under Sections 2430 to 2443, inclusive, of the California Civil Code. This power of attorney is authorized by the Keene Health Care Agent Act and shall be construed in accordance with the provisions of Sections 2500 to 2506, inclusive, of the California Civil Code. This power of attorney shall not be affected by my subsequent incapacity.

3. GENERAL STATEMENT OF AUTHORITY GRANTED. Subject to any limitations in this document, I hereby grant to my agent full power and authority to make health care decisions for me to the same extent that I could make such decisions for myself if I had the capacity to do so. In exercising this authority, my agent shall make health care decisions that are consistent with my desires as stated in this

Note: It is this last sentence in paragraph 2 which is crucial to make this a DURABLE power of attorney.

Q: How does this grant of authority differ from the provisions of a living will – found at Section II. A. of this chapter?

document or otherwise made know to my agent, including, but not limited to, my desires concerning obtaining or refusing or withdrawing life-prolonging care, treatment, services, and procedures.

(If you want to limit the authority of your agent to make health care decisions for you, you can state the limitations in paragraph 4 ("Statement of Desires, Special Provisions, and Limitations") below. You can indicate your desires by including a statement of your desires in the same paragraph.)

4.   STATEMENT OF DESIRES, SPECIAL PROVISIONS AND LIMITATIONS.

(Your agent must make health care decisions that are consistent with your known desires. You can, but are not required to, state your desires in the space provided below. You should consider whether you want to include a statement of your desires concerning life-prolonging care, treatment, services, and procedures. You can also include a statement of your desires concerning other matters relating to your health care. You can also make your desires known to your agent by discussing your desires with your agent or by some other means. If there are any types of treatment that you do not want to be used, you should state them in the space below. If you want to limit in any other way the authority given your agent by this document, you should state the limits in the space below. If you do not state any limits, your agent will have broad powers to make health care decisions for you, except to the extent that there are limits provided by law.)

In exercising the authority under this durable power of attorney for health care, my agent shall act consistently with my desires as stated below and is subject to the special provisions and limitations stated below:

(a) Statement of desires concerning life-prolonging care, treatment, services, and procedures:

_____

_____

Q: How specific should a person be about the medical procedures to be used or withheld? What happens if there are significant changes in the medical technology available?

     (b)   Additional statement of desires, special provisions, and limitations:

_____

_____

(You may attach additional pages if you need more space to complete your statement. If you attach additional pages, you must date and sign EACH of the additional pages at the same time you date and sign this document.)

     5.   INSPECTION AND DISCLOSURE OF INFORMATION RELATING TO MY PHYSICAL OR MENTAL HEATH. Subject to any limitations in this document, my agent has the power and authority to do all of the following:

     (a) Request, review, and receive any information, verbal or written, regarding my physical or mental health, including, but not limited to, medical and hospital records.

     (b)   Execute on my behalf any releases or other documents that may be required in order to obtain this information.

     (c) Consent to the disclosure of this information.

(If you want to limit the authority of your agent to receive and disclose information relating to your health, you must state the limitations in paragraph 4, ("Statement of Desires, Special Provisions, and Limitations") above.

     6.   SIGNING DOCUMENTS, WAIVERS, AND RELEASES. Where necessary to implement the health care decisions that my agent is authorized by this document to make, my agent has the power and authority to execute on my behalf all of the following:

Q: Is it important that an agent have authority to sign these documents?

Note: As to part (3), directing disposition of the body, there may be potential conflict with California law – which provides, (at Health & Safety §7100) "If (such) instructions are contained in a will, they shall be immediately carried out, regardless of the validity of the will in other respects."

Q: How meaningful are these code selections to a layman?

Q: What happens if a layman fills in the date of execution of the form on this line? Can you imagine that such a thing might happen?

(a) Documents titled or purporting to be a "Refusal to Permit Treatment" and "Leaving Hospital Against Medical Advice."

(b) Any necessary waiver or release from liability required by a hospital or physician.

7. AUTOPSY; ANATOMICAL GIFTS; DISPOSITION OF REMAINS. Subject to any limitations in this document, my agent has the power and authority to do all of the following:

(a) Authorize an autopsy under Section 7113 of the Health and Safety Code.

(b) Make a disposition of a part or parts of my body under the Uniform Anatomical Gift Act (Chapter 3.5 (commencing with Section 7150) of Part 1 of Division 7 of the Health and Safety Code).

(c) Direct the disposition of my remains under Section 7100 of the Health and Safety Code.

(If you want to limit the authority of your agent to consent to an autopsy, make an anatomical gift, or direct the disposition of your remains, you must state the limitations in paragraph 4 ("Statement of Desires, Special Provisions, and Limitations") above.

8. DURATION.

(Unless you specify otherwise in the space below, this power of attorney will exist for an indefinite period of time.)

This durable power of attorney for health care expires on

_____

(Fill in this space ONLY if you want to limit the duration of this power of attorney.)

Q: Does this seem appropriate – that divorce will automatically revoke the authority of an ex-spouse? What about authority which may have been granted to someone who was an in-law prior to the divorce?

Q: Why is the principal not allowed to require that two out of her three children, for example, agree on medical decisions? Is this provision for the convenience of the principal or for the convenience of health care providers?

Q: Would it usually be a good idea to nominate the agent as the conservator – particularly if there might be battles between family members and close friends?

9. DESIGNATION OF ALTERNATE AGENTS.

(You are not required to designate any alternate agents but you may do so. Any alternate agent you designate will be able to make the same health care decisions as the agent you designated in paragraph 1, above, in the event that agent is unable or ineligible to act as your agent. If the agent you designated is your spouse, he or she becomes ineligible to act as your agent if your marriage is dissolved.)

If the person designated as my agent in paragraph 1 is not available or becomes ineligible to act as my agent to make a health care decision for me or loses the mental capacity to make health care decisions for me, or if I revoke that person's appointment or authority to act as my agent to make health care decisions for me, then I designate and appoint the following persons to serve as my agent to make health care decisions for me as authorized in this document, such persons to serve in the order listed below.

A. First Alternate Agent _____

_____

(Insert name, address, and telephone number of first alternate agent)

B. Second Alternate Agent _____

_____

(Insert name, address, and telephone number of second alternate agent)

10. NOMINATION OF CONSERVATOR OF PERSON.

(A conservator of the person may be appointed for you if a court decides that one should be appointed. The conservator is responsible for your physical care, which under some circumstances includes making health care decisions for you. You are not required to nominate a conservator but you may do so. The court will appoint the person you nominate unless that would be contrary to your best interests. You may, but are not required to, nominate as your conservator the same person you named in paragraph 1 as your health care agent. You can nominate an individual as your conservator by completing the space below.)

Q: How is a doctor to know whether or not the Durable Power presented by an agent has been revoked by a later document? Would a national registry of Durable Powers be useful – so that it could be quickly ascertained who had the most recently executed Durable Power?

Q: Should instructions on witnesses come at the <u>beginning</u> of document – to prevent the principal from signing and <u>then</u> discovering that only certain people quality as witnesses?

If a conservator of the person is to be appointed for me, I nominate the following individual to serve as a conservator of the person

_____

_____

(Insert name and address of person nominated as conservator of the person)

11.   PRIOR DESIGNATIONS REVOKED. I revoke any prior durable power of attorney for health care.

DATE AND SIGNATURE OF PRINCIPAL

(YOU MUST DATE AND SIGN THIS POWER OF ATTORNEY)

I sign my name to this Statutory Form Durable Power of Attorney for Health Care on _____ at
                                         (Date)

_____ , _____
          (City)   (State)

            _____
              (You sign here)

(THIS POWER OF ATTORNEY WILL NOT BE VALID UNLESS IT IS SIGNED BY TWO QUALIFIED WITNESSES WHO ARE PRESENT WHEN YOU SIGN OR ACKNOWLEDGE YOUR SIGNATURE. IF YOU HAVE ATTACHED ANY ADDITIONAL PAGES TO THIS FORM, YOU MUST DATE AND SIGN EACH OF THE ADDITIONAL PAGES AT THE SAME TIME YOU DATE AND SIGN THIS POWER OF ATTORNEY.)

STATEMENT OF WITNESSES

(This document must be witnessed by two qualified adult witnesses. None of the following may be used as a witness: (1) a person you designate as your agent or alternate agent, (2) a health care provider, (3) an employee of a health care provider, (4) the operator of a community care facility, (5) an employee of an operator of a community care facility, (6) the operator of a residential care facility for the elderly, or (7) an employee of an operator of a residential care facility for the elderly. At least one of the witnesses must make the additional declaration set out following the place where the witnesses sign.)

Q: Do the witnesses both have to be present <u>at the same time</u>? Or could one witness be present when the document is signed, and the other witness be there later, when the principal acknowledges his or her signature? Is there any advantage to have the two witnesses there <u>at the same time</u>?

Q: Is it important that employees of the nursing home not be allowed to act even as witnesses for this document?

READ CAREFULLY BEFORE SIGNING. You can sign as a witness only if you personally know the principal or the identity of the principal is proved to you by convincing evidence).

(To have convincing evidence of the identity of the principal, you must be presented with and reasonably rely on any one or more of the following:

(1)   An identification card or driver's license issued by the California Department of Motor Vehicles that is current or has been issued within five years.

(2)   A passport issued by the department of State of the United States that is current or has been issued within five years.

(3)   Any of the following documents if the document is current or has been issued within five years and contains a photograph and description of the person named on it, is signed by the person, and bears a serial or other identifying number.

(a)   A passport issued by a foreign government that has been stamped by the United States Immigration and Naturalization Service.

(b)   A driver's license issued by a state other than California or by a Canadian or Mexican public agency authorized to issue driver's licenses.

(c)   An identification card issued by a state other than California.

(d)   An identification card issued by any branch of the armed forces of the United States.

(4)   If the principal is a patient in a skilled nursing facility, a witness who is a patient advocate or ombudsman may rely upon the representations of the administrator or staff of the skilled nursing facility, or of family members, as convincing evidence of the identity of the principal if the patient advocate or ombudsman believes that the representations provide a reasonable basis for determining the identity of the principal.)

(Other kinds of proof of identity are not allowed.)

I declare under penalty of perjury under the laws of California that the person who signed or acknowledged this document is personally know to me (or proved to me on the basis of convincing evidence) to be the principal, that the principal signed or acknowledged this durable power of attorney in my presence, that the principal appears to be of sound mind and under no duress, fraud, or undue influence, that I am not the person appointed as attorney in fact by this document, and that I am not a health care provider, an employee of a health care provider, the operator of a

Q: Why do you think at least one of the witnesses must be someone who does not expect to get anything under the terms of the principal's will? What if the witness who signs here is the <u>husband</u> of the housekeeper who is the primary beneficiary of the recently executed will?

Q: Are all patients in a nursing home likely to be able to understand this paragraph? Should this requirement that one witness be a patient advocate or ombudsman be at the <u>beginning</u> of the instructions?

community care facility, an employee of an operator of a community facility, the operator of a residential care facility for the elderly, nor an employee of an operator of a residential care facility for the elderly.

Signature:_____   Residence Address:_____
Print Name:_____   _____
Date: _____   _____

(AT LEAST ONE OF THE ABOVE WITNESSES MUST ALSO SIGN THE FOLLOWING DECLARATION.)

I further declare under penalty of perjury under the laws of California that I am not related to the principal by blood, marriage, or adoption, and, to the best of my knowledge, I am not entitled to any part of the estate of the principal upon the death of the principal under a will now existing or by operation of law.

Signature: _____

Signature: _____

STATEMENT OF PATIENT ADVOCATE OR OMBUDSMAN

(If you are a patient in a skilled nursing facility, one of the witnesses must be a patient advocate or ombudsman. The following statement is required only if you are a patient in a skilled nursing facility – a health care facility that provides the following basic services: skilled nursing care and supportive care to patients whose primary need is for availability of skilled nursing care on an extended basis. The patient advocate or ombudsman must sign both parts of the "Statement of Witnesses: above AND must also sign the following statement.)

I further declare under penalty of perjury under the laws of California that I am a patient advocate or ombudsman as designated by the State Department of Aging and that I am serving as a witness as required by subdivision (f) of Section 2432 of the Civil Code.

Signature: _____
(Added by Stats. 1984, c., 312, § 8. Amended by Stats. 1985, c. 403, § 10; Stats. 1988, c. 1543, § 5; Stats. 1990, c. 331 (A.B.835), § 2 ; Stats. 1991, c. 896 (A.B.793), §4.)

B.   "Living Wills"

"Living Wills" are designated to protect a client from being kept alive, in a vegetative state, after all hope of recovery is gone. Most states now have statutory provisions for such documents, but the statutes vary widely. Many states have statutorily authorized forms for living wills. What is required, or permitted, with regard to such forms also varies from state to state. The only thing that seems consistent in all states, is that if your client does not want to be kept alive in a vegetative state, then the client should put that decision in writing.

BE SURE to check the current, relevant statute before you help a client execute a living will. Frequently there are strict requirements on how many people must serve as witnesses for a living will, and on what relationship, if any, the witnesses may have with the person signing the living will. The purpose for the restriction on witnesses is basically to protect anyone from being pressured into signing a living will. Therefore, it may well be that no nursing home or medical personnel may serve as witnesses – nor may family members – or friends who might be mentioned in the client's will, serve as witnesses on the "living will."

Does your client need to have both a "living will" and Durable Power of Attorney for medical matters? The answer probably is yes. The Durable Power of Attorney gives much more flexibility than the living will. The power may be used in any situation in which the principal is unable to make a decision—including a situation in which the principal is almost certain to recover—but is unconscious because of a serious injury. The living will is only a directive for the end of life.

Normally, the agent under a durable power could make any decision which could be made under the terms of a living will.

But if no agent or successor agent is available, because of death, incapacity, or the like, then the living will can stand alone. Normally, medical personnel are required to implement the directives of a living will—or transfer the patient to a doctor who will do so.[1]

Three sample "living will" forms follow – with comments. Hopefully, these sample forms and comments will help you to become more familiar with some of the variety of provisions that may be included in "living wills."

---

[1] For example, C.R.S. 15-18-113 (5) specifies that:

(5) An attending physician who refuses to comply with the terms of a declaration valid on its face shall transfer the care of the declarant to another physician who is willing to comply with the declaration. Refusal of an attending physician to comply with a declaration and failure to transfer the care of the declarant to another physician shall constitute unprofessional conduct as defined in section 12-36-117, C.R.S.

Sample – Colorado Living Will Form

Q: Would it be a better idea to put the requirement for witnesses at the <u>beginning</u> of the form?

Q: Does this mean that a person who instantly becomes brain dead because of an accident must <u>still</u> be kept on machines for at least seven days? Is that appropriate?

Q: Does this mean that <u>pain</u> killers <u>will</u> still be given? If that is so, why not state that fact clearly?

Q: Does the second sentence in the paragraph seem to conflict with the first sentence? How could this be written <u>clearly</u>?

DECLARATION AS TO MEDICAL OR SURGICAL TREATMENT

I, _____(name of declarant)___, being of sound mind and at least eighteen years of age, direct that my life shall not be artificially prolonged under the circumstances set forth below and hereby declare that:

    1.   If at any time my attending physician and one other qualified physician certify in writing that:

    a.   I have an injury, disease, or illness which is not curable or reversible and which, in their judgment, is a terminal condition, and

    b.   For a period of seven consecutive days or more, I have been unconscious, comatose, or otherwise incompetent so as to be unable to make or communicate responsible decisions concerning my person, then

    I direct that, in accordance with Colorado law, life-sustaining procedures shall be withdrawn and withheld pursuant to the terms of this declaration, it being understood that life-sustaining procedures shall not include any medical procedure or intervention for nourishment considered necessary by the attending physician to provide comfort or alleviate pain. However, I may specifically direct, in accordance with Colorado law, that artificial nourishment be withdrawn or withheld pursuant to the terms of this declaration.

    2.   In the event that the only procedure I am being provided is artificial nourishment, I direct that one of

Q: What is the definition of "artificial nourishment"? Should that be stated somewhere in the form – in plain English?

Q: Is it a good idea to have all three choices on the form – so that it is clear that the signer knew what the options were? Could the choices be stated more clearly?

Q: Is use of only the masculine gender appropriate? How might this be better written?

Q: Should this <u>form</u> also include notice that the witnesses, in accordance with state law, may NOT include possible beneficiaries of the estate, nursing home employees, and the like?

---

the following actions be taken:

    __(initials of declarant)__ a. Artificial nourishment shall not be continued when it is the only procedure being provided; or

    __(initials of declarant)__ b. Artificial nourishment shall be continued for _____ days when it is the only procedure being provided; or

    __(initials of declarant)__ c. Artificial nourishment shall be continued when it is the only procedure being provided.

    3.   I execute this declaration, as my free and voluntary act, this _____ day of _____, 20___.

               By_____

                         Declarant

    The foregoing instrument was signed and declared by _____ to be his declaration, in the presence of us, who, in his presence, in the presence of each other, and at his request, have signed our names below as witnesses, and we declare that, at the time of the execution of this instrument, the declarant, according to our best knowledge and belief, was of sound mind and under no constraint or undue influence.

    Dated at _____, Colorado, this _____ day of _____, 20___.

(WITNESS AND NOTARY)

    SUBSCRIBED and sworn to before me by _____, the declarant, and _____ and _____, witnesses, as the voluntary act and deed of the declarant this _____ day of _____, 20___.

    My commission expires:

                          _____

Minnesota Living Will Form

Note: Notice that this form is <u>mandatory</u> for any living will signed in Minnesota after August 1, 1989. Would a Texas, or Colorado Living Will form be effective in Minnesota – even if it had been properly executed in Texas or Colorado?

Q: How many laymen would really understand the term "designated proxy?"

Q: Is <u>notification</u> of <u>health care providers</u> the only way to revoke a Minnesota Living Will? Must notice be written? Does the statute say that?

MINNESOTA LIVING WILL FORM

A living will executed after August 1, 1989, under this chapter must be substantially in the form of this section. Forms printed for public distribution must be substantially in the form in this section.

"Health Care Living Will"

Notice:

This is an important legal document. Before signing this document, you should know these important facts:

(a) This document gives your health care providers or your designated proxy the power and guidance to make health care decisions according to your wishes when you are in a terminal condition and cannot do so. This document may include what kind of treatment you want or do not want and under what circumstances you want these decisions to be made. You may state where you want or do not want to receive any treatment.

(b) If you name a proxy in this document and that person agrees to serve as your proxy, that person has a duty to act consistently with your wishes. If the proxy does not know your wishes, the proxy has the duty to act in your best interests. If you do not name a proxy, your health care providers have a duty to act consistently with your instructions or tell you that they are unwilling to do so.

(c) This document will remain valid and in effect until and unless you amend or revoke it. Review this document periodically to make sure it continues to reflect your wishes.

Q: Might it be useful to know, from the document itself, how old the person was when he or she signed it?

Q: Does this give any guidance as to <u>how</u> the Living Will may be revoked? Is this part consistent with part (c) of the Notice on the preceding page?

Q: Does this permit a person to make up his or her <u>own</u> definition of "terminal condition"? Would this part allow a person to say the Living Will should go into effect <u>only</u> when three of her five children agree?

(d) Your named proxy has the same right as you have to examine your medical records and to consent to their disclosure for purposes related to your health care or insurance unless you limit this right in this document.

(e) If there is anything in this document that you do not understand, you should ask for professional help to have it explained to you.

TO MY FAMILY, DOCTORS, AND ALL THOSE CONCERNED WITH MY CARE: I, _____ born on _____ (birth date), being an adult of sound mind, willfully and voluntarily make this statement as a directive to be followed if I am in a terminal condition and become unable to participate in decisions regarding my health care. I understand that my health care providers are legally bound to act consistently with my wishes, within the limits of reasonable medical practice and other applicable law. I also understand that I have the right to make medical and health care decisions for myself as long as I am able to do so and to revoke this living will at any time.

(1)   The following are my feelings and wishes regarding my health care (you may state the circumstances under which this living will applies);

_____

_____

Q: Are these blanks more useful for medically trained people than they are for laymen? What if the blanks are not filled in by the person who signs the Living Will? What if the blanks are <u>later</u> filled in by <u>another</u> person? Is there any way to prevent that from happening?

Q: Will the normal layman understand what "artificially administered sustenance" <u>means</u>? Is there a better way to describe the concept?

Q: Is there a way of requesting that feeding be provided for 10 days – and then stopped?

---

(2)   I particularly want to have all appropriate health care that will help in the following ways (you may give instructions for care you do want):

_____

_____

(3)   I particularly do not want the following (you may list specific treatment you do not want in certain circumstances):

_____

_____

(4)   I particularly want to have the following kinds of life-sustaining treatment if I am diagnosed to have a terminal condition (you may list the specific types of life-sustaining treatment that you do want if you have a terminal condition):

_____

_____

(5)   I particularly do not want the following kinds of life-sustaining treatment if I am diagnosed to have a terminal condition (you may list the specific types of life-sustaining treatment that you do not want if you have a terminal condition):

_____

_____

(6)   I recognize that if I reject artificially administered sustenance then I may die of dehydration or malnutrition rather than from my illness or injury. The following are my feelings and wishes regarding artificially administered sustenance should I have a terminal condition

(you may indicate whether you wish to receive food and fluids given to you in some other way than by mouth if you have a terminal condition):

_____

_____

(7) Thoughts I feel are relevant to my instructions. (You may, but need not, give your religious beliefs, philosophy, or other personal values that you feel are important. You may also state preferences concerning the location of your care.)

_____

_____

(8) Proxy Designation. (If you wish, you may name someone to see that your wishes are carried out, but you do not have to do this. You may also name a proxy without including specific instructions regarding your care. If you name a proxy, you should discuss your wishes with that person).

If I become unable to communicate my instructions, I designate the following person(s) to act on my behalf consistently with my instructions, if any, as stated in this document. Unless I write instructions that limit my proxy's authority, my proxy has full power and authority to make health care decisions for me. If a guardian or conservator of the person is to be appointed for me, I nominate my proxy named in this document to act as guardian or conservator of my person.

Q: Is this useful for someone who wants to be allowed to die at home – or in a hospice?

Q: Would it be clear to a layman that "someone to see that your wishes are carried out" really just means "proxy"?

Q: Since this form is mandatory, is there any way a person could name different people as proxies or conservators?

Q: Is this really clear that the <u>proxy's</u> name goes in here? What if the person signing the Living Will puts his or her <u>own</u> name here?

Q: What happens if the signer of this document simply writes "CANCELED" across every page putting a signature and date below each "canceled"? Would this document still be effective? Why or Why not?

Q: What if the organ donor document is signed <u>after</u> this document is signed?

Q: Could nursing home employees serve as witnesses for this document? Is that a good idea?

Name:_____

Address:_____

Phone Number:_____

Relationship: (If any)_____

     If the person I have named above refuses or is unable or unavailable to act on my behalf, or if I revoke that person's authority to act as my proxy, I authorize the following person to do so:

Name:_____

Address:_____

Phone Number:_____

Relationship: (If any)_____

     I understand that I have the right to revoke the appointment of the persons named above to act on my behalf at any time by communicating that decision to the proxy or my health care provider.

     I (have) (have not) agreed in another document or on another form to donate some or all of my organs when I die.

DATE:_____

SIGNED:_____

STATE OF_____

COUNTY OF_____

     Subscribed, sworn to, and acknowledged before me by _____ on this _____ day of _____, 20___.

_____
NOTARY PUBLIC
OR
     (Sign and date here in the presence of two adult witnesses, neither of whom is entitled to any part of your estate under a will or by operation of law, and neither of whom is your proxy.)

Q: How helpful will it be to have the original of a person's Living Will safely tucked away in the person's safe deposit box?

Q: Do the signed copies also have to be notarized?

I certify that the declarant voluntarily signed this living will in my presence and that the declarant is personally known to me. I am not named as a proxy by the living will, and to the best of my knowledge, I am not entitled to any part of the estate of the declarant under a will or by operation of law.

Witness_____Address_____

Witness_____Address_____

Reminder: Keep the signed original with your personal papers. Give signed copies to your doctors, family, and proxy.

Sample – Texas Living Will Form

Note: Notice that this form is <u>optional</u> in Texas.

Q: How much could a Living Will <u>differ</u> from this form and still be recognized?

Q: Would you expect an out-of state Living Will to be more easily implemented in Texas than it would be in Minnesota?

Q: Did the Minnesota form have an exclusion for pregnancy? Is this a good ideas?

A written directive may be in the following form:

"DIRECTIVE TO PHYSICIANS"

"Directive made this ____ day of ____ (month, year).

"I _____, being of sound mind, willfully and voluntarily make known my desire that my life shall not be artificially prolonged under the circumstances set forth in this directive.

"1.   If at any time I should have an incurable or irreversible condition caused by injury, disease, or illness certified to be a terminal condition by two physicians, and if the application of life-sustaining procedures would serve only to artificially postpone the moment of my death, and if my attending physician determines that my death is imminent or will result within a relatively short time without the application of life-sustaining procedures, I direct that those procedures be withheld or withdrawn, and that I be permitted to die naturally.

"2.   In the absence of my ability to give directions regarding the use of those life-sustaining procedures, it is my intention that this directive be honored by my family and physicians as the final expression of my legal right to refuse medical or surgical treatment and accept the consequences from that refusal.

"3.   If I have been diagnosed as pregnant and that diagnosis is known to my physician, this directive has no effect during my pregnancy.

"4.   This directive is in effect until it is revoked.

Q: <u>How</u> could this directive be revoked? In writing? By being burned or torn? Orally? Does anyone have to be notified?

Q: Is this a good idea to allow employees of a nursing home to act as witnesses? Have you ever been in a nursing home?

Q: Does this form ever state how <u>old</u> the declarant and witnesses must be? What happens if the form is signed, but not witnessed?

Q: What happens if the declarant wants to specify certain kinds of treatments which are to be given – or withheld? Is there any way for the declarant to specify that nourishment is to be withheld? Will this document have any effect on the use of pain killers?

"5.   I understand the full import of this directive and I am emotionally and mentally competent to make this directive.

    "6.   I understand that I may revoke this directive at any time. Signed_____

(City, County, and State of Residence)

I am not related to the declarant by blood or marriage. I would not be entitled to any portion of the declarant's estate on the declarant's death. I am not the attending physician of the declarant or an employee of the attending physician. I am not a patient in the health care facility in which the declarant is a patient. I have no claim against any portion of the declarant's estate on the declarant's death. Furthermore, if I am an employee of a health facility in which the declarant is a patient, I am not involved in providing direct patient care to the declarant and am not directly involved in the financial affairs of the health facility.

Witness_____

Witness_____ "

C. CONCLUSION

Because "Living Wills" are so likely to be tightly restricted by particular state statutes, if may be <u>dangerous</u> not to use the specific Living Will form authorized by the jurisdiction in which your client is domiciled.

However, because state law is changing so rapidly in this area, it may well be appropriate to add an <u>addendum</u> to the standard Living Will form – stating what your client's wishes would be as to euthanasia, for example if such actions should later become legal – either because of change of law or change of domicile by your client.

Among the most dramatic of the recent changes in law in this area is the reaffirmation by Oregon voters, in November 1997, of the legality of assisted suicide. Many elderly or terminally ill people state that they would very much like to be able to exercise the option of assisted suicide if it were legal to do so.

Including individual requests, such as this, as an <u>addendum</u> to a standard Living Will form would seem to be appropriate if so requested by your individual client. Care must also be taken to coordinate the final provisions of the Living Will with the provisions of the Durable Power of Attorney for Medical Matters.

All five documents discussed in this book – Wills, Trusts, Durable Powers for Financial Matters, Durable Powers for Medical Matters, and Living Wills, should be thoughtfully and carefully drafted to accomplish the goals of each individual client.

LAST WILL AND TESTAMENT
OF
GEORGIA O'KEEFFE

I, GEORGIA O'KEEFFE, residing in Abiquiu, County of Rio Arriba, State of New Mexico, do hereby make, publish and declare this to be my Last Will and Testament, hereby revoking all Wills and Codicils heretofore made by me.

FIRST: I direct that all my debts (other than any mortgage or other secured indebtedness) and funeral and administration expenses be paid out of my estate as soon after my death as convenient.

SECOND: I direct that all estate, inheritance, legacy, succession, transfer and other death taxes (including any interest and penalties thereon) imposed by any domestic or foreign laws now or hereafter in force with respect to all property taxable under such laws by reason of my death, whether or not such property passes under this my will or any codicil hereto and whether such taxes shall be payable by my estate or by any recipient of such property, shall be paid by my Executor out of my Residuary Estate without apportionment. This Article shall not be construed to apply to the tax on "adjusted taxable gifts" (Section 2001). The aforesaid reference is to the Internal Revenue Code of 1954, as amended, and shall be deemed to refer to corresponding provisions of any subsequent Federal tax law.

THIRD:

A. I give the sum of Three Thousand ($3,000) Dollars to INEZ OSSENDORF, if she is then living. If she is not then living, I direct that this gift shall lapse and become part of my Residuary Estate.

B. I give the sum of Thirty Thousand ($30,000) Dollars to JACKIE SUAZO, if he is then living. If he is not then living, I direct that this gift shall lapse and become part of my Residuary Estate.

C. I give the sum of Three Thousand ($3,000) Dollars to each of the following, if he or she is then living. If he or she is not then living, I direct that this gift shall lapse and become part of my Residuary Estate.

1. CANDELARIA LOPEZ
2. IDA ARCHULETA
3. AGAPITA LOPEZ
4. ESTIBEN SUAZO
5. MARGARET WOOD

D.   I give the sum of One Thousand ($1,000) Dollars to each person who shall be in my employ in Abiquiu, New Mexico at the time of my death (other than those named above in this Article THIRD) provided that such person shall have been in my employ for a continuous period of one year prior to my death.

FOURTH: I hereby forgive and cancel any outstanding balance of the indebtedness in the amount of Thirty Thousand ($30,000) Dollars evidenced by the Promissory Note executed by ROSALIA and JOHNNY JARAMILLO in my favor along with any interest thereon. I also forgive and cancel any and all indebtedness owed to me at the time of my death by JOHN BRUCE HAMILTON along with any interest thereon. I further direct my Executor to deliver to them all evidence of their indebtedness and to execute whatever instrument or instruments which are appropriate to evidence such cancellation.

FIFTH: I give all my right, title and interest in and to my real property located in Abiquiu, New Mexico, subject to any mortgages, liens or encumbrances of any kind, consisting of a house and lot originally obtained from St. Thomas The Apostle Roman Catholic Church and any adjoining lots and parcels owned by me and located in Abiquiu, New Mexico, along with all the furnishings located in said real property (but, in no event, to include any works of art) and the equipment used in connection therewith, not otherwise specifically bequeathed in this my Will or any Codicil thereto, and together with any and all improvements on said properties and any and all appurtenances thereto to either the NATIONAL PARK SERVICE or the NATIONAL TRUST FOR HISTORIC PRESERVATION IN THE UNITED STATES, both presently located in Washington, D.C. as my Executor, in his sole and absolute discretion, shall select. The aforesaid bequest is conditioned upon the recipient being an organization described in both Section 170(c) and 2055(a) of the Internal Revenue Code of 1954, as amended (or any corresponding section of any tax laws of the United States from time to time in effect).

If the aforesaid condition is not met and neither organization is selected by my Executor to receive this devise or if the property, furnishing, equipment, improvements and appurtenances to such charitable organizations or institution as shall be selected by my Executor provided that such organization or institution shall be an organization described in both Section 170(c) and 2055(a) of the Internal Revenue code of 1954, as amended (or any corresponding section of any tax laws of the united States from time to time in effect).

SIXTH: I give my right, title and interest to my ranch, consisting of a house and acreage located outside of Abiquiu, in the county of Rio Arriba and Sate of New Mexico, which was formerly part of the "Ghost Ranch" and was acquired by me from Arthur Peck, together with the furnishings located therein (but, in no event, to include any works of art) and equipment used in connection therewith, not other wise specifically bequeathed in this my Will or any Codicil thereto and together with any and all improvements on said property and any and all appurtenances thereto and together with any transferable policies of insurance relating thereto, to my friend, JOHN BRUCE HAMILTON, or if he does not survive me, to THE UNITED PRESBYTERIAN CHURCH IN THE UNITED STATES OF AMERICA, located at 475 Riverside Drive, New York, New York, for its general purposes.

SEVENTH: If my friend, JOHN BRUCE HAMILTON, shall survive me and qualify as Executor of my estate, I give him the following works of art created by me:

A.   Any six (6) works of art from among my oil paintings on canvas.

B.   Any fifteen (15) works of art from among my drawings and/or water colors and /or pastels.

C.   Notwithstanding the foregoing, JOHN BRUCE HAMILTON shall make his selection from works of art other than those specifically bequeathed elsewhere in this my Will or any codicil thereto.

EIGHTH: I give the following works of art created by me, if they are owned by me at the time of my death, as follows:

A.   To THE ART INSTITUTE OF CHICAGO, presently located in Chicago, Illinois:

1. Abstraction—White Rose III   1927
(also known as: Ballet Skirt or
Electric Light)
    Oil on Canvas 36 x 30
2. Black Rock with Blue Sky
And White Clouds   1972
    Oil on Canvas 36 x 30
3. Cliffs Beyond Abiquiu   1943
    Oil on Canvas 30 x 24
4. From a Day with Juan IV   1977
    Oil on Canvas 48 x 36
5. It was Yellow and Pink III   1960
    Oil on Canvas 40 x 30
6. Pelvis III   1944
    Oil on Canvas 48 x 40
7. Sky Above Clouds IV   1965

Oil on Canvas 96 x 288

8. White Patio with Red Door   1960

Oil on Canvas 48 x 84

9. White Shell with Red   1938 ca.

Pastel   22 x 28

B.   To the MUSEUM OF FINE ARTS, presently locate in Boston, Massachusetts:

1. Shell and Old Shingle No. 1   1926

Oil on Canvas 9 x 7

2. Shell and Old Shingle No. II   1926

Oil on Canvas 30 x 18

3. Shell and Old Shingle No. III   1926

Oil on Board   10 x 6

4. Shell and Old Shingle No. IV   1926

Oil on Canvas 9 x 7

5. Shell and Old Shingle No. VII   1926

Oil on Canvas (21 x 32)

or (32 x 21)

6. Fishhook From Hawaii #2   1939

Oil on Canvas 36 x 24

7. Grey Hills II   1936

Oil on Canvas 16 x 30

8. Sunflower   1937
(also known as: A Sunflower
From Maggie)

Oil on Canvas 15 x 20

9. The Lawrence Tree   1929

Oil on Canvas 31 x 39 ¼

C.   To THE BROOKLYN MUSEUM, presently located in Brooklyn, New York:

1. Dark Tree Trunks   1946

Oil on Canvas 40 x 30

2. Fishhook From Hawaii No. 1   1939

Oil on Canvas 18 x 14

3. Green, Yellow and Orange   1960
        Oil on Canvas 40 x 30
4. Red Hills with Pedernal—   1936
        New Mexico
        Pastel   21 ½ x 27 ¼
5. Rib and Jawbone   1936
        Oil on Canvas 9 x 24
6. Yellow Leaves   1928
        Oil on Canvas 40 x 30

D.   To the CLEVELAND MUSEUM OF ART, presently located in Cleveland, Ohio:

1. Cliffs Beyond Abiquiu –
        Dry Waterfall   1943
        Oil on Canvas 30 x 16
2. Dead Tree with Pink Hill   1945
        Oil on Canvas 30 x 40
3. It was Yellow and Pink II   1959
        Oil on Canvas 36 x 30
4. Sunflower, New Mexico I   1935
        Oil on Canvas 20 x 16
5. White Pansy   1927
        Oil on Canvas 36 1/8 x 30 1/8

E.   To THE METROPOLITAN MUSEUM OF ART, presently located in New York, New York:

1. Grey Line with Lavender and Yellow   1923 ca.
        Oil on Canvas 48 x 30
2. Grey Tree—Lake George   1925
        Oil on Canvas 36 x 30
3. New York East River   1928
        Oil on Canvas 12 x 32
4. Red and Yellow Cliffs – Ghost Ranch   1940
        Oil on Canvas 24 x 36

F. To THE MUSEUM OF MODERN ART, presently in New York, New York:

1. An Orchid   1941
        Pastel   27 x 212
2. From a Day with Juan II   1977
        Oil on Canvas 48 x 36 (dark)
3. Ladder to the Moon   1958
        Oil on Canvas 40 x 30
4. Patio with Black Door—Large   1955
        Oil on Canvas 40 x 30
5. Summer Days   1936
        Oil on Canvas 36 x 30

G. To NATIONAL GALLERY OF ART, presently located in Washington, D.C.:

1. Jack-in-the-Pulpit #II   1930
        Oil on Canvas 40 x 30
2. Jack-in-the-Pulpit #III   1930
        Oil on Canvas 40 x 30
3. Jack-in-the-Pulpit #IV   1930
        Oil on Canvas 40 x 30
4. Jack-in-the-Pulpit #V   1930
        Oil on Canvas 40 x 30
5. Jack-in-the-Pulpit #VI   1930
        Oil on Canvas 36 x 18
6. Black and White   1930
        Oil on Canvas 36 x 24
7. Cow's Skull on Red   1931-1936
        Oil on Canvas 35 x 40
8. Line and Curve (Abstraction)   1927
        Oil on Canvas 32 x 16 1/8
9. Shell No. 1   1928
        Oil on Canvas 7 x 7
10. Sky Above White Clouds I   1962 ca.
        Oil on Canvas 60 x 80

H.   To the PHILADELPHIA MUSEUM OF ART, presently located in Philadelphia, Pennsylvania:

1. Birch and Pine Tree No. I   1925
   Oil on Canvas 35 x 22
2. From the Lake No. 3   1924
   Oil on Canvas 36 x 30
3. Orange and Red Streak   1919
   Oil on Canvas 27 x 33
4. Two Calla Lilies on Pink   1928
   Oil on Canvas 40 x 30

J. Notwithstanding the foregoing, I authorize and direct my Executor in his sole and absolute discretion to cancel the bequest of any or all of the works of art bequeathed to any one or more organizations named in this Article EIGHTH and/or to substitute different works of art created by me for the ones designated herein. In no event shall my Executor be required to make any such substitution or cancellation unless, in his sole and absolute discretion, he desires to do so. If my Executor does cancel any such bequest, I direct that the work or works of art affected thereby shall pass in accordance with Article NINTH of this will.

NINTH: All other works of art created by me, other than those specifically bequeathed in this my Will and other than those which must be sold by my Executor to defray the cost of taxes and administration expenses an including any which are subject of any bequest under Article EIGHTH of this Will which is canceled by my Executor shall be given to such charitable organizations or institutions as shall be selected by my Executor, including any institution or organization or institution shall be an organization described in both Section 170(c) and 2055(a) of the Internal Revenue Code of 1954, as amended (or any corresponding section of any tax laws of the United States from time to time in effect). In making this selection, I direct my Executor to include the UNIVERSITY OF NEW MEXICO and the MUSEUM OF NEW MEXICO, MUSEUM OF FINE ARTS, presently located in Santa Fe, New Mexico, provided such institutions are willing to comply with the conditions and restrictions which my Executor may impose in accordance with Article TENTH below.

TENTH: I specifically authorize my Executor to impose any conditions or restrictions in respect to any bequest made under Articles EIGHTH and NINTH of this my Will relating to the manner and frequency of the exhibition of the works of art so bequeathed as well as any other matters related to such works of art. Notwithstanding the foregoing, I direct that my Executor shall not impose any conditions or restrictions which will prevent said bequest from qualifying as a charitable bequest for the purpose of being able to deduct the same on my Federal Estate Tax return.

ELEVENTH: I give to the NATIONAL GALLERY OF ART all photographs of me taken by my late husband, ALFRED STIEGLITZ, which are presently on loan to said institution.

TWELFTH: A. I give all of my letters, personal correspondence and clippings to YALE UNIVERSITY, presently located in New Haven, Connecticut. This bequest is subject to the same terms and conditions as apply to the papers previously received by YALE UNIVERSITY from the estate of my husband, ALFRED STIEGLITZ.

B. I give all of the rest of my writings and papers, together with all copyrights thereon and rights of publication thereto to JOHN BRUCE HAMILTON. If he does not survive me, I give the same to YALE UNIVERSITY.

THIRTEENTH: I give all photographs, prints, negatives and other photographic material owned by me at my death, not otherwise specifically bequeathed herein, to such charitable organizations or institutions as shall be selected by my Executor provided that each such organization or institution shall be an organization described in both Section 170(c) and 2055(a) of the Internal Revenue Code of 1954, as amended (or any corresponding section of any tax laws of the United States from time to time in effect).

FOURTEENTH: A. I give all of my books, phonograph records, dogs and automobiles, as well as all of the balance of my tangible personal property, including any works of art not created by me which are not otherwise specifically bequeathed, to JOHN BRUCE HAMILTON, if he survives me.

B. I give to JOHN BRUCE HAMILTON, if he survives me, all of my right, title and interest in and to all of my copyrights and any right to royalties thereon as well as the right to renewals and extensions of the same, including, without limitation, all royalties and rights under the Agreement between myself and The Viking Press dated July 22, 1975.

FIFTEENTH: I direct that all expenses related to the storage, packing, shipment and delivery of any tangible personal property, whether works of art or otherwise, disposed of in this my Will shall be paid by my Executor as an administration expense of my estate.

SIXTEENTH: All the rest, residue and remainder of my estate, wherever situated, including any lapsed gifts (herein called my "Residuary Estate"), I give to such charitable organization or institution as shall be selected by my Executor proved that such organization or institution shall be an organization described in both Section 170(c) and 2055(a) of the Internal Revenue Code of 1954, as amended (or any corresponding section of any tax laws of the United States from time to time in effect).

SEVENTEENTH: A. I appoint JOHN BRUCE HAMILTON as Executor under this my Will. If JOHN BRUCE HAMILTON fails to qualify or ceases to act, I appoint GERALD DICKLER to act as Executor in his place. I authorize my last living duly qualified Executor under this my Will to designate, by an acknowledged written instrument, his successor to act as sole Executor in his place.

B. I direct that JOHN BRUCE HAMILTON shall not be entitled to any commission or other compensation for his services as Executor, notwithstanding the existence of any statute to the contrary. The bequests made to him in Article SEVENTH are in lieu of all compensation or commissions to which he would other wise be entitled as Executor.

If JOHN BRUCE HAMILTON fails to qualify or ceases to act as Executor for any reason whatsoever, I direct that his successor, whether named herein or otherwise appointed, shall be paid a fee of Two Hundred Thousand ($200,000) Dollars for his or her services as Executor and shall not be entitled to any other commission or compensation for said services, notwithstanding the existence of any statute to the contrary.

C. Whenever under any of the provisions of this Will, any fiduciary is authorized in such fiduciary's discretion to take any action or make any determination or decision, any such action, determination or decision shall be final and binding upon any one interested in my estate or any trust hereunder and such fiduciary shall not be held accountable in any court or to any person with respect thereto.

No fiduciary shall be liable or responsible for the loss or depreciation of any security, investment or other property which may be received, purchased, made or retained by such fiduciary in good faith in accordance with the provisions of this Will, or with respect to any of the funds held by such fiduciary hereunder, or for any loss incurred in any enterprise undertaken or participated in by such fiduciary with respect to any of the funds held by such fiduciary hereunder, or for any act, deed or loss, no matter how incurred, arising from any matter with respect to any of such funds, undertaken by such fiduciary in good faith pursuant to the provisions of this Will.

No person dealing with any fiduciary acting hereunder shall have any duty to inquire into the propriety or validity of any action taken by any such fiduciary, or be required to see to , or be liable for , the application of any money paid or property transferred or delivered to any such fiduciary.

I direct that no bond or other security shall be required of any fiduciary serving under this my Will in any jurisdiction, and no such fiduciary shall be required to render periodic accounts.

EIGHTEENTH: In addition to any powers conferred by law, my Executor hereunder shall have the following powers, authorities and discretions with respect to any property, real or personal, at any time held under any provisions of my Will and may exercise the same without the order or approval of any court:

1. To retain any such property, including but not limited to, so-called "tax-shelters," without regard to the proportion any such property or similar property held may bear to the entire amount held and without any obligation to diversity the same, whether or not the same is of the kind in which fiduciaries are authorized by law or any rule of court to invest funds.

2. To invest and reinvest in and to acquire by purchase, exchange or otherwise, property of any character whatsoever, foreign or domestic, or interests or participations therein, including by way of illustration and not of limitation: real property, mortgages, bonds, notes, debentures, certificates of deposit, capital, common and preferred stocks, and shares of interests in investment trusts, mutual funds or common trust funds, without regard to the proportions any such property or similar property held may bear to the entire amount held and without any obligation to diversify, whether or not the same is of the kind in which fiduciaries are authorized by law or any rule of court to invest funds.

3. To invest in securities producing tax-exempt income without any liability to any person for any decline in value resulting from such investment.

4. To sell any such property upon such terms and conditions as may be deemed advisable, at public or private sale, for cash or on credit, for such period of time as may be seemed advisable, or partly for cash an partly on credit, and with or without security, and the purchase of such property shall have no obligation to inquire as to the use or application of the proceeds of sale; to exchange any property held hereunder upon such terms and conditions as may be deemed advisable; and to grant options for any of the foregoing.

5. To lease or to sublease any such property, including any oil, gas or mineral property, for such period of time and to grant such covenants or options for renewal as may be deemed

advisable without regard to the duration of nay trust; and to mortgage, pledge or otherwise encumber any such property upon such terms as may be deemed advisable.

6. To partition, repair, manage, improve or otherwise alter any such property for such price and upon such terms as may be deemed proper.

7. To be a partner or joint venture in, or officer, director or stockholder of any business enterprise.

8. To participate in and to consent to any plan of reorganization, recapitalization, consolidation, merger, combination, dissolution, liquidation or similar plan and any action thereunder, including by way of illustration and not of limitation: the deposit of any property with any protective, reorganization or similar committee, the delegation of discretionary powers thereto, the sharing in the payment of its expenses and compensation and the payment of any assessments levied with respect to such property; and to receive and retain property under any such plan whether or not the same is of the kind in which fiduciaries are authorized by law or any rule of court to invest funds.

9. To exercise all conversion, subscription, voting option and other rights of whatsoever nature pertaining to any such property and to make payments in connection therewith and to grant proxies, discretionary or otherwise, with respect thereto; to appoint voting Trustees under voting Trust Agreements and to delegate to such voting Trustees the power to vote and all other powers, authorities and discretions usually conferred upon trustees under voting trust agreements.

10. To borrow such sums of money at any time and from time to time for such periods of time upon such terms and conditions from such persons or corporations (including any fiduciary hereunder) for such purposes as may be deemed advisable, and to secure such loans by the pledge or hypothecation of any such property held hereunder, and the decision with respect thereto shall be final and binding upon all persons interested hereunder; and the lender shall have no obligation to inquire as to the application of the sums loaned or as to the necessity, expediency or propriety of the loan.

11. To register and hold any property of any kind, whether real or personal, at any time held hereunder in the name of a nominee or nominees an tot hold any such personal property in any State; and to receive and keep any stocks , bonds or other securities unregistered or in such condition as to pass by delivery.

12. To extend the time for payment of any claim or obligation; and to abandon, settle, compromise, renew, modify, release, adjust or submit to arbitration in whole or in part and without the order of any court any and all claims or obligations whether the same shall increase or decrease the value or aggregate of the property held hereunder.

13. To distribute in the exercise of sole and absolute discretion any property in kind at market value unless otherwise directed herein or in cash, or partly in kind and partly in cash, and to allocate among the recipients the property distributed in kind, including carryover basis property, without any obligation to make proportionate distributions or to distribute to all recipients property having an equivalent Federal income tax cost and without regard to equality of treatment of the recipients, without any need to make any adjustment and without being subject to question by any person.

14. To decide in the exercise of sole and absolute discretion whether to exercise any income, estate or gift tax option, including whether to claim executor's commissions, attorneys' fees and other administration expense in my estate as estate tax or income tax deductions and whether to make any adjustments between income and principal because of any such decisions, and any such determinations shall be final and binding upon all beneficiaries hereunder.

15. To retain, employ and compensate at any time, including in advance of the final settlement of my estate, such agents and service (including investment counsel, accountants, attorneys, custodians, stockbrokers and other agents) as may be deemed advisable.

16. To do all such acts and exercise all such rights and privileges, although no specifically mentioned hereunder, with relation to any such property as if the absolute owner thereof and to make, execute and deliver any and all instruments or agreements.

NINETEENTH: In the event that any person, who would be a beneficiary under any provision of this my Will if he or she survives me or survives some other beneficiary hereunder, should die under such circumstances that there is not sufficient evidence to determine whether or not such person survived me or survived such other beneficiary, as the case may be, I direct that for the purposes of this my Will such person shall be deemed to have predeceased me or to have predeceased such other beneficiary, as the case may be.

TWENTHIETH: Wherever appropriate in this my Will and unless otherwise provided to the contrary herein, the masculine, feminine and neuter genders shall be deemed to include the others; the singular shall be deemed to include the plural, and vice versa; the term "fiduciary" shall be construed to mean and include a guardian, trustee, executor or administrator C.T.A.;

reference to any fiduciary shall be deemed to include any successor, whether named herein or otherwise appointed; and the terms "person" and "individual" shall be construed to mean and include an individual, a trust, estate, partnership, association, company or corporation.

IN WITNESS WHEREOF, I have hereunto set my hand this <u>22</u> day of August, 1979.

Georgia O'Keeffe
Georgia O'Keeffe

We, the undersigned, do hereby certify that at <u>Abiquiu</u> on the day of the date hereof, the foregoing instrument consisting of 19 pages, not including this attestation, was in our presence and in the presence of each other signed by GEORGIA O'KEEFFE, as testatrix, who is known to each of us and the same was by her then and there to each of us declared to be her Last Will and Testament, and, at her request and in her presence and in the presence of each other in evidence of such fact and in evidence of the fact that the Testatrix is now of sound and disposing mind and memory, we do hereby append our signatures respectively.

Louise Talbot Trigg   residing at_ [address]
Jean M. Seth   residing at_ [address]

Adam Seth   residing at_ [address]

STATE OF *New Mexico*   )

                                :ss.:

COUNTY OF *Rio Arriba*   )

Each of the undersigned, individually and severally being duly sworn, deposes and says:

The within Will was subscribed in our presence and sight at the end thereof by GEORGIA O'KEEFFE, the within named Testatrix, on the 22 day of *August* 1979, at Abiquiu, *New Mexico*.

Said Testatrix at the time of making such subscription declared the instrument so subscribed to be her last Will.

Each of the undersigned thereupon signed his name as a witness at the end of the said Will at the request of said Testatrix and in her presence and sight and in the presence and sight of each other.

Said Testatrix was, at the time of so executing said Will over the age of 18 years and, in the respective opinions of the undersigned, of sound mind, memory and understanding and not under any restraint or in any respect incompetent to make a will.

The Testatrix, in the respective opinion of the undersigned, could read, write and converse in the English language and was suffering from no defect of sight, hear in or speech, or from any other physical or mental impairment which would affect her capacity to make a valid will.   The will was executed as a single, original instrument and was not executed in counterparts.

Each of the undersigned was acquainted with said Testatrix at such time and makes this affidavit at her request.

The within Will was shown to the undersigned at the time this affidavit was made, and was examined by each of them as to the signature of said Testatrix and of the undersigned.

The foregoing instrument was executed by the testatrix and witnessed by each of the undersigned affiants ~~under the supervision of~~ _____. Attorney-at-law.

Louise Talbot Trigg

Jean M. Seth

Adam Seth

Severally sworn to before me
This _22_ day of _August_ 1979.

  Glenn F. Wade
  Notary Public
My Commission Expires Feb. 11, 1980

FIRST CODICIL
TO
LAST WILL AND TESTAMENT
OF
<u>GEORGIA O'KEEFFE</u>

I, GEORGIA O'KEEFFE, residing in Abiquiu, County of Rio Arriba, State of New Mexico, do hereby make, publish and declare this to be the First Codicil to my Last Will and Testament dated August 22, 1979.

FIRST: I hereby revoke Article FIFTH of my said Will and add a new Article FIFTH to read as follows:

FIFTH: I give all my right, title and interest in and to my real property located in Abiquiu, New Mexico, subject to any mortgages, liens or encumbrances of any kind, consisting of a house and lot originally obtained from St. Thomas The Apostle Roman Catholic Church and any adjoining lots and parcels owned by me and located in Abiquiu, New Mexico, along with all the furnishing located in said real property (but, in no event, to include any works of art) and the equipment used in connection therewith, not otherwise specifically bequeathed in this my Will or any Codicil thereto, and together with any and all improvements on said properties and any and all appurtenances thereto to such charitable organizations or institution as shall be selected by me Executor provided that such organization or institution shall be an organization described in both Section 170(c) and 2055(a) of the Internal Revenue Code of 1954, as amended (or any corresponding section of any tax laws of the United States from time to time in effect. Notwithstanding the foregoing, I direct that my Executor shall have the right, to be exercised in his sole and absolute discretion, to sell the aforesaid real property and personal property and to pay over the proceeds of said sale to whichever said institution he shall select in accordance with the terms of this Article.

<u>SECOND:</u> I hereby revoke Article SEVENTH of my said will and add a new article SEVENTH to read as follows:

<u>SEVENTH:</u> If my friend, JOHN BRUCE HAMILTON, shall survive me, I give him the following works of art created by me regardless of whether he qualifies and serves as Executor of my Estate:

A. Any six (6) works of art from among my oil paintings on canvas.

B. Any fifteen (15) works of art from among my drawings and/or water colors and or pastels.

C. Notwithstanding the foregoing, JOHN BRUCE HAMILTON shall make his selection from works of art other than those specifically bequeathed elsewhere in this my Will or any Codicil thereto.

THIRD: I hereby revoke article SEVENTEENTH paragraph B and add a new Article SEVENTEENTH, paragraph B to read as follows:

B.   I direct that JOHN BRUCE HAMILTON shall be paid a fee of Two hundred Thousand ($200,000) Dollars for his services as Executor and shall _ _ t [sic] be entitled to any other commission or compensation for said services, notwithstanding the existence of any statute to the contrary.

If JOHN BRUCE HAMILTON fails to qualify or ceases to act as Executor for any reason whatsoever, I direct that his successor, whether named herein or otherwise appointed, shall be paid a fee of Two Hundred Thousand ($200,000) dollars for his or her services as Executor and shall not be entitled to any other commission or compensation for such services, notwithstanding the existence of any statute to the contrary.

FOURTH: As thus amended, I hereby ratify, confirm, redeclare and republish my said Will.

IN WITNESS WHEREOF, I, GEORGIA O'KEEFFE, have hereunto subscribed my name and affixed my seal this 2 day of *November*, 1983.

Georgia O'Keeffe
Georgia O'Keeffe

SIGNED, SEALED, PUBLISHED AND DECLARED as and for the First Codicil to her LAST WILL AND TESTAMENT by the above-named Testatrix, GEORGIA O'KEEFFE, in the presence of us, who, at her request, in her presence, and in the presence of each other, have hereunto subscribed our names as witnesses on the day and year last above written.

Laurel Seth	___*[address]*___
Cynthia Black	___*[address]*___
Mark Dawson Jamison	___*[address]*___

STATE OF *New Mexico*   )
) ss.
COUNTY OF *Santa Fe*   )

Each of the undersigned, individually and severally being duly sworn, deposes and says:

The within Codicil was subscribed in our presence and sight at the end thereof by GEORGIA O'KEEFFE, the within Testatrix, on the 2 day of *November, 1983*, at

       (left blank in original)

Said Testatrix at the time of making such subscription declared the instrument so subscribed to be her First Codicil to her last Will.

Each of the undersigned thereupon signed his name as a witness at the end of said Codicil at the request of said Testatrix and in her presence and sight and in the presence and sight of each other.

Said Testatrix was, at the time of so executing said Codicil, over the age of 18 years and, in the respective opinions of the undersigned, of sound mind, memory and understanding and not under any restraint or in any respect incompetent to make a codicil.

The Testatrix, in the respective opinions of the undersigned, could read, write and converse in the English language and was suffering from no defect of sight *except some impairment,* hearing or speech, or from any other physical or mental impairment which would affect her capacity to make a valid codicil. The Codicil was executed as a single, original instrument and was not executed in counterparts.

Each of the undersigned was acquainted with said Testatrix at such time and makes this affidavit at her request.

The within Codicil was shown to the undersigned at the time this affidavit was made, and was examined by each of them as to the signature of said Testatrix and of the undersigned.

The foregoing instrument was executed by the Testatrix and witnessed by each of the undersigned affiants under the supervision of *Oliver Seth*, an attorney-at-law.

Laurel Seth

Cynthia Black

Mark Dawson Jamison

Severally sworn to before me this 2nd day of *November,* 1983.

Rosemarie Benavidez

       Notary Public

My commission Expires 11/17/1986

SECOND CODICIL
TO
LAST WILL AND TESTAMENT
OF GEORGIA O'KEEFFE

I, GEORGIA O'KEEFFE, hereby make, publish and declare this to be the Second Codicil to my Last Will and Testament executed by me on August 11, 1979.

FIRST: Paragraph J. of Article EIGHTH is hereby revoked in its entirety.

SECOND: Article NINTH is hereby revoked in its entirety.

THIRD: Article TENTH is hereby redesignated as Article NINTH and the reference therein to Article NINTH is deleted.

FOURTH: Article ELEVENTH is hereby redesignated as Article TENTH.

FIFTH: Article TWELFTH is hereby redesignated as Article ELEVENTH and paragraph B thereof is hereby deleted in its entirety.

SIXTH: Article THIRTEENTH is hereby redesignated as Article TWELFTH.

SEVENTH: Article FOURTEENTH is hereby deleted in its entirety.

EIGHTH: Article FIFTEENTH is hereby redesignated as Article THIRTEENTH.

NINTH: Article SIXTEENTH is hereby redesignated as Article FOURTEENTH and amended in its entirety to read as follows:

FOURTEENTH: All the rest, residue and remainder of my estate wherever situated, including any lapsed gifts, shall constitute my residuary estate. I give my residuary estate to my friend, JOHN BRUCE HAMILTON. If John Bruce Hamilton fails to survive me, I direct that my residuary estate shall instead be distributed to such person or persons and upon such estates or conditions in such manner, and at such times as John Bruce Hamilton shall appoint by Will. In default of effective exercise of this power of appointment, my residuary estate shall instead by distributed among the heirs of John Bruce Hamilton as if he died intestate.

TENTH: Articles SEVENTEENTH, EIGHTEENTH, NINETEENTH and TWENTIETH are herby redesignated as Article FIFTEENTH, SIXTEENTH, SEVENTEENTH and EIGHTEENTH.

ELEVENTH: a new Article NINETEENTH is hereby added which reads as follows:

NINETEENTH: Should any person entitled to share in my estate either as heir at law or as a legatee or devisee under this Will contest or seek to set aside this Will, or establish any legal right to share in my estate other than as herein approved and provided, I hereby give and bequeath the sum of ONE DOLLAR ($1.00) only and expressly direct that he shall receive no other or further share in my estate. Any property forfeited by the operation of this article shall be distributed as part of the residue of my estate, to be disposed of by my Personal

Representative, and each interest shall pass and vest under this Will in the same manner, as if such contestant had died without issue prior to the date set for the distribution of my estate.

TWELFTH: Except as hereinabove amended, I hereby ratify confirm and republish my aforesaid Last Will and Testament and prior Codicils thereto.

IN WITNESS WHEREOF, I have hereunder set my hand this _8th_ day of August, 1984.

Georgia O'Keeffe

WE, the undersigned, do hereby certify that GEORGIA O'KEEFFE, on the day of the date hereof, in our presence, we being in the presence of each other, signed, published and declared the above instrument as and to be her Second Codicil to her Last Will and Testament, and that we, on the same occasion, at her request, in her presence, and in the presence of each other, have hereunto signed our names as attesting witnesses.

Judy Lopez, residing at   [address]

Benjamin Sanders, Jr. residing at [address]

Ursula Sanders residing at   [address]

STATE OF _New Mexico_   )
) ss.
COUNTY OF _Santa Fe_   )

We, GEORGIA O'KEEFFE, Judy Lopez, Benjamin Sanders, Jr., and Ursula Sanders, the testatrix and the witnesses, respectively, whose names are signed to the attached or foregoing instrument, being first duly sworn, do hereby declare to the undersigned authority that the testatrix signed and executed the instrument as her Second Codicil to her Last Will and that she signed willingly, or directed another to sign for her, and that she executed it as her free and voluntary act for the purposes therein expressed; and that each of the witnesses saw the testatrix sign or another sign for her at her direction, and in the presence of the testatrix and in the presence of each other signed the Second Codicil to the Will as witness and that to the best of his knowledge the testatrix had reached the age of majority, was of sound mind and was under no constraint or undue influence.

Georgia O'Keeffe

Judy Lopez

Benjamin Sanders, Jr.

Ursula Sanders

Subscribed, sworn to and acknowledged before me by GEORGIA O'KEEFFE, the testatrix, and subscribed and sworn to before me by _Judy Lopez, Benjamin Sanders, Jr., and Ursula Sanders,_ witnesses, this 8th day of August, 1984.

Ava L. Williams
Notary Public, My Commission Expires: 9-22-84

LAST WILL AND TESTAMENT OF ELVIS A. PRESELY, DECEASED
FILED AUGUST 22, 1977

LAST WILL AND TESTAMENT
OF
ELVIS A. PRESLEY

I, ELVIS A. PRESLEY, a resident and citizen of Shelby County, Tennessee, being of sound mind and disposing memory, do hereby make publish and declare this instrument to be my last will and testament, hereby revoking any and all wills and codicils by me at any time heretofore made.

ITEM I
Debts, Expenses and Taxes

I direct my Executor, hereinafter named, to pay all of my matured debts and my funeral expenses, as well as the costs and expenses of the administration of my estate, as soon after my death as practicable. I further direct that all estate, inheritance, transfer and succession taxes which are payable by reason of my death, whether or not with respect to property passing under this will, be paid out of my residuary estate; and I hereby waive on behalf of my estate any right to recover from any person any part of such taxes so paid. My Executor, in his sole discretion, may pay from my domiciliary estate all or any portion of the costs of ancillary administration and similar proceedings in other jurisdictions.

ITEM II
Instruction Concerning Personal
Property: Enjoyment in Specie

I anticipated that included as a part of my property and estate at the time of my death will be tangible personal property of various kinds, characters and values, including trophies and other items accumulated by me during my professional career. I hereby specifically instruct all concerned that my Executor, herein appointed, shall have complete freedom and discretion as to disposal of any and all such property so long as he shall act in good faith and in the best interest of my estate and my beneficiaries, and his discretion so exercised shall not be subject to question by anyone whomsoever.

I hereby expressly authorize my Executor and my Trustee, respectively and successively, to permit any beneficiary of any and all trusts created hereunder to enjoy in specie the use or benefit of any household goods, chattels, or other tangible personal property (exclusive of choses in action, cash, stocks, bonds or other securities) which either my Executor or my Trustee may receive in kind, and my Executor and my Trustee shall not be liable for any consumption, damage, injury to or loss of any tangible property so used, nor shall the beneficiaries of any trusts hereunder or their executors or administrators be liable for any consumption, damage, injury to or loss of any tangible personal property so used.

ITEM III
Real Estate

If I am the owner of any real estate at the time of my death, I instruct and empower my Executor and my Trustee (as the case may be) to hold such real estate for investment, or to sell same, or any portion thereof, as my Executor or my Trustee (as the case may be) shall in his sole judgment determine to be for the best interest of my estate and the beneficiaries thereof.

ITEM IV
Residuary Trust

After payment of all debts, expenses and taxes as directed under ITEM I hereof, I give, devise, and bequeath all the rest, residue, and remainder of my estate, including all lapsed legacies and devises, and any property over which I have a power of appointment, to my Trustee, hereinafter named, in trust for the following purposes:

(a) The Trustee is directed to take, hold, manage, invest and reinvest the corpus of the trust and to collect the income therefrom in accordance with the rights, powers, duties, authority and discretion hereinafter set forth. The Trustee is directed to pay all the expenses, taxes and costs incurred in the management of the trust estate out of the income thereof.

(b) After payment of all expenses, taxes and costs incurred in the management of the trust estate, the Trustee is authorized to accumulate the net income or to pay or apply so much of the net income and such portion of the principal at any time and from time to time for the health, education, support, comfortable maintenance and welfare of: (1) my daughter, Lisa Marie Presley, and any other lawful issue I might have, (2) my grandmother, Minnie Mae Presley, (3) my father, Vernon E. Presley, and (4) such other relatives of mine living at the time of my death who in the absolute discretion of my Trustee are in need of emergency assistance for any of the above mentioned purposes and the Trustee is able to make such distribution without affecting the ability of the trust to meet the present needs of the first three numbered categories of beneficiaries herein mentioned or to meet the reasonably expected future needs of the first three classes of beneficiaries herein mentioned. Any decision of the Trustee as to whether or not distribution shall be made, and also as to the amount of such distribution, to any of the persons described hereunder shall be final and conclusive and not subject to question by any legatee or beneficiary hereunder.

(c) Upon the death of my father, Vernon E. Presley, the Trustee is instructed to make no further distributions to the fourth category of beneficiaries and such beneficiaries shall cease to have any interest whatsoever in this trust.

(d) Upon the death of both my said father and my said grandmother, the Trustee is directed to divide the Residuary Trust into separate and equal trusts, creating one such equal trust for each of my lawful children then surviving and one such equal trust for the living issue collectively, if any, of any deceased child of mine. The share, if any, for the issue of any such deceased child, shall immediately vest in such issue in equal shares but shall be subject to the provisions of ITEM V herein. Separate books and records shall be kept for each trust, but it shall not be necessary that a physical division of the assets be made as to each trust.

The Trustee may from time to time distribute the whole or any part of the net income or principal from each of the aforesaid trusts as the Trustee, in its uncontrolled discretion, considers necessary or desirable to provide for the comfortable support, education, maintenance, benefit and general welfare of each of my children. Such distributions may be made directly to such beneficiary or to any person standing in the place of a parent or the guardian of the person of such beneficiary and without responsibility on my Trustee to see to the application of any such distributions and in making such distributions, the Trustee shall take into account all other sources of funds known by the Trustee to be available for each respective beneficiary for such purpose.

(e) As each of my respective children attains the age of twenty-five (25) years and provided that both my father and grandmother then be deceased, the trust created hereunder for such child shall terminate, and all the remainder of the assets then contained in said trust shall be distributed to such child so attaining the age of twenty-five (25) years outright and free of further trust.

(f) If any of my children for whose benefit a trust has been created hereunder should die before attaining the age of twenty-five (25) years, then the trust created for such child shall terminate on his death, and all remaining assets then contained in said trust shall be distributed outright and free of further trust and in equal shares to the surviving issue of each deceased child but subject to the provisions of ITEM V herein; but if there be no such surviving issue, then to the brothers and sisters of such deceased child in equal shares, the issue of any other deceased child being entitled collectively to their deceased parent's share. Nevertheless, if any distribution otherwise becomes payable outright and free of trust under the provisions of this paragraph (f) of this ITEM IV of my will to a beneficiary for whom the Trustee is then administering a trust for the benefit of such beneficiary under the provisions of this last will and testament, such distribution shall not be paid outright to such beneficiary but shall be added to and become a part of the trust so being administered for such beneficiary by the Trustee.

ITEM V
Distribution to Minor Children

If any share of corpus of any trust established under this will becomes distributable outright and free of trust to any beneficiary before said beneficiary has attained the age of eighteen (18) years, then said share shall immediately vest in said beneficiary, but the Trustee shall retain possession of such share during the period in which such beneficiary is under the age of eighteen (18) years, and, in the meantime, shall use and expend so much of the income and principal of each share as the trustee deems necessary and desirable for the care, support and education of such beneficiary, and any income not so expended shall be added to the principal. The Trustee shall have with respect to each share so retained all the power and discretion had with respect to such trust generally.

ITEM VI
Alternate Distributees

In the event that all of my descendants should be deceased at any time prior to the time for the termination of the trusts provided for herein, then in such event all of my estate and all the assets of every trust to be created hereunder (as the case may be) shall then be distributed outright in equal shares to my heirs at law per stirpes.

ITEM VII
Unenforceable Provisions

If any provisions of this will are unenforceable, the remaining provisions shall, nevertheless, be carried into effect.

ITEM VIII
Life Insurance

If my estate is the beneficiary of any life insurance on my life at the time of my death, I direct that the proceeds therefrom will be used by my Executor in payment of the debts, expenses and taxes listed in ITEM I of this will, to the extent deemed advisable by the Executor. All such proceeds not so used are to be used by my Executor for the purpose of satisfying the devises and bequests contained in ITEM IV herein.

ITEM IX
Spendthrift Provision

I direct that the interest of any beneficiary in principal or income of any trust created hereunder shall not be subject to claims of creditors or others, nor to legal process, and may not be voluntarily or involuntarily alienated or encumbered except as herein provided. Any bequests contained herein for any female shall be for her sole and separate use, free from the debts, contracts and control of any husband she may ever have.

ITEM X
Proceeds From Personal Services

All sums paid after my death (either to my estate or to any of the trusts created hereunder) and resulting from personal services rendered by me during my lifetime, including, but not limited to, royalties of all nature, concerts, motion picture contracts, and personal appearances shall be considered to be income, notwithstanding the provisions of estate and trust law to the contrary.

ITEM XI
Executor and Trustee

I appoint as Executor of this, my last will and testament, and as Trustee of every trust required to be created hereunder, my said father.

I hereby direct that my said father shall be entitled by his last will and testament, duly probated, to appoint a successor Executor of my estate, as well as a successor Trustee or Trustees of all trusts to be created under my last will and testament.

If, for any reason, my said father be unable to serve or to continue to serve as Executor and/or as Trustee, or if he be deceased and shall not have appointed a successor Executor or Trustee, by virtue of his last will and testament as stated above, then I appoint National Bank of

Commerce, Memphis, Tennessee, or its successor or the institution with which it may merge, as successor Executor and/or as successor Trustee of all trusts required to be established hereunder.

None of the appointees named hereunder, including any appointment made by virtue of the last will and testament of my said father, shall be required to furnish any bond or security for performance of the respective fiduciary duties required hereunder, notwithstanding any rule of law to the contrary.

ITEM XII
Powers, Duties, Privileges and Immunities of the Trustee

Except as otherwise stated expressly to the contrary herein, I give and grant to the said Trustee (and to the duly appointed successor Trustee when acting as such) the power to do everything he deems advisable with respect to the administration of each trust required to be established under this, my last will and testament, even though such powers would not be authorized or appropriate for the Trustee under statutory or other rules of law. By way of illustration and not in limitation of the generality of the foregoing grant of power and authority of the Trustee, I give and grant to him plenary power as follows:

(a)   To exercise all those powers authorized to fiduciaries under the provisions of the Tennessee Code Annotated, Sections 35-616 to 35-618, inclusive, including any amendments thereto in effect at the time of my death, and the same are expressly referred to and incorporated herein by reference.

(b)   Plenary power is granted to the Trustee, not only to relieve him from seeking judicial instruction, but to the extent that the Trustee deems it to be prudent, to encourage determinations freely to be made in favor of persons who are the current income beneficiaries. In such instances the rights of all subsequent beneficiaries are subordinate, and the Trustee shall not be answerable to any subsequent beneficiary for anything done or omitted in favor of a current income beneficiary, but no current income beneficiary may compel any such favorable or preferential treatment. Without in anywise minimizing or impairing the scope of this declaration of intent, it includes investment policy, exercise of discretionary power to pay or apply principal and income, and determination of principal and income questions;

(c)   It shall be lawful for the Trustee to apply any sum that is payable to or for the benefit of a minor (or any other person who in the judgment of the Trustee, is incapable of making proper disposition thereof) by payments in discharge of the costs and expenses of educating, maintaining and supporting said beneficiary, or to make payment to anyone with whom said beneficiary resides or who has the care or custody of the beneficiary, temporarily or permanently, all without intervention of any guardian or like fiduciary. The receipt of anyone to whom payment is so authorized to be made shall be a complete discharge of the Trustee without obligation on his part to see to the further application thereof, and without regard to other resources that the beneficiary may have, or the duty of any other person to support the beneficiary;

(d)   In dealing with the Trustee, no grantee, pledgee, vendee, mortgagee, lessee or other transferee of the trust properties, or any part thereof, shall be bound to inquire with respect to the purpose or necessity of any such disposition or to see to the application of any consideration therefore paid to the Trustee.

ITEM XIII

Concerning the Trustee And the Executor

(a) If at any time the Trustee shall have reasonable doubt as to his power, authority or duty in the administration of any trust herein created, it shall be lawful for the Trustee to obtain the advice and counsel of reputable legal counsel without resorting to the courts for instructions; and the Trustee shall be fully absolved from all liability and damage or detriment to the various trust estates or any beneficiary thereunder by reason of anything done, suffered or omitted pursuant to advice of said counsel given and obtained in good faith, provided that nothing contained herein shall be construed to prohibit or prevent the Trustee in all proper cases from applying to a court of competent jurisdiction for instructions in the administration of the trust assets in lieu of obtaining advice of counsel.

(b)   In managing, investing, and controlling the various trust estates, the Trustee shall exercise the judgment and care under the circumstances then prevailing, which men of prudence, discretion and judgment exercise in the management of their own affairs, not in regard to speculation, but in regard to the permanent disposition of their funds, considering the probable income as well as probable safety of their capital, and, in addition, the purchasing power of income distribution to beneficiaries.

(c)   My Trustee (as well as my Executor) shall be entitled to reasonable and adequate compensation for the fiduciary services rendered by him.

(d)   My Executor and his successor Executor shall have the same rights, privileges, powers and immunities herein granted to my Trustee wherever appropriate.

(e)   In referring to any fiduciary hereunder, for purposes of construction, masculine pronouns may include a corporate fiduciary and neutral pronouns may include an individual fiduciary.

ITEM XIV
Law Against Perpetuities

(a)   Having in mind the rule against perpetuities, I direct that (notwithstanding anything contained to the contrary in this last will and testament) each trust created under this will (except such trusts as have heretofore vested in compliance with such rule or law) shall end, unless sooner terminated under other provisions of this will, twenty-one (21) years after the death of the last survivor of such of the beneficiaries hereunder as are living at the time of my death; and thereupon that the property held in trust shall be distributed free of all trust to the persons then entitled to receive the income and/or principal therefrom, in the proportion in which they are then entitled to receive such income.

(b)   Notwithstanding anything else contained in this will to the contrary, I direct that if any distribution under this will becomes payable to a person for whom the Trustee is then administering a trust created hereunder for the benefit of such person, such distribution shall be made to such trust and not to the beneficiary outright, and the funds so passing to such trust shall become a part thereof as corpus and be administered and distributed to the same extent and purpose as if such funds had been a part of such trust at its inception.

ITEM XV
Payment of Estate and Inheritance Taxes

Notwithstanding the provisions of ITEM X herein, I authorize my Executor to use such sums received by my estate after my death and resulting from my personal services as identified in ITEM X as he deems necessary and advisable in order to pay the taxes referred to in ITEM I of my said will.

IN WITNESS WHEREOF, I, the said ELVIS A. PRESLEY, do hereunto set my hand and seal in the presence of two (2) competent witnesses, and in their presence do publish and declare this instrument to be my Last Will and Testament, this _3_ day of _March_ , ~~1976~~ 1977

s/ Elvis A. Presley
ELVIS A. PRESLEY

The foregoing instrument; consisting of this and eleven (11) preceding typewritten pages, was signed, sealed, published and declared by ELVIS A. PRESLEY, the Testator, to be his last Will and Testament in our presence, and we, at his request and in his presence and in the presence of each other, have hereunto subscribed our names as witnesses, this _3_ day of _March_ , ~~1976~~, 1977 at Memphis, Tennessee.

s/ Ginger Alden   residing at __(Omitted)__

  s/ Charles F. Hodge   residing at __(Omitted)__
s/ Ann Dewey Smith   (Omitted)

STATE OF TENNESSEE   )
)ss.
COUNTY OF SHELBY   )

     S/ Ginger Alden, Charles F. Hodge   and s/ Ann Dewey Smith   after being first duly sworn, make oath or affirm that the foregoing Last Will and Testament was signed by ELVIS A. PRESLEY and for and at that time acknowledged, published and declared by him to be his Last Will and Testament, in the sight and presence of us, the undersigned, who at his request and in his sight and presence, and in the sight and presence of each other, have subscribed our names as attesting witnesses on the __3__ day of ___March___ , ~~1976~~, 1977 and we further make oath or affirm that the Testator was of sound mind and disposing memory and not acting under fraud, menace or undue influence of any person, and was more than eighteen (18) years of age; and that each of the attesting witnesses is more than (18) years of age.

s/ Ginger Alden

s/ Charles F. Hodge

s/ Ann Dewey Smith

     SWORN TO AND SUBSCRIBED before me this _3_ day of __March__ , ~~1976~~. 1977

s/ Dayton Bucher Smith II
    Notary Public

My commission expires:
August 8, 1979

ADMITTED TO PROBATE AND ORDERED RECORDED AUGUST 22, 1977;
JOSEPH W. EVANS, JUDGE
RECORDED AUGUST 22, 1977; B.J. DUNAVANT, CLERK; BY: JAN SCOTT, D.C.

LAST WILL AND TESTAMENT
of
MARK ROTHKO

I, MARK ROTHKO, of New York, N. Y. being of sound mind and memory, hereby make, publish and declare this to be my Last Will and Testament, hereby revoking all wills and other testamentary dispositions by me at any time heretofore made.

FIRST: I direct my Executors to pay all my just debts, funeral and administration expenses as soon after my decease as is convenient.

SECOND: I give and bequeath to the TATE GALLERY, London, England, five (5) paintings of their choice of those paintings which were created by me for the Seagram Building, New York in 1959.

THIRD: I give, devise and bequeath to my wife, MARY ALICE, the real estate owned by me at 118 East 95th Street, New York, together with all of the contents thereof.

FOURTH: I hereby bequeath to my wife, MARY ALICE, the sum of Two Hundred Fifty Thousand ($250,000) Dollars.

FIFTH: In the event of the death of my wife or the simultaneous death of myself and my wife, I give, devise and bequeath the sum of Two Hundred Fifty Thousand ($250,000) Dollars together with the real property at 118 East 95th Street, New York, and all the contents thereof, in equal shares to my children, KATE and CHRISTOPHER.

SIXTH: All the rest, residue and remainder of my property, I give and bequeath to the Mark Rothko Foundation, a non-profit organization, incorporated under the laws of the State of New York. The Directors of the Foundations are to be: WILLIAM RUBIN, ROBERT GOLDWATER, BERNARD J. REIS, THEODOROS STAMOS AND MORTON LEVINE.

SEVENTH: In the event of the death of my wife or the simultaneous death of my wife and myself, I appoint as Guardians of my children, MR. and MRS. MORTON LEVINE, of New York.

EIGHTH: I hereby nominate, constitute and appoint MORTON LEVINE, BERNARD J. REIS and THEODOROS STAMOS as Executors of this will. I direct that my Executors shall not be required to furnish any bond, undertaking or security for the faithful performance of their duties. In the event of the death of either one or two of them, the remaining person or persons shall serve as Executor.

IN WITNESS WHEREOF, I have hereunto set my hand and seal this 13th day of September 1968.

Mark Rothko (L.S.)

On this 13th day of September, 1968, the above-named Testator, MARK ROTHKO, in our presence, subscribed and sealed the foregoing instrument, and at the time of such subscription, published and declared the same to be his Last Will and Testament, and thereupon we at such time, at the request of the above named Testator, in his presence, and in the presence of each other, signed our names thereto as subscribing witnesses.

Louis Meyer   residing at   (omitted)

Mary Ann Harten   residing at   (omitted)

Ruth B. Miller   residing at (omitted)

Sample Memo Form and Instructions for UPC Memorandum Disposition of Tangible Personal Property:

Pursuant to the terms of my Will, I hereby make this Memorandum of Disposition of Tangible Personal Property as permitted by Colorado law (C.R.S. 15-11-513).

Description of Item of Tangible Personal Property	First Beneficiary	Second Beneficiary (if the first beneficiary is not alive when I die)
_____	_____	_____
_____	_____	_____
_____	_____	_____
_____	_____	_____
_____	_____	_____
_____	_____	_____
_____	_____	_____

If the first beneficiary and the second beneficiary die before I do, the gifts listed for these people shall be distributed in accordance with the terms of my Will.

_____   _____

Signature   Date

Sample Instructions:

Instructions should be as short, clear, and un-technical as possible. Here is one possibility, which would be appropriate in a state which has adopted the newest version of the UPC memo statute—allowing use of the memo for gifts of any tangible personal property other than money. If your state still has more restrictions on what can be bequeathed by memo, you should include a summary of those restrictions—translated to plain English, if possible.

INSTRUCTIONS: Your will states that you may make a list giving away certain items of tangible personal property. You may use the attached form, or any piece of paper, to make the list of the special items to be given away.

1. If something is already mentioned in your will, do not include that same thing on this list. You cannot change anything in your will by using this list.

2. Do not include money or land on this list.

3. Put a number beside each item you are giving away, and then describe that item so that everyone will know which item you mean.

4. Beside the description of the item write the name of the person you would most like to have the item, (the "First Beneficiary"), and then write the name of the person you would like to have the item if the first person you named is not alive when you die. The second person you name for reach item is the "Second Beneficiary," and will get the item only if the "Fist Beneficiary" is not alive when you die.

5. When you have written down all the items you want to include on the list for now, just sign and date the list.

6. You can add to, or change the list any time you like, just by tearing up the old list and making a new one.

7. You do not need to have any witnesses when you make and sign the list.

8. Keep the list in the same envelope in which you keep your will—but DO NOT ATTACH IT TO THE WILL! You can change the list anytime you like, but you cannot change your will while you are living in (state name) without (insert summary of state legal requirements).

9. Feel free to call me at any time, if you have any questions. (Name, address, and phone number of attorney).

Breinigsville, PA USA
20 August 2009
222524BV00004B/4/P

9 781600 420757